Praise for **ACTOR**

"Fourteen leading American actors come alive as human beings and as artists in an exchange of intimacies about their individual ways of working, their lives in the theater, and how they happened to be drawn into it. Conversations sensitively led by the authors circle this thing called 'acting,' a mysterious process of being me/not-me while others are watching and also a craft that can be taught and learned. If you have ever felt serious about this process and the talented, committed people who risk it, read this one-of-a-kind book. I couldn't put it down."

—ZELDA FICHANDLER, Chair, Graduate
Acting Program, Tisch School of the Arts, NYU

"It's so wonderful to finally read a collection of anecdotes where the practices and experiences of actors are described so uniquely, yet depict how each individual ultimately performs the same job. From a casting director's point of view, it was delightful to find actors such as John Lithgow, Marian Seldes, and Patti LuPone so eloquently and clearly describing their performances in a manner in which I could relate and truly understand. It was almost as if I were getting an individual lesson in 'succeeding in show business' from each of the interviewees. By providing a myriad of different actors' perspectives, processes, triumphs, and failures, what clearly emerges is the need for a strong sense of true individualism—something that I believe is crucial for newcomers, as well as veterans. Rosemarie Tichler and Barry Jay Kaplan's compilation of dialogue is something that will certainly be of infinite value for so many in the performance industry and should be a necessity for all those breaking into the business. For any actor who strives for success in theater, film, or television, this book is an educational and intellectual goldmine."

—BERNIE TELSEY, casting director

"Because of their provocative, empathetic, and insightful interview techniques, coauthors Rosemarie Tichler and Barry Jay Kaplan manage to reveal both the working methods and the deeply personal perspectives of fourteen of America's most gifted actors. In the book's depth of purpose as well as in its sheer entertainment value as a great reading experience, *Actors at Work* sets a standard that subsequent actor-interview books will be hard-pressed to match." —RON VAN LIEU, Lloyd Richards Chair of Acting, Yale School of Drama

"*Actors at Work* is an amazing resource and inspiration for anyone who loves theater or film and certainly for anyone interested in actors and acting. The interviews, conducted with great sensitivity and knowledge by Rosemarie Tichler and Barry Jay Kaplan, give the reader a rare glimpse and a deeper understanding of an actor's process and struggles. This book is an invaluable read." —ELLEN LEWIS, casting director

"*Actors at Work* not only offers a fascinating insight into the personalities of these extraordinary actors but also provides a glorious read for anyone interested in an artist's ineffable creative process." —JAMES LAPINE, author of *Sunday in the Park with George*

Rosemarie Tichler and Barry Jay Kaplan
ACTORS AT WORK

ROSEMARIE TICHLER was Casting Director and Artistic Producer at New York's legendary Public Theater, where she worked with the country's major playwrights, directors, and most gifted actors, many of whom are interviewed in this book. She teaches at NYU's Graduate Acting Program and has taught workshops at the Juilliard School, the Actors' Center, Yale Drama School, and Columbia University. She is the recipient of the Casting Society of America's Apple Award, the Villager Award for Excellence in Casting, and two Tony Award Producing nominations. Ms. Tichler founded the Shakespeare Lab, now in its thirteenth year, and she is on the board of directors of New York's Classic Stage Company.

BARRY JAY KAPLAN's work as a playwright has been supported by grants from the Drama League, New York State Council on the Arts, and, through New Dramatists, the Frederick Loewe Foundation and the Cameron Mackintosh Foundation. He is the recipient of the Joe Callaway Award and the Whitfield Cooke Best Play Award for *Bananas and Water*. He is also the author of two bestselling historical novels, *Black Orchid* (with Nicholas Meyer) and *Biscayne*.

ACTORS
AT WORK

ACTORS
AT WORK

Rosemarie Tichler and
Barry Jay Kaplan

FABER AND FABER, INC.

AN AFFILIATE OF FARRAR, STRAUS AND GIROUX

NEW YORK

FABER AND FABER, INC.

An affiliate of Farrar, Straus and Giroux

19 Union Square West, New York 10003

Distributed in Canada by Douglas & McIntyre Ltd.

Printed in the United States of America

First edition, 2007

Library of Congress Cataloging-in-Publication Data

Actors at work / [interviews] by Rosemarie Tichler and Barry Jay Kaplan.— 1st ed.

    p. cm.

ISBN-13: 978-0-86547-955-5 (pbk. : alk. paper)

ISBN-10: 0-86547-955-0 (pbk. : alk. paper)

    1. Acting. 2. Actors — Interviews. I. Tichler, Rosemarie, 1939– II. Kaplan, Barry Jay.

PN2061.A33 2007

792.02'8 — dc22

                                                2007004329

Designed by Cassandra J. Pappas

www.fsgbooks.com

1 3 5 7 9 10 8 6 4 2

For Ellen, Theo, and Harvey
RT

For Ron
BJK

We want to thank our agent, Emily Forland, and our editor, Denise Oswald, for their help in bringing Actors at Work into being. The book, of course, would not exist without the participation of fourteen extraordinary actors. We want especially to thank each of them for their generosity, their unfailing good humor, and their willingness to answer our questions and share their hard-won wisdom about the elusive art of acting.

CONTENTS

FOREWORD

by Mike Nichols

One thing is clear: they do not know how they do it and they don't want to know. Interviews with actors are interesting games of hide-and-seek. When asked about how he did his acting, Paul Muni, the beloved American actor of the 1930s and 1940s, was known for recounting his mother's response when asked how she made latkes: "Well, I clean the kitchen table very carefully. I get my board and scrub that too. Then I put a little flour on it, get out the potatoes, eggs, and all the ingredients. Then I make latkes."

People in the theater love the story about John Gielgud, who was asked by someone, "Any hints you can give me about playing King Lear?" Gielgud said, "Get a small Cordelia." This was excellent advice, since Lear has to carry the dead Cordelia around the stage for an entire scene.

Eileen Atkins was about to do her first play in London, and she asked Ralph Richardson whether he had any advice about acting on the stage. He said, "Try to get a nap in the afternoon."

These stories are not about evasiveness, but about true helpfulness. The secret of acting, if there is one, cannot be told. That is the main thing about it. You can't catch an actor revealing "how I do it." They don't know, and if they did, they would never tell, because certainly that would be the surest way to lose it.

I once congratulated the great French actor Marcel Dalio on a brilliant long take in a movie I was directing, and he said, "Well, I was saying to the makeup man, 'If you are an actor, you have to pray every day for a small miracle, because you can't make it come. You can only pray it will come one more time.'"

Of course, this doesn't mean there's nothing to be learned from great actors. There are things they can tell you. The other actor is everything. In connecting with the others on the stage with you, you are halfway there, and as Phil Hoffman points out, if you are looking Meryl Streep or Vanessa Redgrave in the eye, you are more than halfway there. In that case my advice would be to know your lines very well and keep looking.

There are, of course, some things we know about what actors do. There is the audience. There is no denying that the presence of an audience is important to actors. You won't hear them talking about that either. I am a director, and I get to think about the audience openly: Are we clear? Can the story be followed? Are we telling as much of it as we can? And so on. That is my job, and as part of it, I often think of things the actor is doing as asking unspoken questions: Does this happen to you too? Do you know someone like this? A series of questions in our minds, all of them beginning with, Do you also . . . ?

But no, actors won't talk about that either.

I asked Meryl, "How the hell did you ever think of making Ethel Rosenberg funny?" She said, "Well, you never know what you're going to do till you do it." I don't know a better lesson in acting.

This book is full of similar useful things, but you have to figure them out. That's what makes it so interesting and instructive. In these fourteen conversations, the varied and brilliant actors are speaking not with a journalist who has a list of searching questions, but with two fellow artists who live where they do. Seldom are these performers so open and honest. They reveal how they approach a script, prepare for rehearsal, work with other actors and directors, and work in film or TV versus the stage, and they talk about key roles in their careers. Their varied experiences, differing sensibilities, and ways of working will be a resource, help, and guide to young people who are drawn to the theater and will be fascinating for fans as well. Have a look. You will be richly rewarded.

PREFACE

I fell in love with acting when I was a teenager in the 1950s, watching live television drama and going to the Broadway theater. I watched Kim Stanley, Geraldine Page, Julie Harris, and Rod Steiger, and I was overcome. People I didn't know allowed me to know what they were thinking, and revealed to me their secret passions and their pain. For a young woman whose world was books, this was an extraordinary gift. I saw actors who were truly alive in their work, and they awakened an aliveness in me to another's humanity and to the ridiculousness, sweetness, and horror of living. I knew that writers were the poets and organizers of the theater experience, but the actors were the flesh and blood, the pulsating bearers of the writers' imaginings, and I was hooked. Years later I became a casting director and have been privileged to work with many of the actors in this book. I hope their stories will give young actors information and insight and give the general reader an appreciation and respect for the glorious art and craft of acting.

—Rosemarie Tichler

Because I am a playwright, the participation of the actor is crucial to the realization of my work. I once believed that my plays were actor-proof, written with such care that all any actor had to do was say the words. I was quickly disabused of that notion. What came to fascinate me about actors is that I get to see them at work. When I do it's as if I'm watching one of my dreams come alive before my eyes. And not only do the actors make my dream live, somehow they are able to reveal more to me about what I've written than I knew. They become my partners in telling my story. The better the actor—the ones with wit and imagination and intuition—the better my plays become.

—Barry Jay Kaplan

The book you're about to read is a series of interviews with prominent stage and film actors. We hope the interviews capture the spontaneity of conversation at the same time that they explore the ways in which actors work: how actors approach a role, the ways in which they work with directors and fellow actors, the ways in which they use or don't use their own personal lives in their work, their influences, their idols, their fears.

These interviews with major film and theater artists cover the craft of acting, the uses of training, acting's roots in ordinary life, and the paths to work and success. The actors tell us what they did while they were looking for work and how they auditioned for roles, how they cope with obstacles in the rehearsal process, and how they manage to carve out personal lives at the same time. The focus of the interviews is the job itself of acting.

ACTORS
AT WORK

Marian Seldes

The New York City apartment in which Marian Seldes lives is on Central Park South and has, as one would expect, a magnificent view. The walls of the small balcony are glass, so the view is not impeded from anywhere in the living room. At the time of our interview it is a late afternoon in December, and not only has the light gone but it is raining. Marian opens the door herself, though there is an assistant somewhere in the apartment. She welcomes us into a long, narrow living room oddly bare of paintings. Leaking pipes from the apartment next door have necessitated temporarily removing them, she explains. She guides us to a small table near the terrace, around which she has arranged three chairs, and for a moment we three jockey for positions, each of us deferring to the other. Marian, a disarmingly youthful seventy-eight, is physically imposing on the stage and no less so in person. She is tall and lean, and though modest about her appearance, she has the classic look of someone who was a great beauty in her youth, and she wears her years well and with good humor. Her manner is gentle, thoughtful, witty, and theatrical. Her gestures are eloquent, particularly in the way she uses her long arms to embrace a person or an idea or to describe an entire era of New York theatrical history. She is a child of the city, her father the eminent writer of theater criticism and social history Gilbert Seldes. Her childhood was one of privilege and culture; the great theater figures of the day were in and out of the Seldes household on a regular basis.

We'd like to cover how you started, your beginnings, who you worked with, how you got here. And we'll talk about the working part of it—the approach to roles. So, to begin. You grew up in New York?

I was born here, and my birth in the theater was early because my father was a theater critic. And so going to the theater, which is so difficult for young people now, was simple. I assume it must be like how film is. I could go by myself to movies and things, but I saw more theater than films. The theater was a family thing. Sadly, I look around now, and I don't see families at the theater, because they don't want to go or can't afford to.

Did school encourage your theatrical interests?

I think one of my great faults is not having a lot of ambition. I'll explain that later to you. Our schooling was based on the great teachings of Maria Montessori. Students were allowed to develop at their own rate, in a sense. You had to get the work done, but if it suited you to get it done earlier in the month or later, and you had what was called a unit card, you just kept up to date. I loved that. I loved the discipline of that. And I say that because I love the discipline of the theater. I love checking in and being there and doing it.

It seems like the opposite of discipline.

Well, it's giving the responsibility of it over to you.

But it's a risk, isn't it?

It is. My brother, Timothy, did not enjoy it as much as I did. I don't think he would say these words at all, although he got a very good education there. But their way of teaching history courses was to do all the reading and all the essays and whatever, and then we always wrote a play. Every year you did something that you created from the raw material. I'm talking about this at length because theater and writing and learning were all one thing to me then and still are. When I read a play, I love to read a book about the era the play was in. I don't have to. I love to. I want to look at the pictures the real people saw.

Did you also do contemporary plays there?

They were all about history. Or you would do Shakespeare. I'm sorry you missed my Shylock.

Did you see this as something you could do for your life?

I saw it as something I wanted to do. I lacked a certain confidence in the way I looked. Actresses were these beautiful creatures. Katharine Cornell. Somebody radiant.

Did you relate what you saw when you went to the theater to what you were doing in school?

No. That was private, wonderful. So much more. I had a marvelous father. Those blue books on the shelves there are all the issues of *The Dial*, the great culture magazine of the twenties. You can imagine the people that came in and out of the apartment. My father knew everyone. The entire 1920s with my mother and father were golden times. And I think both Timothy and I would tell you that we liked their friends almost more than our friends. Because the people were so wonderful with children. And when we grew up, they were still our friends.

And did you think about training? That that's what would be needed?

I knew I would go to school. And I didn't really want to go to college. I wanted to learn. This is going to sound awful, but I knew at the age I was that I had to prepare myself to be in the theater and on the stage on Broadway. I knew instinctively it would take me some time to settle, look, and be like an actress, because I was quite shy about that kind of thing. And also there was one part of me that wanted dancing. I did study ballet when I was still at Dalton. I wasn't a good enough dancer to be a dancer, but I don't regret one second. I loved it so. I studied at the School of American Ballet at the time of Balanchine. The first time I was ever on a real stage, a New York stage, was at the old Metropolitan Opera House in 1942. The great choreographer Michel Fokine had just died that August. It was September. I don't know how that was arranged, but someone from the Metropolitan got in touch with the school and said they needed people to be seen in the street area of *Pétrouchka*. I was not supposed to go out on a school night. I was also rather disciplined at home, and I never asked to, because that was the rule. Something made me call my mother, and she said, "Of course you must do it." So that night I went down to the Metropolitan Opera. Gorgeous, gorgeous old theater. People told us what to do and everything of course. Among the other people in the crowd dancing in the background were Jerry Robbins and the impresario Sol Hurok dressed as a bear. Everyone wanted to be there on the stage to honor him. I was just transported.

Why did you feel you weren't good enough to dance?

You *know*. You know when you look around. And I believe that even though I was always so very strong, I was not strong enough to be a classical ballerina.

You played Isadora Duncan in a play, didn't you?

Yes, but that's not dance. That I could excel at because after Dalton I went to the Neighborhood Playhouse and the great teacher of dance was Martha Graham. She had as much influence on me as a dancer as she did as an actress. I mean equally powerful. I thought her use of the body on the stage was as thrilling as anything I had ever seen in the theater. And there was a dancer that I loved—Nora Kaye— who did the ballets, and she too had a kind of clarity and strength in using the body that never occurred to me as an actress.

I have been socked in the gut by Martha Graham, so I know where it comes from. It comes from inside. So I'm telling you . . . I certainly was prepared. I had been prepared by wonderful teachers. I had one of the greatest acting teachers, Sanford Meisner. Just an amazing, amazing teacher. And lucky for me, because all my dreams of doing Shakespeare and the Greeks were just laughable to him. He wanted me to do realistic plays. I mean none of this grand gesture sort of thing. And this was good because the theater was changing and people didn't want to see Greek plays or Shakespeare unless they came over from another country. The greatest influence Meisner had on me was to disenchant me of my "idea" of what acting was. Meisner's approach to teaching and to acting was just based on the truth in the situation the playwright gave you. But for the whole first year of the Neighborhood Playhouse training, you hardly used any scripts at all. And all my acting—I was a high school student—had been based on plays, not on exercises, and not on any kind of talking about acting. So it was a marvelous and scary shock to me that my idea of acting was, to put it bluntly, wrong.

What were you scared of?

I thought I was perhaps in the wrong place, but it didn't take me very long to be so fascinated by him as a teacher—and so fascinated by him as a person—to simply let my old-fashioned ideas go at the age of sixteen or seventeen and embrace the way he was teaching. Which was not only to find the truth in the situation, but to depend on your partner. Now, it's fifty, sixty, seventy years later, and people will say to me sometimes, "Ah, but the way you listen . . ." But what else could I do? Apparently, there's a kind of actor who is involved in something else, who doesn't depend on his partner. But for me it's essential. I can't think of a partner I didn't adore acting with, man or woman. And when I became a teacher at Juilliard, I could pass this on to the students—the dependence on each other. Of course, in an ideal situation you would have a company that worked together. We don't have it in America, and we don't seem to want it. We want companies that are pulled together quickly with famous people and attractive people, and we want the theater "business" to thrive and sell tickets. But when you're learning to act and learning to be part of the theater, those things really have nothing to do with the training. I think it was something I did instinctively, because in life, and as an actress, I depend on people for everything. If I can't look in your eyes when we talk, then I can't talk to you. And I'll be hurt if you don't listen to me and won't converse with me. What I had to get rid of was a sort of search for beauty and elegance and speaking beautifully and moving beautifully and feeling immense tragic thoughts. I'm making fun of myself because I have to, but that was my dream. And do you know, later in my life, when I did quite a lot of comedy, it's sending up that part of myself that makes people laugh.

That's brilliant.

So I can even use the very thing that kept me back. Meanwhile, at the very time I was being taught by Sandy Meisner, I was being taught by an equally great teacher, and that was Martha Graham. And in her class, where there were no words, I was able to hold on to that other dream I had, of that kind of power, the reason to listen to the actor beyond the part he's playing. Something that is so compelling that you don't know how to describe it, and of course, that's what people are talking about when they talk about Brando or Laurette Taylor. They can't describe it, but even when you're in a restaurant and looking around at the people, or sitting in the park or whatever you're doing, someone interests you and other people don't. And it's just a basic human attraction to something. And when that attraction is powerful in the theater, in a play, it makes the experience you expect go up to another level. And we've all seen it, and we've all had performances we've adored. And I don't necessarily mean the famous actors that we go to that don't disappoint us. I mean you go to the theater and someone you've never seen before is that person, and you begin to look at that person and be fascinated by that person. One more thing to say about this kind of fascination is that the playwright had better love the character and love writing the character and love you being interested in the character. When you begin your career, if you don't have interesting characters, everything I'm saying is almost without merit, because you simply must fulfill, you simply must solve a kind of everyday problem—who are you, why are you there, what do you want, how are you going to get it? With a great part, it's so much more than that; it's living a life in front of an audience. Nothing can compare to that.

You are a major transitional figure in the American theater in acting because you came from the classical tradition of Katharine Cornell and

Judith Anderson and then you went to the naturalism of Meisner and then went on.

I don't see myself that way. When you say it, I can see what people now call the journey, and I can see that had I not been willing to learn, and were I not inspired by actresses and actors, I would never have been as lucky as I am now. I mentioned Brando, also Geraldine Page and Kim Stanley and Colleen Dewhurst, and now there's Cherry Jones—people who can simply take a piece of material and make it real and not give up the things I love that are still wonderful and beautiful and strange and imaginative. Because I think, to mention Meisner again, one of the great things about his teaching was that if you followed what he was asking you to do, it freed your own imagination. If you simply look for the truth and follow the truth in the situation, then there's no struggle in a sense to make the audience believe. You believe it, they'll believe it, and at the same time, you are free to move the way you move, to touch a piece of furniture or a flower or something that's in the room, or your own clothing or the face of your partner, in a way that only you could do. I never remember a situation in which a really fine director told you how to do something like that. The behavior is yours.

And he gave you just the tools to search for the truth . . .

Exactly. The perfect way of saying.

And it frees you to use those tools to find your way.

And to be available to your partner. And truly, truly when the evening is over and you've played the play, you've played it for the other actor as much as for the audience. And I'm an actress who adores the audience. I want them there. It would never occur to me to criticize an audience. The fact that they get there amazes me, and that they get there in a group and they stay there and, except in very rare circumstances, they follow the play and want the play.

So when you studied with this great teacher of naturalistic acting, it was at a time of a theatrical revolution.

Exactly. The theater was changing. And the people I grew up seeing—Katharine Cornell, Judith Anderson, Ina Claire—they were going away. And their kind of acting was going away. To me, all that acting had enormous reality. Because the plays they were in were quite elegant plays by Behrman, Philip Barry. Judith Anderson . . . I thought she was great. And all the femininity of the women on the stage. It's hard to speak for another actress of course, but I felt the certainty in her acting. There was no question, there was no other way to do it than the way she did it, and she had an amazing voice, beautiful diction, and a marvelous body. She certainly depended on all of us in the play, and I mean this as a great compliment, not a criticism, but she could have done it alone.

My impression was that the commitment to her choices was so fierce that it was a total world.

And remember: Medea is in a sense a madwoman, and the other people in the play, except for the nurse and the children, are people who have betrayed her, or will betray her, and she's fighting for her life. And Judith just did that so completely and so utterly focused, and I never saw her give a bad performance. Ever. She was great. I played Electra to her Clytemnestra, and in that too she was extraordinary. There, it was a different person, not the madwoman at all, but someone in jeopardy all the time. And she was extraordinary in that too. I saw her in *The Chalk Garden*. I wish I'd seen her in everything. I saw her do Lady Macbeth. I saw her do Olga in *The Three Sisters*, and there was no greatness in Olga. Olga was that headmistress, that sister. I thought she was absolutely wonderful. To be with Cornell and Judith Anderson—I not only dreamed of the kind of actress I wanted to be, but I certainly felt that my career would be in the classical theater. And when I woke up to the idea that those kinds of plays were not being produced, my gratitude toward the Meisner teaching was increased a thousand times.

Who were the other actors you studied alongside?

What's so odd to me is . . . I'm seventy-eight. Richard Boone was in my class, and Margaret Feury, who became a beautiful teacher in Los Angeles. And Kathleen Maguire. And I can't believe I'm saying that to you, because we were all in class together. The person who became my lasting and close friend, Anne Meacham, was brilliant. She did *Hedda Gabler* on Broadway. I saw her performance many times. I thought she was remarkable. And I thought she was making the same transition from classical theater to naturalism that I was. She had an idea of theater, that it must be grounded in reality. Even today, there's no script that I receive that I don't send to her. She was wonderful, fearless.

What does it mean when you say an actress is fearless?

It means that if something occurs to them in rehearsal, they are strong enough to do it, to show it. It can be embarrassing. It can be so overdone that it's embarrasing, and it can be so reserved that it doesn't mean anything. And a wonderful director can see where it's going and say, "Try that, try that, try that." Encourage. That's what teaching is too. We'll talk about teaching sometime. It's encouraging the impulse, the very basic impulses. So that the brilliant thing about Anne Meacham's Hedda was that she was so clever that her husband, whom she didn't love, and Judge Brack, who was always judging her, and the silly aunt who comes in and takes off her hat, and you believed Hedda as real; you can't go too far when you're Hedda. She's not mad, she's not crazy, she's just on fire. And that's what Anne did. It was quite wonderful. So she and all those others, that was my class.

What was your first play on the New York stage?

Medea with Judith Anderson. I was a black servant. You couldn't do it now, because you would have a black actor. And of course I understudied the chorus. The head of the Neighborhood Playhouse sent me to see John Gielgud, who was acting in *Love for Love*. She said, "You can see him right after the matinee." I'd already seen him in *The Importance of Being Earnest*, one of the best productions I'd ever seen in my life. I adored it. And she said, "He'll expect you." I got as dressed up as I knew how. I think I was seventeen. And so I got all ready and I went to see him. It was at the Royale Theatre. I went through an alley, and no one was there. But I was on time for the play. I'd forgotten that the Theatre Guild, which was producing this, gave their matinees on Thursday. Every other company did them on Wednesday. And I was twenty-four hours too soon. So I went back the next day. Oh, I remember that day. It was so wonderful. Gielgud was so generous as a person and so knowing what it's like to be on trial. He asked me to sit down, and he said, "Before we speak of the future, tell me about your father." And he'd read *The Seven Lively Arts* and he wanted to talk about my father. And he wanted to know what Greek parts I'd played. I said, "I've workshopped them, but I've never been in a Greek play." He said, "Is that your dream?" And he paid attention and took me seriously. I didn't have to audition. He just took me. The production got under way that summer, and they sent for me. I had hoped to get the part of the youngest woman in the chorus. And Robert Whitehead, the great, great producer, this was his first production. He did it with another man named Oliver Rea. A very very nice man. And Oliver had just fallen in love with a young pretty actress. So I didn't play that part. But I was happy about it because the rehearsals were absorbing. I didn't mind, because I could observe and figure out how to do it my own way. And watching Judith Anderson create this part that Robinson Jeffers had adapted for her to do—it was wonderful. Gielgud, by the way, did not want to play Jason. He did it because she had played Gertrude to his Hamlet, which *she* had not wanted to do. "She did that for me," he said, "so I'll do this for her." That left an impression on me.

I have seen you in parts where I thought that Marian doesn't need to do that. She could be doing other more interesting parts.

I know. Because of commitment. It makes you happy. If you really want to do theater. If you don't want to, go out and do something else.

Did you also want to be in the movies?

No. It never occurred to me. I was in an accident when I was about six years old and I had scars on my face, and I never considered being in a movie, much less being a star. The scars were much more noticeable then. I should have said that to you sooner, when I told you that's how I looked. I never talk about it to anybody, but I felt that people could see it. But I don't think people see it. I remember going downtown in a taxicab with Harold Clurman to see Charlie Chaplin in *Monsieur Verdoux*, and he said, "Can I touch your face without bothering you?" He said, "You have powder on your nose." And he tried to get it off. And it was the scar. He didn't mean anything, but those aren't things you just get over.

What was the step after Medea?

When *Medea* closed, I went to summer stock and then got a telegram from the Whitehead office saying would I like to go on tour in *Medea*.

I didn't have an agent, so I sent a wire back: IS IT A SPEAKING PART? And apparently he broke down laughing. Most of learning comes from being directed, from being able to be directed. No one tells you that. To be able to take an idea and run with it. I did all the understudy rehearsals for the whole year we were on tour. Oh, it was wonderful to do it. There was a lot more work available for an actress like me in those days. I worked all the time. But I worked without ambition. I didn't try to get parts. People just called me because they were at the theater. And they said, "Marian, would you like to do this or that?" Eventually, I did get an agent. He was in the class above me at Neighborhood Playhouse. His name was George Morris. And he was so dear. His phrase was "What will be will be." And he was wonderful. I stayed with him I think until he died. He died too young. And then I tried a few other people. I don't think agents have ever gotten me jobs in the theater.

Was there a moment or a role where you thought you clicked?

I'll answer you, but I hope not to embarrass myself. I knew in high school. And "click" is such a funny word. You know it's in the wonderful *Cat on a Hot Tin Roof*, when Brick always hears the "click." I know in rehearsal that I'm getting there. And I know in rehearsal when I'm good. People come and look at me funny, like, That's it. I do know.

You got some of your fame, if you will, from A Delicate Balance. *Was there something extraordinary about that experience?*

In *A Delicate Balance*, I didn't have that much confidence. It was about the writer of that part. That Julia is some part. I was stunned and thrilled that they even noticed me. But I think the answer to your question was *Painting Churches*. Because that was a leading part with a glorious actor, Donald Moffat. And written by a poet, Tina Howe. I think that's the first time I was ever called Seldes in a review. I loved it. I really loved that part. I loved that play. It was my dream of what an actress could do. I think *Chalk Garden* was good for me too. Because it was such a beautiful play. But it didn't set me up at all.

Did you think in those terms?

Yes. I wanted to be a great actress or I didn't want to be an actress. I wanted to be a great ballerina and couldn't. I want to excel and it makes me very nervous and anxious.

But isn't that ambition?

Yes, but I didn't show it. It's how you use yourself to the fullest. And not to be, as I was in *Deathtrap*, offstage for the second act. I had to be offstage. Whereas when I was in *Equus* I was onstage all night, I was perfectly happy.

You gave a record number of performances in Deathtrap. *Tell me why you stayed with it so long.*

Well, I'll tell you why. And I'll tell you honestly. I was not offered a single play, a single television show during that period. I had an agent. I taught at Juilliard and loved it. My class would be over at six o'clock and I'd go to the theater. That was it, and I was in bliss. Between *Deathtrap* and *Equus* I was on Broadway for eight years continuously. Extraordinary plays. And all the time I was teaching. Back in those years I didn't see parts that I—I don't see myself in parts that I can't completely play. Do you know what I mean? I don't see something and think, Oh I wish I'd done that. I see other things. I once went to see Geraldine Page in a play called *Midsummer*. And the character she played had children. She came home from a restaurant and took food out of her handbag. It was food she should've eaten, but instead she brought it home for her children. And it was so true and so beautifully done. I remember thinking, I can't do that. I might as well give up. That's how beautiful it was. I see what's good, what's wonderful. Then of course I saw everything. But I don't think that's my part. I do know that. So long as you can say that that is extraordinary acting, but you still know what you can touch. I tried very hard to do different things and to explore where I would not expect to go. There was another play I was offered recently where I first thought of the actress who created the role. I just thought, God, I can't take that from her. And the other thing I thought was, I don't know if I have the strength. You see. It's a world, and I don't know how to do it. I don't know. Coming into it late, the cast all know what they're doing, and I'd be standing there. But on the other hand, I turned down a play this morning because I thought I was too old for it and that the part should be much sexier, much more dying for sex. Your body has a lot to do with that. I'm not dying for sex. And if I did it, I would be less than the part. And I just didn't want to do that. A two-character play. Wonderful. You're onstage all night, acting and acting. But I just knew it wasn't right. And then on another level I thought that the characters were feckless and brought nothing to my understanding of another human being.

So for you a part must be—

It must be a real experience, something you won't forget. Now, I won't say I got it every time. But pretty much if you were to go down the characters I've played and the playwright and the play, you'd say, Oh I wish I'd seen that. That's interesting. There are a few odd ones. I wanted to work with Herman Shumlin. I knew Herman Shumlin had directed *Little Foxes*. So I got to be in a very uninteresting play, but I got to work with Herman Shumlin. Oh, I just loved him. I just loved this man. And I learned a lot. During the run, he called me up one night and said, "Marian, how are you?" And I said, "Fine." "Not ill?" "No." "Then why did you turn the page of the newspaper on a different line than you usually do?" I never worked with anyone like that—so precise.

How do you do it?

It can be just as fresh if it's on the same line. But my god. It was amazing. And if someone is wonderful and talented, making you take two steps and turn is fine. If they have no talent, you just say, Well, I'll take these two steps and turn, and then tomorrow at rehearsal I'll just do what I should do.

Is that how you work with a director who turns out to be not very interesting?

Yes. You just bring it in better. I've never had an argument with a director on how to do something. I just find a way to do it that isn't against what he's told me but is bearable for me. And most of it is physical. Many people come on the stage, to a place they've never been before, and sit down. Even if they're not supposed to look around, a person looks around. Don't they? You did when you came in here. So when a director says come in and sit down, if I don't think the character is in a hurry, I think, Well, I've got to find something that makes her hurry. So I have this thing that makes her do it faster. You see, I think we never finish the learning process of acting. Ever, in fact. As I get older and older and older, I feel I have more and more to learn. And no matter how much you prepare before the first rehearsal of a play, if you are not open to the director's concept of your character, it will be a confrontation rather than a learning experience. That is not to say that I always agree with the director, but I don't ever argue with one. I don't think there's time and I don't think it's valuable to the other actor who's in a scene with you. I think that is part of what we call homework. You've got to go home and think, Ah, I didn't think of it this way. I don't agree with it. Why did he say that? And I'll tell you that if you really look into the play again and into your part again, and maybe think more about the part than you playing the part, you can usually accommodate what the director wants.

And that's something that's crucial for an actor.

Yes. If you don't believe that the director is the leader, then you shouldn't be in a play, you should do solo acting. Because it isn't one person. The greatest plays are about a lot of people.

Have you ever had a time when whatever you had to have the character do was opposed to what you believed?

Yes. But I did it anyway. And I thought, A lot of the people who were in this play—it was quite recent—were in this play because I'd said I'd do it. And if I say I'm not doing it, it isn't as if they can't replace me. We all can be replaced. Everyone can be replaced. We know that. But I just couldn't do it. I feel that when you're in a play, it's against the gods of the theater to complain about it. Get out of it or shut up. Don't say, I hate this person. No. Make it work.

In the world of the theater there's so much complaining.

This is a life that's so much better than anything. And really if you don't like your job, really you do have to get away. Because you don't know it, but you're making it hard for someone else who may be working in the next cubbyhole.

Can you give an idea of how a director works with you and helps you be your best?

Yes. By suggesting other ways to do it. In a way that is uncritical. That is helpful. And sometimes it can be a word. Oh, here's a piece about George Cukor. He said—he used to work his jaw so funny. I think he had trouble with his teeth. He used to say, "Marian, I'm going to tell you something I'd tell Kate Hepburn. Don't do anything you wouldn't do, do you understand?" And I did understand. He wants me to be me. I never had another moment of doubt in the whole rehearsal or during the performances, and they fired him. But of course David Selznick fired him from *Gone With the Wind*. Oh, you're around such funny things.

In terms of how you approach a role . . . You're sent the script, right? And you say, "I'd love to do it." So when you start rehearsal, what do you come into it with?

I've already read the whole play. All the parts. But not having decided how to play the part. At the Public and with Tony Kushner, I read lots of things just for him. Because he asked me to. And certainly when he directed Ellen McLaughlin's *Helen*. And I know what I want to do. But I don't know how it's going to come out. And sometimes I wait until the first reading, and I think, I wonder what she will sound like. And it comes out with what she sounds like, and I know it. I can't explain it. If I come in there with the performance—I don't understand that. Even in a great part. Even in a classic part. You do have the idea. But you have to see what the whole thing is.

Have you worked with actors who work differently from you? I mean, if someone does come in with the performance?

That's fine with me.

But they're never going to respond to what you do, because they've already got their role. What do you do?

You go out for coffee. You do something. Because that's it. You've just got to. There's a way. There's always a way. And then, in my other life in television and film, there's no complaining and I do everything I'm told. I'm like a marionette. Do this, do that. I have no control. And I'm just very careful with what they do with the back of my hair. Because I say the shot's going to be over my shoulder a lot—and it is— in that the focus is wherever the camera eye goes, your eyes go. I don't like to do anything if I don't have a good line. Just be still.

In film, how do you work?

Live television I loved. It was like theater. I did a lot of *Studio One*'s. I did a lot of matinee theaters in Hollywood. I worked with a lot of extraordinary people. I worked with Fay Bainter, who was in *Lysistrata*, my father's version. I worked with Frances Farmer, that beautiful actress. I worked with these people, these dreams I never would have worked with. And it was live. And so the urgency was always there. And I began to get good parts. As soon as it went to film, it stopped. Then I was always a murderess, or someone who was picked up in a stagecoach. But lucrative. No complaints. I didn't have to do it, but I did. I didn't live in Hollywood for more than three years. My first husband got a job working for CBS out there, and there was no question that I go. And when I came back, people knew me. They didn't know my name, but they knew me. I'd be in a store, and they'd say, "Oh, you smiled." Because I never smiled on film. Killer people are sad or neurotic or—if I did a *Murder She Wrote*—you know I did it. Just think of black hair.

You have such a wonderful attitude toward auditioning.

Oh, I love it.

People say no, don't audition.

It's an opening night for me. I love it. A chance to do my work. And you don't know who's sitting there. You don't know if the young man who checked you in or the young woman who took your coat will be the head of the studio. You don't know if it's the director or a casting person. You never know. And if you don't do it, it comes back to you. Learn it, do it, make up for it. Put on something funny.

So many actors of all ages complain about the audition process—about how dehumanizing it is. How rude directors are.

They are rude in the subway too. People are people. In every profession. And you'd ask about an actor who's hard to work with or a casting person who makes you feel like dirt—you have to do better than that. You have to. Or else it is so sickening. But again not in the theater. I've very rarely been treated badly in an audition in the theater.

In television or film?

Yes. It's so sad, it's so sad. And why shouldn't they yell at you? They're twenty-three years old. They've never sat in a theater.

Let's go back to Painting Churches.

I had to audition for that three times. I think they wanted Nancy Marchand, and you could see why. She was a huge TV star at the time. And I was so thrilled that Frances Conroy played the daughter. Marvelous actress. You know she brings her own originality to that part in *Six Feet Under*. I don't want to watch *Six Feet Under* unless I see her. I think she's remarkable. And in that play *The Lady from Dubuque* she had cancer. I could almost not look at the stage. I also did it with Elizabeth McGovern. It certainly crossed my mind that if that part had been given to me when I was in my late teens, early twenties, I'd have had a different career. I'd have made a mark somehow on that part. I loved it. I loved that part. Tina Howe said she's writing another play with a part for me. Time is of the essence. Let's go. Let's get into rehearsal.

Can you speak of the affinity you have for Albee's characters—and maybe how you approached the role in Three Tall Women?

I think he's such an extraordinary writer, whether you're fortunate enough to create a part or it is a script already presented. In our modern theater, there are a lot of examples where you will talk to an actor or an actress and he or she will say, "Well I improvise, and I actually use what I say." No, no. The blueprint is there, and once again, it is your task to find in the text what he saw when he was writing it. I think the greatest experience you can have as an actor is to be in a play with a living playwright, and know that he's there. It is the most daunting and the most satisfying thing to do. Daunting because perhaps you will never get what he saw when he wrote the play. Perhaps you'll never get exactly what he wanted, and you'll never know that. But there's always for me a sense of—no matter how many times I've played the part—if the playwright comes and sees it, again, a sense of, Is this really what he wanted? I feel very shy to admit that, but I feel it. But that's not your concern when you are rehearsing a new play. You just go for it, and you must make choices. Edward is so professional, he will not speak to you and tell you what to do or ask you what to do. He will speak to the director, and you'll get the note from the director.

Do you feel that the connection between his love of your work and your love of his is that the architecture of his plays is classical and he cares so much about language that you don't feel shy to speak well?

Yes. I mean, early in my career, especially when I started in television, I would in a sense mess up my speech so that they believed I was an American. Taxi drivers used to ask me if I was British. A play is like a score. You must say those notes, and they have a shape and they have a music, and when you get it, get the rhythm of his speech, it's like flying. In the plays of Albee's that I've done, I feel this terror before I go on, and the minute I hit the stage, it's like flying. It takes care of itself, the part is there. I don't think there's a part he's written that isn't a wonderful part. I mean his plays, I'm not thinking for myself. I mean, he amazes me. He just amazes me. He's written a play called *Occupant*, about the amazing brilliant American sculptor Louise Nevelson, and it's a two-character play between a man who is talking to her—and that man, he's not called Edward Albee, but you know it's Edward—and this amazing, articulate, brilliant, egotistical woman. I talk about it this way because I've done it twice with him, and he'll never play the part, of course, but for benefits and things we've done it, and it's, well, I'm almost blushing for him because Edward is not what we think of as an actor. But I've also played scenes with him. I did *Counting the Ways* for him in Washington at a PEN benefit. And he's of course a marvelous actor because he has nothing to prove. And this goes back to the acting thing. And someday we're going to do it in New York. I don't know where or when, but we're going to do it. It was written four or five, six years ago, and it was rehearsed—but never opened—with the wonderful Anne Bancroft. Her final illness was what prevented it from opening.

I saw that!

You were one of the few people. Don't you think it's an amazing piece of work?

Amazing.

And all it is, is a man and a woman. And you know he doesn't up and write about a real person. I mean of course he wrote about Bessie Smith, but he creates these people who are now in the lexicon of American life. You talk about Martha in *Virginia Woolf*, and she represents an entire kind of woman in America. And you ask me about *Three Tall Women*, which of course was about a real woman, his adoptive mother, and that play, which is so special, had absolutely universal appeal to people. It was their mother, or their grandmother, or the woman who influenced them most in their life. It is such a special play, it's so focused on a kind of woman in America today or then, and it's, I think, a very daring play.

I always thought you played her with great abandon and fun.

Well, I think all his people are witty too. Even when they're suffering, they're funny. And I played two parts in that play. The middle-aged woman is the part I started in, and then the brilliant Myra Carter simply felt she could not play the old woman anymore. It was pulling her apart, and I appreciated it because her performance was so cruelly real, her use of herself in the part was so amazing. Well, it eventually fell to me to play it. I went all across the country playing that part, and that's why I feel I can say how the audience has reacted to it. And to think of a play without a famous star actor going all across the country in the big cities, it's because of Edward Albee. They love to see what he writes. He's a star playwright, and it's very hard to be that in America now. And there were times when they weren't interested in him, and he kept writing plays. He has a new play now. He's always writing.

When you began to teach, did you find yourself repeating things that you had learned as a student?

I didn't think that ever, but of course I did. I am everything everyone taught me. John Houseman at Juilliard didn't ask how I would do it or what I would do. I knew how to teach.

As a teacher, what kind of things about your technique were you able to bring to the students? Or didn't you work that way?

I think what I brought to a class was a sense that it was all about them. I used to let them, whenever I could, choose the scenes they would do, because I wanted them to read plays. You've got to learn how to read a play if you're going to be an actor. And it's not an easy thing to learn how to do. The only way to do it is to do it. I think that my students knew, and still know, that I trusted their instincts more than mine, that I gave them faith and confidence in themselves. I don't know how to work if someone destroys my confidence. Or destroys my confidence in the piece of work we're doing. It just destroys me. But encouragement is very important. Of course they all want to be actors, they've made up their minds. But you can hurt that, you can make it harder for them to be even student actors if they don't have the sense that the possibility is always there. I never had a student that I didn't believe could grow. Well of course Juilliard was a wonderful school. They had to audition for the school; they had probably done quite a lot of acting before they went to the school. And they were young men and women, they weren't kids anymore.

You are known for that part of your teaching work—the kindness and the encouragement and the safety that you brought to the room. Frances Conroy told us about a scene she was doing for you from Mary Stuart, and she couldn't be a queen, so you—

I remember it perfectly. It was actually the scene in *Elizabeth the Queen* between Mary and Elizabeth, and the two actresses had brought candles and the candles were burning and the wax was coming off the candles. I threw my aunt's mink coat toward Franny, and of course the wax got all over it, and I didn't care. I saw her transform. Sometimes I was able to just say something at the right time, while they were acting. I would say, "Kill her, kill her" or, "Go after her, do something physical." And they would. They knew I would do this occasionally, and sometimes I would just sit there and never say a word. But you have no idea what people can do. And we are talking about someone who is so talented, and her growth as an actress is enormous. Henry Stram was the same way. These are people who just had to be actors and who still amaze me when I go to see them. But I was always careful because I thought, This is perfect, this student and me. I say to my students before I begin with them, "If I ever say something that I think is funny to make you laugh and it hurts you, tell me. I would never hurt you. So you tell me." Because you know sometimes people say something, and you get a big laugh from the crowd, and you see someone go, Ohhhh.

One of your former students told me that when she was in class, students would be doing some scene that was just terrible, and you would go over and whisper something in their ears and they would be brilliant. So what did you say?

It was always different. But I could see what they were playing at, and I'd let them go a long time. You know when it's not working. And they know. And they think, Will she ever stop this thing? And just as a painting teacher or an artist might say it needs more red—as simple as that. And ah yes—right there, that was the place to be better, or whatever. I can find a way to tell you what to do. And I'll take your arm, and I'll take you away from the other people so you're not being criticized, you're being helped. And you can't wait to get back into it. Because the people there are all talented. So I felt that everyone who was in this class I owe. They don't owe. I've got to get it, make it like— maybe it comes from dancing—if you work on the muscle, you don't think about it anymore. You don't say, Oh, I'm making a lovely ges- ture when I dance. The audience would go out of the theater. But if you include it in the character, it's thrilling. And that's what I would do. And I would go to see their other classes too, see where they were having trouble—possibly speech. They come from all over the coun- try now to give four years at Juilliard. It's extraordinary.

Is four years too much?

Maybe it is in a world that constantly worships youth, that says, Get on, get famous, you're so pretty, I'm about to get a movie. Two years doesn't feel so much. And I remember I was very young, too young for my class. But it didn't matter. I learned so much from watching other people. I loved to go to rehearsal and watch. Of course I wanted to play, but I love to watch people rehearse.

What do you learn from watching actors rehearse?

If I'm in a play and I can put my attention on the other actors in re- hearsal when I'm not in the scene, I can learn a lot about the director and what we're going for. Because it's not focused on me. Being a teacher and directing two or three plays a year when I was at Juilliard taught me so much about rehearsal. And of the responsibility the di- rector has to everyone in the play. I used to try, particularly when I had the first-year students at Juilliard, the incoming class, to work with someone every day. I tried always to involve them and to let them work every day. I tried to do as many scenes in a scene class as I could and then send them away to work on them and bring them back, and when they would come back, of course, I would just—we would all just watch them. And I could look around at the faces of my students and see that they were learning from their fellow students. And that's what I do in rehearsal too. I can learn from that.

I see that. I never thought of that. No one's mentioned it.

And I'm going to say something wicked too. I've never felt this in my professional career since I came to work in New York City, but in summer stock I sometimes felt it. When you do six or seven different plays every year and different actors come in from the movies and television, you can also learn what not to do, what is destructive, what is selfish, what kind of behavior turns the rehearsal into a mockery. And I think that every actor has the responsibility to make the rehearsal work. We have a lot of things we must do, and just to come in and act your part, to me it's not enough. If you believe in the theater, you have to make the theater better wherever you are—if it's in a classroom or a rehearsal or an audition. You have to make the other person feel okay. Theater is my real life, my real life is theater. It's almost equal. You know, I can't walk down the street without being fascinated by someone or something, even if it's a dog. Sandy Meisner was always telling us to look at animals.

In your work and in your teaching and in your life, you do seem to embody the sense of the ideal of what the theater could be.

I want to. That's what I've always wanted.

Billy Crudup

★

The office we've borrowed for the interview with Billy Crudup is on the sixteenth floor of the building that houses Actors' Equity. It is a corner office with tall windows looking west and south, at the intersection of Broadway and Forty-sixth Street. The setting sun is just visible between buildings, and when it is gone completely, the lights flickering below us on Broadway take on a technicolor clarity that seems perfect for the occasion. Billy Crudup arrives early for the interview. At age thirty-five, just ten years since he starred in *Arcadia* at Lincoln Center and walked away with a handful of awards, he is at an enviable stage of his career, balancing starring roles in film and onstage. This evening he is wearing a fur-trimmed blue parka, jeans, a plaid shirt, a T-shirt, and a sweatshirt. In his looks, manner, and dress, he resembles a graduate student at Columbia, just out of class and rushing to an interview with his thesis adviser. Before we begin talking, he takes a moment to bring out his PalmPilot and show us a picture of his year-old son. He smiles as we remark on the child's adorableness. Billy's face at that moment, which movie reviewers have often described as chiseled, is softer and friendlier. Then he flings his backpack down, throws off his coat, and takes a chair at the head of the long table. Throughout our conversation he speaks with the confidence of a man who knows he's good at what he does. He rarely hesitates, though he occasionally lets a question hang in the air while he considers his answer. His answers are articulate and spontaneous. He is a professional actor who loves acting, takes his work seriously, has thought a great deal about it, and is eager to do well what he is there to do. On this night, it's conversation.

Did you see something as a child, a performance in a movie or a play that made you think, I want to do that?

I saw Fisher Stevens in *Brighton Beach Memoirs*, and I was very impressed with his talent and with his confidence. I remember Michael J. Fox in the *Back to the Future* movies. I kind of wanted to be him—not necessarily that I wanted to give that performance, but I wanted to be popular like he was, and entertaining and funny. And I saw *Fences* with Courtney Vance and James Earl Jones. I still have all my Playbills. I was starstruck at the theater. When I started to act more regularly as an undergraduate, I started to focus more on actors like Daniel Day-Lewis and William Hurt and Meryl Streep. One of the things I liked about Daniel Day-Lewis and William Hurt was their ability to be surprising. And not just in terms of their work in a film, but the characters they were developing were surprising to me. I never knew exactly what I was going to get. And I appreciated that transformational quality. And Meryl Streep obviously is one of our seminal actors, period, also with respect to being able to transform. And I think that was exciting to me—being able to be so expressive.

Because you saw them as transformational, did you feel that there was some craft that you needed to learn?

There was something about just being *able* to do it that made me want to do it. When I was in high school, in each class there was inevitably some point at which you would perform, whether it was to get up front and read a book report, or maybe in social studies classes, where you would have to impersonate somebody from history and do some kind of performance. In my senior year, there was an English class I was taking in which we were asked to memorize the "to be or not to be" soliloquy. And for whatever reason, I could internalize much more than anybody and much quicker. It was kind of impressive to people. And I liked that I had something impressive to offer. So I think that sort of piqued my interest. It wasn't just that I was like, Hmmm, must join creative forces with the Bard. I don't remember what I was doing with "to be or not to be." I might have been just fucking around. I wasn't a nervous wreck the way other students were who were standing in front of people performing it. So that was another thing.

What were you getting from it early on?

People told me I was good at it, so that made me want to do it more. Because I wanted to be good at something. When I was in college, I wasn't a drama major. I didn't know anybody who was involved in drama. So I studied speech and communications because it was the only thing I could do that allowed me to continue performing while getting a semi-comprehensible degree. Basically, it was all interpretive, a performance of nondramatic work. And I loved it. I had a great time doing it. One of my mentors was a wonderful teacher named Paul Ferguson.

Did you think, Aha, I'm going to be an actor?

Not right away. I thought what I would do was teach, because I really enjoyed this discipline and I thought I might be able to teach. I liked the academic environment. But by the time school was over, I was really drawn to acting and I was doing it all the time. And I thought, I want to pursue it. I was cautious, though, because no one I knew had done it. Then I thought the way to do it was to get my master's so I could teach if I couldn't get work as an actor.

Did it seem like a very faraway thing for you to be onstage?

Oh yeah. Completely foreign. When Ron Van Lieu called to say I'd been accepted at NYU, that was the most exotic thing that possibly could have happened. I never imagined that I would be able to go to such an esteemed institution. It was mind-blowing. It took me a long time to adjust to being an actor in New York. I couldn't comprehend it really. Some people talk about knowing from an early age: I knew I was going to do this, I knew I was going to do this, as soon as I got on the stage I knew it. And I didn't. I really fought it for a long time. I mean, the clear obstruction to this desire in me to *not* be a part of it was the fact that I was so comfortable in it. I was never more comfortable than when I was in graduate school. When the lights go down and the curtain comes up in the theater, I calm down and I know what I'm doing.

How did your parents view all this?

My mom was thrilled because she'd exposed me to theater since I was a little kid. I played the piano, and she always enjoyed my performances, so she was thrilled that I was pursuing it. I think it was more strange to my father. He didn't really understand it until I started to make a living at it. And my grandfather was convinced until he died that I was getting my M.B.A. So he never really got it. My grandmother was fantastic about it. She was terrified in the beginning because she had a stepson who pursued acting and it was dreadful for him, so that's what she associated with it. It took her a long time to not fear for my safety. Now she just sees everything. Almost nothing I do appeals to her taste, and still she sees everything. She even sat through four hours of *Oedipus* that we did off-Broadway. She sat there, and she could be like this: [he claps enthusiastically]. She was thrilled. And it was pretty far-out there, that production. She's a queen as far as I'm concerned. All of my family has been incredibly supportive.

When you started out, did everything that you learned in school start to come to the fore? Was it all there just waiting for you?

There is a certain element that's there, but you have to put it into use. I couldn't have done *Arcadia* at all without the training I got at NYU. The text analysis, the voice, the speech, the dialect. It was all too exotic. I'm not in possession of it in a way that would enable me to do it all on my own. I have to do vocal warm-ups. I have to do extensive dialect work with a coach like Liz Smith or Deb Hecht. I think there's a kind of attack I have on material that I got out of going to school that's sort of in my bones. But the actual process that you go about continues to be a kind of practice.

Can you describe this "attack"?

It's a twofold approach. Whenever we were confused by a scene, Ron asked questions that instilled in us the responsibility to always ask questions when we read material, to take nothing for granted. Why is the writer giving the character that particular thing to say? It's a more aggressive rather than passive approach. Nora Dunfee had a different approach, which was that the way we communicate with

each other has been defined by the musicality of language. In order
to communicate an emotional understanding of the text, we must
understand the music of it. There is an inherent, intuitive sense of
communication. When we focus on rendering behavior, we forget
the inherent music of communication. So you need to begin to look
for ways of communicating that have nothing to do with behavior,
psychology, physical life. Nora focused on Noël Coward and Shaw,
good writing that accesses the inherent musicality of communication. The way we communicate emotion through words has a code.
We don't have to do anything to discover this but stay out of our own
way and not be self-conscious. I remember I did something from
Spoon River Anthology. I was interested in who the character might
have been and in creating a mood, and therefore I was not creating
the basic sense of the language. When I was finished, I asked Nora
what I was doing wrong. "Everything," she said, and she proceeded
to give me line readings. I didn't want line readings in my first year
of training. Ron's work was easier. I preferred pursuing an objective. It took me a while to learn where the two approaches met.

Okay. You get a script. What's the first thing you do?

It varies with the material. Take *Elephant Man*. The play takes place
over months and in different locations. So you have a where, when,
and how. Who are the characters? It takes patience and rereading.
You take nothing for granted. You ask all the questions, but only
rudimentary ones. Next, I worked on the dialect, breaking down the
phonetics of it. Then, when I began rehearsing, I had a rudimentary
understanding and could begin to explore nuance of interaction with
other actors. I had to eliminate the obstacles that kept me from in-
teracting with other actors. I also prepared physically beforehand. I
was not sure how it would be made manifest, so I started exercising,
stretching, yoga, to be as limber as possible. You don't always need that.
In the film *Dedication* that I just did with Dianne Wiest, my prepara-

tion work was to observe people and have a psychological take on the character, also based on discussions with the director. The character was terrified of this world, and this manifested itself in aggression and self-protection. He was unavailable to outside stimuli, which he saw as threatening. I observed people on whom I could project this. I looked for behavior I was associating with the character.

In the case of a film role, where there might not be any rehearsal, how do you prepare for the shoot?

Depends on the role. With no rehearsal, mostly I do a lot of the breaking down of scenes myself. I make choices prematurely so I have a point of view. You don't want to be unprepared. I can always let it go in the playing if I find something more interesting. I'll go line by line, break down the beats of the scenes, like I would for an audition, make definitive and maybe simplistic choices just to have some control. I direct myself, and hopefully that will leave me available to other stuff. If I don't do that, it becomes generalized. I *prefer* to discover in the space of other actors and the director, but if you haven't made choices, if you're not in control, you're not going to be available to the other person. Well, *I'm* not.

How important are the performances of the other actors?

In film, I used to think the rapport was vital. Then I discovered that the scenes were cut in such a way that didn't attend to that at all. They create the chemistry in the editing. In the theater, the other actors are a significant part of your performance, based on rehearsals, on a constraining or a liberating environment, on how interested they are in playing—a much more vital relationship than in film. It's always great to have actors who are in control, making choices and available. In film, you're busy with a lot of details not related to the present moment; you're standing on an apple box. You're trying to remember what you did in the take before. There are a number of constraints that keep you from being available. In a play, you can put up a fourth wall. In film you can't ignore the distractions of sight lines, where you're standing, the presence of the camera, continuity, all things that keep you from being available.

What do you think it is in your personality that has allowed you to have a career? Certainly there are lots of people with talent for whom the career doesn't seem to happen.

I think it's a confluence of events, as it is in most people's careers. The fact that I went to a conservatory and had a depth of training that enabled me to pursue a lot of different things—the sort of shotgun approach to getting into the business. I wasn't only able to do a certain kind of TV. I wasn't only able to do Broadway musicals. I think that enabled me to find a foothold. Timing plays a big part. For example, when I auditioned for *Arcadia*, which was my first big thing, the casting director Daniel Swee didn't call me back after the first time. He said, "You were fine, you're just not what we're looking for." And I told my agent I fucked up the audition. I knew what the director wanted as soon as I left. I just needed another ten minutes. And my agent was like, "Yeah, we hear that a lot." I called Daniel Swee myself, and he said, "I understand, but you just weren't right for it." I kept working on it anyway because it's a great part and I had a friend who liked reading the role of Thomasina. Two weeks later Daniel Swee called me because he didn't find anybody. Not because he was pursuing me, but because he didn't find anybody, so he opened the door again. And just by chance I had been working on it, and I knew the material through and through and I went in and got it. So there was an element of timing in there. I also think too, on a sort of crass, superficial level, the way I look made many more opportunities possible for me. And I happened to come of age in a time when being a leading white man in his twenties was a very lucky thing to be. So very early on I chose discriminately and both consciously and unconsciously was able to create a market for myself.

You seem to choose things that interest you. A lot of your films are character studies.

I'm not entirely sure where that came from, but I think it alludes to something I was talking about before with the actors that were exciting to me early on, Hurt and Day-Lewis. I really latched onto those guys. I think in many respects too that my attraction to them was about wanting to be regarded seriously myself, independent again of my aesthetic taste. I wanted to be taken seriously for something. So I thought, Who do they take seriously out there and what do they do? Consequently, what happens is you begin to develop your own aesthetic within that.

How have you expressed that in the real world?

Very early on I was at Purchase doing my first job out of school. The director hired me to play this sort of lurking butler in a Sherlock Holmes mystery, and I was having a good time. I got my Equity card. And I got a call from my agent in response to having begrudgingly auditioned for a horror film that was the sequel to the sequel to the sequel or something. And I got an offer for it: they were going to pay me forty thousand dollars to work for two months on this movie. I'd have to leave the play of course. Forty thousand dollars! I was making $260 a week in the play. I was fixated on how that would enable me. And I remember the moment where I thought, I don't think that's what I'm going to be doing. I was enjoying my time there at Purchase. I was enjoying exploring things with these people. And I was getting by. I wasn't starving by any means. I was getting enough work to sustain. So I turned the movie down.

What did that do for you?

It generated an internal authority. I was thirty thousand dollars in debt, but in some sense I knew I could find my way through it. I suppose there is a kind of hubris in it too. I don't know where I got that from exactly. But I guess I had gotten enough good feedback to feel like there'd be other chances to be in horror movies. And if at a certain point I wasn't doing the kinds of things that I wanted to do, then I'd have to broaden my horizons a little bit. But I wanted to see if I could pursue a career with a narrow focus. And strangely enough, that created a kind of market for me. When I turned stuff down, I got more offers.

No regrets about things you turned down?

No.

Have people advised you on what roles to choose?

Not so much anymore. My first agents bore the brunt of my vigilance at the beginning of my career. But my agent now knows what I'm going to do most of the time, so he doesn't take it personally. He represents me despite the fact that I'm not going to earn him the money that another actor in my position might be able to earn. I think he sort of takes that as a given. One of the things too that has shaped my career and allowed me to make some of these choices is a voice-over campaign for MasterCard that I got seven years ago. And the consistent income from that has provided me with a kind of freedom and liberty to make choices. And that's played a significant role in my career.

You don't feel any need to be in Los Angeles?

I know there's a sense that I'm not in L.A., that I'm not joining the game. That's an issue that any serious actor who wants to do serious work has to think about. But there are hundreds of actors out there with big opportunities who make what they think are calculated moves that just wind up having no significant effect, and they end up doing a disservice to themselves in any number of different ways. So I always felt like there was no way for me to be able to control being wanted and being in something successful. The only thing that I can control is trying to do the best that I can at the stuff that appeals to me for what I'm offered. And consequently, when things would come up and the agents would say, "You really need to do something. You need to be out there," I just kept saying, "I know, but I can't be out there in something that I don't want to be out there *in*," because if I'm popular for something, I'm only going to get hired for more stuff like that. And if that something is something I don't like, that means I'm going to have to keep doing things I don't like in order to maintain my presence. And that doesn't make any sense to me for any number of reasons. When will I be doing the stuff I want to? Also, I'm getting all the jobs I want. I have had unbelievable opportunities. So that's always been my sort of counterargument.

Would anything change that position? A role? An amount of money?

I can't just *do* things. I'm not built that way. It's not going to work. And I'll resent it. And I won't have any fun. Maybe it would change if I reach the point at which I stop being able to work on the things that are really interesting to me. Maybe I'll need to reconsider this, but that hasn't happened yet, in part because of MasterCard. The six months here or the eight months there that I haven't been working or looking for work, I haven't been filled with the kind of desperation that so many actors are: "I need to get a fucking check in here quick because my rent's due!" I have had a pretty steady job with them.

When you started acting in films, were you satisfied with what you saw of yourself?

I actually just thought of a moment in *Without Limits*. Robert Towne was the director, and at the end of the scene in which I'd done this monologue, he said something while the camera was still rolling. And I was really angry about it. And I just turned to him and started cursing him. I mean it was sort of tongue-in-cheek. But he used that moment in the film for a moment when my character was talking to the coach. So there is actually a moment when I the actor am butting heads with the director that is literally there in the film. And Towne got a big kick out of it. It was cracking him up that he used it and it worked. But when you see it there is a difference between the person who said, *"Oh fuck"*—that was Billy Crudup—and the person who was in the scene who was the character. There's a fine line. And of course the artiste in me was appalled because I'm a firm believer that the real craft of acting comes from creating and making it appear that it's happening for the first time. I'm not as much a believer in making things happen for the first time and filming them. There's less artistry in it as far as I'm concerned, though I'm a bit of a hypocrite, because I often cherish moments that just happen. I think you have to leave yourself open to that. This is part of a kind of dogmatism that I'm trying to wrench myself out of.

What do you mean by dogmatism?

I think you can make a lot of mistakes because of the responsibility you bear. I have had incredible opportunities. And since I have viewed them as incredible opportunities, consequently I've viewed them as responsibilities too, whether that's intentional or unintentional. It's been kind of an internal mechanism driving my desire to get that experience right because it's such a great opportunity. And I think that has in times before created a kind of internal panic that made me less available to mold myself with a director.

How did this dogmatism come to be?

I think it was born out of the fact that when I was just out of school and I started to work frequently, I found myself in circumstances where I was asked to define my way of working. Whether it was going back to NYU to talk to students, or in an interview with a magazine or something, I found myself with a need to define my process. I'm actually just working this out right now, but I think I wanted to define it with a level of respect to the craft. That then informed my process. My philosophical attempts to articulate it sort of defined my craft. So that's where some of that dogmatism comes from, out of my need to articulate it.

Since you have pretty much chosen your roles, do you feel that there's a sense of autobiography in your work?

I think it's a creative scrapbook. I think you're right, in that each piece of work marks where you were in your life. But the reason I wouldn't say autobiography is because it doesn't fully take into account the other aspects of my life. It takes into account my creative life, and it takes into account where I was in the development of my craft. If I could trace each job back to where that inspiration came from in my personal life, you could extrapolate some kind of journey. But I think the work that you would have to do in order to try to understand that would just be too ornate to make sense. It's up to other people I think to interpret it. I wouldn't waste my time going back.

You've already lived it.

Precisely.

In Inventing the Abbotts *and in* Big Fish *you could have played either of the leading male roles.*

I really wanted to play the heavy in *Abbotts*. He was the tough kid. I was feeling a little rebellious at the time, and he was not a sympathetic character. You hear a lot very early on about what you need to do in order to shape your career. You hear a lot about playing parts that are sympathetic and about not being pigeonholed. I think there was a part of me that was testing that. I wanted to see how big of a prick I could play and still try to make him human and still try to not be pigeonholed as a certain kind of actor.

That's why you did it?

I don't think that's entirely why I did it. I mean, I mostly liked the director, Pat O'Connor, and I liked the script, and it was a very nice offer. But I think there was a part of me too that was excited by taking a bit of a risk. And then that became a way for me. I thought, God, I really like this challenge of taking on people that I don't fully trust, people that I don't have faith are good people somehow. I mean in some ways there's a good and bad kind of person. But I like the idea of taking a chance to explore people who we would ordinarily dismiss and to see if there are opportunities to elaborate on who they are as people. So then I tried to take as many of those kinds of parts as were offered. I mean there were a lot. *Jesus' Son*. Even *Measure for Measure*.

You chose to do the heavy, Angelo, instead of the sympathetic Claudio.

The roles that are somehow interesting to me are always somebody trying to fight his way through. Solyony in *Three Sisters* was the more interesting part in many ways than Tusenbach. But it's funny, because as I've grown out of that rebellious era, I've noticed how beautiful Tusenbach is in a different way, and I've wanted to be in possession of that kind of part. So I think in that way it stands as a kind of autobiographical reference point.

The Elephant Man *was a completely sympathetic character.*

That spoke to a different point in my evolution. In the first couple of years out of school I would not have been as interested in that. I mean I might have been interested in trying to explore the physical life of that part, but I would have thought, Why doesn't he berate the nurses, or why doesn't he spit on anyone? Where's the conflict here? It's hard to find goodness in characters. The harsher characters—somehow we get them. Goodness we are sort of suspicious about. And that became the challenge of going in. How do you not create a caricature? I think that the Elephant Man aspired to something beautiful.

Are there roles in literature that you want to do?

I've spoken about Tusenbach but that's the only one that is of any interest to me. I don't feel there is a particular part. I think I'm sort of past that stage. I so rarely think like that. That Shakespeare thing: I want to do a *Hamlet* before I'm forty. I've considered that, but just in the way that everyone considers that. When will I do my Hamlet? But not because I have a particular drive to play Hamlet.

Do you ever think about when you're fifty? What other roles you might play in terms of the arc of your career?

I don't have any idea. When I am in my golden years, I want to be able to look back at my résumé and know that each thing I did, I did because I thought it had the potential to be something interesting. And I've been very lucky to have been successful at that, by my own standards, for most of the time. And I want to try to continue that as long as I can. So there's no role, there's no big role.

Is there anything you feel shifting in terms of choices you want to make?

Definitely. I used to feel that if I just tried as hard as I could doing the kinds of things that I wanted to do, then the material would find an audience. And that hasn't been the case. It hasn't been as easy as that. *Stage Beauty* is a good example of a trend over the last five years for me. Why it didn't do better, I don't have a clue. I don't have a clue about why any of the stuff that I've done hasn't done better commercially. *The Elephant Man* closed after two months, and then Kate Burton and I were nominated for Tonys. So even if we both won, the show had already closed. We couldn't find an audience. And so there's a lack of some of that confidence and arrogance that allowed me to make those decisions before. Because I did feel—not that I articulated it to myself—I think I did feel somewhere that if I just tried to stay true to what I wanted to do, these things would find an audience.

Do you feel comfortable with the kind of career in which you are offered things? Do you develop projects?

Recently someone was talking to me about development. Did I want to develop ideas or develop a project? It's not like that for me. I want to do good stuff. So my answer is, Yeah, develop some of that. But in terms of the work I wanted to do, I couldn't come up with something that had dramatic value. So I want to be associated with people who can. I've always felt that I do best when I'm serving a director's piece of work. That doesn't mean I don't have my own opinions of how it's going, but I'm not the primary artist in this craft, either in theater or film. In film it's much more clear. I think the primary artist is the writer. They create the original.

Don't you feel a sense of randomness then?

Oh yeah. I love that. Just what comes my way. I mean, you have a choice because there isn't just one script that comes your way. And sometimes you just need to work. Actually *Big Fish* was a case when I hadn't worked for a while and I needed to work. It was a chance to work with Tim Burton. I don't think I would have developed that project with me playing that part. It was just an opportunity that arose to work with some good actors on a nice script with a good director. I am at my best, my most useful, when I am being directed. When I'm a tool. And by no means do I take that lightly, nor do I think I'm subservient. I generate ideas about characters that I play. I don't generate ideas about material. So in a certain sense there's not much for me to do. I look back to when I did *Arcadia*. I didn't understand what ninety percent of it meant, much less could I have created those ideas. Much less could I have said, You know what I think I'd really like to do is a play that involves chaos mathematics and landscape gardening. Or, You know what I'd love to do is play some kind of ironic tutor. I wouldn't have a clue. But when Trevor Nunn said, "This is how you do it. This is how this moment works," that was igniting. I didn't know it existed before. So I think that's when I'm at my most useful.

What if you come up against a director who just works in ways that are counter to the ways you believe in or has bad ideas?

Certainly there were directors who worked a different way. Mary Zimmerman is a very creative and articulate director and a smart woman. And we spent a great deal of time during *Measure for Measure* trying to find a vocabulary that was helpful for each other. And we both worked hard at explaining ourselves, and we got as far as we could and no further. I've gone through many phases in my short career about dogmatism and rigidity, and I have not always . . .

mmm . . . acquitted myself in the best way. I've been sort of dog-matic about my process. "I need these things. Don't say those kinds of things to me. They're not helpful. It's not useful." And I think that was more out of insecurity and fear on my part. I think I have a process, but I wouldn't be in this business if I didn't understand and enjoy that it's a collaborative process. I like that. I cherish that. We all have to deal with our egos, and it's quite difficult sometimes to deal with directors. But you try to recognize that the process may be difficult from their perspective as well. I've never said, This is just not working and bye-bye. You have to find a way. And you always do. Because the show must go on. There is no out clause.

You just finished doing The Pillowman *on Broadway. How was it to work on that production?*

That was a special experience. John Crowley is the kind of director you want, especially with complicated material, or you feel awash in all the nuances. You can do more harm than good. If the material is really dynamic, with different objectives, characters not saying what they mean, behavior that must be manifested . . . If I make choices and have no director to refine them, the work becomes unfocused and the performance becomes incoherent. You need a director to say this is the event of the scene, this is important and this isn't. Like in the first scene, when we're saying nothing that we mean. It's all about what's not being said. You need someone to shape it. On the other hand, I remember seeing the film of *Without Limits*, and something seemed really awkward about the two scenes at the end. And then I realized that the director had reversed them. And it made much more sense from a narrative point of view. But everything I was doing—all the nuance I thought I was bringing to it—was now completely ir-relevant. And not only that, but it was destructive, because the time that I used trying to be forceful about it could have been used in just being in the moment. But acting is acting, you know?

Estelle Parsons

Estelle Parsons has been temporarily displaced. Leaks into her top-floor apartment on West End Avenue have caused her and her husband to sublet a friend's apartment fifteen blocks downtown while repairs are being made. The friend's penthouse apartment is in a state of semi-chaos. "Time Warner's been here three times," Estelle complains as she stows our coats in an overstuffed hall closet. "The telephone company's been here. Cable TV has been here. Nothing works right." She manages to close the closet, then leads us into the dining area, warning us not to hit our heads on the overhead light fixture. The telephone keeps ringing. At one point she takes a call from an agent and makes plans for a project she's doing in Los Angeles with Al Pacino and Dianne Wiest. At the same time, the maid comes in and starts unpacking groceries and cleaning up in the kitchen. When the phone call is finished, we settle in at the dining table, placing Estelle at the head. Her hair is cropped as short as a boy's, a mix of brown and blond and silver. Her skin is smooth. At a very youthful seventy-eight, her speech still retains traces of her girlhood in Marblehead, Massachusetts. Her hands and fingers move rhythmically as she speaks, as if she is impatient to get to the next thought. What she says is uncensored, intuitive, spontaneous, surprising. She is not trying to protect any-one—least of all herself—nor is she trying to sculpt an image or suit a public perception of herself. Her famous energy is in full force in the interview; she is full of stories and plans for the future. She could have talked all night.

When you saw people on the stage when you were a little girl, when did you come to think, I'd like to do that?

I started acting when I was six or seven, as a frog in a play with the Tavern Players. There was this great community theater run by a very wonderful woman, Marian Benvie, who was known all over New En-gland. My father really hated it. Everything that went wrong with me he'd say was because I was in the theater, so that was really really bad. I would be hauled in front of him to explain, I don't know what—I cried myself to sleep, I wet the bed, or god knows what—I'd be called in front of him, and he'd say it was because I was in the theater. And I was tap-dancing—I thought I could be another Shirley Temple, you know—blue satin skirt, tap dancing and ballet, and all that stuff, from the very beginning.

You understood that there was a place for you on the stage.

Absolutely. And then I played leading roles in *A Christmas Carol*, where this little invalid girl dies in the end, so I knew I could get love. I knew I was moving the audience to tears, because I'd hear the pocketbooks open and hear the sniffles. I really understood the re-lation between actor and audience from the beginning, which people who go to school and don't apprentice don't really under-stand: you're a totally different person in front of an audience than you are in front of a teacher or five students. My mother realized that it was something I'd like to do. There was a little theater company. Everybody who was anybody on the North Shore, where we lived in Marblehead, Massachusetts, was in this company, so my mother of course took me and my sister there. My father was a very depressed person, so it wasn't that he was raving about it, but it was a kind of silence. He came to see me in a leading role I had, in which I thought I was so wonderful, everybody told me I was so wonderful. And he came, and when it was over, he walked up these six stairs from the audience to the stage and never said one word. Not one word, not one word; I've never forgotten it.

Did this help you in some way?

I think it was very bad, because my anxiety knows no bounds in the theater, both acting and directing, but mostly acting. I don't suppose it affects me directing. But acting: there's just no boundary to the size of my anxiety, even now, even though I do have an understanding of it, and at least I can cope with it now. Before, it caused me to threaten to quit every two minutes every show.

What was at the base of the anxiety?

Well, I think the fact that I did it as a kid, and the fact that my father didn't like it. I didn't think you grew up and kept doing it. I thought it was something you did as a kid, as part of this family situation. It never occurred to me that I could grow up and do it. But I was not a stupid person, and I'm sure that it was just my father's disapproval. And also we were in Marblehead, and what we got from news magazines and newspapers was that there were really no good role models for being an actress. Judy Garland was a drughead. Other people, like Rita Hayworth, were too sexy for their own good. And mostly it was movie people, and women held up as sex objects—and all of this might have been of interest to me but was just too frightening and too threatening. I didn't think I could end up as Betty Grable, with my bottom sticking out as a pinup. I maybe would have liked to, but I mean it just didn't seem to be something a nice girl from Marblehead did.

How did you get into it, then?

I went to Connecticut College, and there always seemed to be people from show business in New York who came up there—boyfriends of girls there or whatever. And I was singing in bars and singing with bands, and so people would say, "My god, you should be in New York; here's my card. When you come down . . ." And then I sang with a double octet, which I actually put together with a couple of other people and wrote the arrangements and directed and everything, and I had these solo parts, and I got such a response when I did all these solos, I was just the toast of the town.

What did you sing?

I sang, "Just take it slow and easy if you wanna get along with me [she sings]. I said go slow." So I was doing all this sexy stuff in my music, you know. They loved me.

Then how did you start acting?

I was in college, you see, doing this stuff, singing in bars, getting paid with a bottle of champagne or whatever, but every time I saw my father I'd say, "Look, I'm getting these offers to visit so-and-so in New York. Can't I quit school and go down there and start?" I wasn't thinking of serious acting. I wanted to do musicals. I loved to do musicals and sing, and here I had these opportunities, but my father said, "No, no, no. You finish college." And obviously I'm not a revolutionary spirit, so I dutifully finished college. In boarding school I had got all these cups for being the smartest person in school, the smartest person in my class and everything, and when I got to college, I just turned into a mediocrity. I felt that I was losing my creativity. I tried to audition for the Old Howard—that's the burlesque company in Boston. They needed chorus girls, and I thought, This is a great beginning. I can sing and dance, and I'll audition for a chorus girl. I wasn't going to be a stripper. That wasn't in my vision, but I thought I could get started—you know, like comics did in burlesque. Who knows? I could have been Fanny Brice or something. But my father said, "No, no, no—don't do that." He didn't stop me, but my own fears did.

So you never studied acting exactly?

Study! How can you study acting?

Well, there are those who believe that you can study acting.

Well, look, I went to the Actors Studio forever, and I was in Lee Strasberg's private classes. I was by then a perfectly seasoned actor and at that point was perfectly good. Professional studying is one thing, but to not be an actor and try to learn to study is . . . it makes no sense to me. But I know you have to do it now; I know you have to.

How so? Do you mean practically?

When I started, and all the time I was in college and even in high school, I apprenticed in summer stock. First I paid to go. My father wanted to buy me a convertible. I said, "No, I want the money; I'm going to go to this summer theater," where the woman who ran our company was actually teaching, where Paul Newman first went. And I went there. Gerry Friedman and a lot of people came from the profession, and I worked in a class-A summer stock company. I was in a play with Jane Powell, Veronica Lake, and Roddy McDowall. Jack Lemmon was an apprentice too, and we played these small parts. But already my anxiety was so high.

Do you think any of the anxiety would relate to perhaps not knowing quite what you were doing?

No. I knew what I was doing.

When you would get roles, how did you know what to do? When you looked at the script, how did you know what to do?

Same way I know now.

Well, what is that way?

You read the script, and it tells you all you need to know. And then you start saying the words, and they tell you something. And then you get with the other people, and that tells you something.

You don't read the script and see something already there? You find it as you go along?

A movie script, you read it and you respond; I mean they're very accessible. You read a movie script, you know who that woman is. Unless you don't, in which case you don't take the job. But basically, you can read a movie script, because you know you do them without rehearsals, so you read a movie script and it's all there. It's all there emotionally. All you have to do is get up and do it. But in the theater you read a script, and the better the script, the more you think, What in god's name is this? And you just keep working on the script and it gives you the clues. Reading it out loud over and over, and wondering why this person is saying this, and how could this person possibly be saying that. It's all in the script, isn't it? You don't need anything else.

But obviously some of this studying of acting teaches you how to examine a script, how to break down a script—

Oh, I don't know—

You do that intuitively.

Apparently. I mean I die when someone says, "Well this whole first act is exposition." I feel like saying, Well then, go home. Because if this act is not human beings functioning in reality, theatrical reality, then you're just going to go out and say this is exposition. If that's where your mind is, go on home, because your job is to do this thing for the audience. This person is real, they don't know it's exposition, the character doesn't know that. That attitude is just closing doors to creativity or interpretation. So I don't think it's helpful. I don't know a beat from a non-beat.

But when actors talk that way with you in a scene—

Oh, they don't—

They don't dare, or they don't?

No, if they do, I probably don't—

Don't hear—

. . . listen. Or maybe I try to; I mean, why would they talk to me?

Don't they say, "Well, after this beat I probably should do this or that, should really get up . . ."? I mean, they tell you what some action is at this beat.

Well, that's maybe a little more modern than what I'm used to.

But your acting is very modern.

I don't like people talking to me that way. Maybe that's their home-work. Maybe they talk that way. I'm probably not paying attention to them. I'm probably busy in one room doing my stuff. My anxieties are probably in full bloom.

What do you do at home after the rehearsal? Is there a way for you to work on it at home, when you're not actually engaged?

It depends on the script really. I used to prefer to do everything on my feet. I used to barely read a script. I'd read it enough to say I want to do it or don't want to do it. And then I would put it aside until the re-hearsals began. When I did *Galileo* at Lincoln Center, John Hirsch was going to do three or four days of films and background and research, and I thought, Oh, let's get up on our feet and find out what this is about. But people like to do that. I used to really just want to get on my feet and get started. My thought—I think my whole frame of refer-ence—came from vaudeville. Not that I have a clue what vaudeville was, except from what I saw in the movies. But it was the idea that you just get up and get out there. And I did understand that I'm a com-pletely different person in front of an audience. My ability in front of an audience is very different; my inhibitions are gone when I'm someone else in front of an audience. Consequently, the way to get from me to that complete lack of inhibition, that ability really to function creatively, is a very difficult thing because I'm inhibited lots of times. I've been the despair of directors because I would look like I wasn't capable of doing anything, because I would be inhibited until the audience came, because I'm a completely different person when there's an audience and I have to do it. That's why I was so good when I was in *Miss Margarida's Way*, because I had no choice.

Well, how are you then in rehearsal? Difficult?

Terrible. I don't know. What do you mean?

Well, are you inhibited in front of the other actors until there's an audience?

Probably. To some extent. But basically, I'm just trying to remember the lines.

Have you known the actors to complain about you: "Oh, well, she's not giving me enough in rehearsal"?

I think that they probably do. Never easy, the rehearsal period. I always thought I was in the wrong business anyway, until I worked with Arthur Penn, and then it just felt like all the notes fell into place on the piano, because up until then . . . You know, directors will say, Move here and move there, don't do this, why are you doing that, and I wouldn't know; I'd just go there every day and I'd do what came to me. I wouldn't censor what I was doing; I was on this journey to find whatever. That's the way I worked when I did my first play, *Mrs. Dally Has a Lover*. They'd already had two people do it, and I guess they were wrong for the part and it was the perfect part for me.

In what way?

I'm really a tragicomedian. I'm not all tragedy and I'm not all comedy. And if one falls in that area, and if they get somebody who isn't like me, then it becomes a different thing. It's why I can do your work, Barry, when a lot of people can't. It's a funny thing we're born with, right? The way you write, and the way I play. And I can play other things; I can play pure tragedy if I have to. I've done that a lot. And pure comedy. I love that. I loved *Roseanne*. But basically I have this other thing, and I think that's what *Mrs. Dally* needed.

Can you elaborate on that a bit?

Mrs. Dally Has a Lover was about a woman who was in her late thirties, and her only child had been drowned in a swimming pool when her husband wasn't watching. And she's married to a taxi driver, this ordinary, brutish guy who had let the kid die. Anyway, she was having an affair with this teenage delivery boy from the grocery store, played by Bobby Drivas. So at one point in rehearsal, I put Bobby on my back and was playing around the kitchen with him on my back, and the director said, "Oh no, you can't do that, you can't do that." So, you know, I was chagrined. I just did it, it just came to me, and you can see it resonates perfectly whether it ended up in the play or not. As part of the rehearsal, it was a perfectly good idea, it was the baby that died, you know, and at the same time sexy.

I did *Mrs. Dally Has a Lover* when I was thirty-two, and I went to the Berkshire Theater Festival at forty to work with Arthur Penn in the summer of 1966. Annie Bancroft did *The Miracle Worker*, and I thought, I really want to work with this director, and Arthur hired me, and we did *Skin of Our Teeth* with Annie Bancroft. She'd just married Mel Brooks then, and she played Sabina, and I played Mrs. Antrobus, and Alvin Epstein played Mr. Antrobus. Frank Langella played the son, and Frank's girlfriend, whose name I've forgotten, played the daughter. And it was this experimental rehearsal technique, which was, you read the scene and then you got up and did it in your own words. It was like the actor's nightmare. You have to play the scene when you don't have a clue what's in it—Arthur Penn's point being that if you've got talent, then when you read the script, you absorb much more than you know you've absorbed about what the whole play is about. It's kind of the way I work now, I guess, because you basically just read it, but through that you've absorbed an awful lot of the play. And he felt that if you don't bring yourself up front, if the actor doesn't bring himself up front—rather than trying to create the character immediately—if you don't do that work up front, he feels you've lost your contribution. What makes your Hamlet different from someone else's Hamlet. It is what you bring up front.

I'm not sure I agree with that, but in any case, this was a way to be forced to bring yourself to the play. You would play the scene as yourself in your own words, and then you'd go back and read the script again and see what you'd left out, and then you'd begin to think, Why did I leave that out, and little by little, you would have a very full production with very full characters. It just opened my eyes; I mean it was the first time I really felt alive in the whole space—not just on the stage, but in the whole space, with the audience there. In other words, it created some kind of confidence that I could just sit there as Mrs. Antrobus, perfectly happy in this theater in Stockbridge, see the reality of where I was, and still be playing this character in an imaginary world, which is what, of course, Lee talks about in The Method: that you cannot move away from yourself into a character, but you have to combine the reality and the imaginary world, because only by bringing the imaginary world to the basic reality do you get the excitement and aliveness.

Sometimes I think there are different ways of describing the same process. I mean, an actor who brings himself so alive—you do it, what great actors do—so alive in the moment . . . and also is so available to the imaginary events.

Did you see Vince Young play this game against USC? He plays football for Texas. He's like a superhuman person. I mean this man is so phenomenal, you wouldn't believe it. And the coach said, in this little interview, "I watched this guy in the beginning and started sort of molding him, and then I realized what this guy was, and I just encouraged him to find his own way." And this guy is at this point the greatest football player ever. And this coach, when he saw what this guy was, said, "Do your thing." And the guy has led the team that just beat USC, which hasn't been beaten in a couple of years.

Arthur Penn freed you in this way—

Instead of thinking everything I'm doing is wrong—Oh, if you told me to go there, why can't I go there? It used to be that I pulled myself through the rehearsal period. I'd learn everything I had to do, and then when the audience came, I would come alive, and then I would start really doing my work. So I said, Just let me get through the rehearsal, just let me get through, let me get through it. And then people would think I wasn't going to be able to do it. You know, the director would come, and the producer would come and take me out to dinner, and they'd think I wasn't going be able to do it, and then when the audience came, it was, "Oh, oh, well, okay, you know, you can do it." So it was very hard, because it offended my sense of theatrical truth somehow, I think. I wasn't ready to do the things these directors wanted me to do, and that's just me because, you know, I'm not very typical of theater actors. I mean they seem to be willing to get up there and do what people say, and I don't seem to be able to do that. I just really march to my own drummer. I do in real life as well. You know, I just do. I've always been that way.

But then how have you managed to thrive with directors who don't necessarily see things your way?

Well, I probably don't work for them more than once. I don't know, and this is just from my point of view; directors may not have had as big a problem with me as I had with them. I don't know, because I always work. Well yes, I have some talent; I can't help that. It comes out whether you want it to or not.

How did the anxiety you experienced affect your work?

Oh, well, the anxiety is about the work; it's not *in* the work.

Could you explain that a little more?

Well, I mean it's like . . . I had this maid's dress and I never ironed it. I was perfectly okay when I went out on the stage as the maid, but I never ironed the dress. I just somehow could not face the reality that I was going to be acting, so I couldn't take the dress home and iron it—or do it at the theater—and be prepared to work. It's like I'm horrified that I have to go out on a stage. When I did that Tennessee Williams play *Seven Descents of Myrtle*, I had not a clue what I was doing. Tennessee Williams is hard; it's naturalism with lyricism, you know? And I had never dealt with that kind of material before, so I learned the thing and I was on the stage the entire time. So I'd have a shot of vodka, and I'd stand there with my suitcase, and then I'd march out and do the play. But I don't even remember any of the work I do. People come up and quote lines from plays, and I won't even know I was in them. Eileen Heckart came up to me and said, "Blablablablablabla, hahaha, Estelle," and I didn't know what she was talking about, and it was some line that I had in a play that I had done rather well in. But I don't remember anything I do, and that's what the anxiety is about.

Is that still true?

Oh, it's much less. I've been in therapy all my life; I'm in analysis now.

What kind of response did you have to making movies?

Well, I was working in Stockbridge for Arthur Penn, and I had sublet my New York apartment. I had my trunks packed, and I was moving to San Francisco. John Hancock was starting a rep company there. This had been my dream, to be in a rep company, and I never could get to be in one. Stephen Porter had tried to get me into the Phoenix, and they hired Rae Allen. I mean, they wanted a different kind of actress, you know, so I was heartbroken. I cried and cried and cried. I tried to get with the Living Theatre. I tried to get with Peter Brook. I couldn't get with anybody; nobody wanted me. Not at these theaters. So I was doing Murray Schisgal's play called *Fragments* with Gene Hackman and Dusty Hoffman and a guy named Graham Jarvis, who died last year, and Marty Fried was directing it, and it was part of this summer in Stockbridge, and Arthur said to me, "I've got a script I want you to read, a movie script." And then I got the call from John Hancock saying the money had fallen through and we weren't going to San Francisco, and here I was without an apartment, and two kids, and without a job, and you know I read this script, and as I was reading along, I thought, Why doesn't he get Madeleine Sherwood? I'm not interested in movies. I'd had offers before, you know, for these supporting roles in movies, and I'm just not interested in movies. I'm interested in theater, that's what I'm interested in. So I read and read, and then I thought, My gosh, this part is getting good, this part is getting really good. This is a really good secondary role. And I had nothing to do, because I'd lost my job. So I said—and I loved working with Arthur so much—I would go anywhere to do anything with him, because he means the world to me. Not personally of course, but just to work with, you know. It's not true of everybody. I like Arthur, and Stephen Porter I like a lot, and Richard Block, who did my *Happy Days*. I've only done *Happy Days* with him, but that's the hardest play in the world, and he was really really good.

How was Arthur's work? Was it different in the movie than onstage?

Oh yeah, yeah, sure, it was. We just did it in the movie; we didn't rehearse; we just did it. But since I had this great awakening with him, it carried over into the movie.

Did you use the Actors Studio to work on material?

Yeah.

Do you pick other actors from there?

Well, I read in the paper that all the best work was coming out of the Studio.

This was in the fifties.

Then I was with NBC on the *Today* show and the *Home* show, so I auditioned. I got someone at NBC to read the other part [laughing], and I auditioned with Emily from *Our Town* for Elia Kazan, and I didn't get in of course, so they suggested that I go to Lee Strasberg—he had private classes—and that would be a good thing for me and then from there I could get into the Studio. So it had nothing to do with my thinking I had anything to learn, mind you. It was just that the jobs were coming out of there, and it was the place to be. So I had this little meeting with Lee Strasberg, and he said, why did I want to act, and I promptly cried for about four minutes, and he said, "Okay, I'll take you." So that's how my anxiety comes out, you see.

Well, it was useful.

Well, it probably always is; I don't know. I was in class with him then for a few years, and he kept saying, "Oh, do that scene for a Studio audition." And Paula, Lee's wife, was particularly high on me; she just thought I was fantastic. And in improvisatory stuff I was particularly good. Then I took these scenes and I'd do them at the Studio, and I'd fail because I'd get so frozen up; I just couldn't work there. I was so . . . just couldn't work there at all when I went to do these auditions.

But you got into the Studio at some point.

Eventually I got in, because I drank a lot before I did this audition. I was doing a play with Bill Traylor, it was Terrence McNally's first play. Edward Albee had this series at the Cherry Lane Theatre for new playwrights, one of whom was Terrence McNally. So Bill Trayler and I were doing one of Terrence's plays. It was about a man who stayed locked in his room, playing records, and I was the wife. I had to cook a chicken, I had to feed the little boy, who was going to get dressed up as Carmen Miranda to go to school for something. It was one of those plays. So I did a scene from it with Bill Traylor at the Studio. I don't think I drank too much—I don't want to suggest I'm a drunk—I just want to confess I was so frozen when I went there that it's a little medication, if you will. If I could have had antidepressant pills, they might have done the job; Dexamyl or something would have done the same thing. Or it maybe had nothing to do with it. So I went in and did it with Bill Traylor, tore his shirt in the course of the audition, and I got in.

What do you see has happened to the Actors Studio? I mean, they seem to be teaching how to act.

I'm not there anymore. Well, not really. Now, I use it. We're going to do a series of readings on the West Coast. And I did a wonderful set of readings of all the Group Theatre plays, which had never been gathered together and done. And there were experts there, people who had written books about the Group Theatre. It was a wonderful festival we had for about a month, and then I did another one on plays that had been developed at the Actors Studio and gone to Broadway. So much stuff from there went into the commercial mainstream that we could do only the Broadway ones. So I did do some wonderful stuff there, but I was there five years, and that was . . . enough.

But actors still kept coming to the Studio.

I don't really think Lee could see the difference between talent and neurosis. You know, there was an actor there who's a perfect example, Chad Burton—you've probably never come across him—but he was untrained and he was taken in and he was wonderful. I mean, when we did *Cherry Orchard* at the Studio with Arthur Penn, every producer in town wanted it. Lee said it was like a symphony orchestra getting up to work. We did it with this experimental technique. But Chad Burton was in that, and when he fell off the chair as Pishchik, everybody thought it was real. But he couldn't do eight performances a week; he was just not an actor. He had either this gift or this neurosis to be real and alive, but only when it was in this once-in-a-while situation. Lee didn't really seem to have the kind of toughness Kazan did, or just the knowledge. He thought, These people are hot, get them in here. So it began to change when Kazan left, and it began to become . . . I don't know what. It was still Lee; Lee was getting older but . . . I found him invaluable. I think he changed my whole attitude toward theater. Not quite sure how. I've been thinking about it all these years, but . . . I think in really looking for all the details and the inner life in this thing that I call now theatrical truth, 'cause it's not necessarily real-life truth, it's what works when I am directing. I say, "What is it, whatever you're doing, you have to make it get out here to me, because I don't know what it is out here, and I have to know what it is out here, because art is communication," and I think in a lot of ways, actors have forgotten that. Lee used to say, "A great actor acts with the audience and the other actor; a good actor acts with the audience." But he never said, A good actor acts with the other actors. I mean it's communication with the audience, which I think has gotten a little bit lost, frankly.

It's interesting that you said that. I would think he would want you to act with the other actor and not the audience—

Oh, why? That's not acting!

I know that, but that's because he wasn't interested in communicating past the proscenium.

Oh, I would not agree with that.

Well, you know better than I.

No, no. I thought his theatrical ideas were so sound; they were always misinterpreted, as they always are. But you know, to be there year after year after year with him . . . Listen, he didn't treat me nice. When we were doing this *Cherry Orchard*, and we were invited to do it everywhere, and I said, "Would you like it if we just continued here and maybe opened it to the public here?" he looked at me and said, "What, is this a vanity production for you?" And I'd waited like six or eight months to work with Arthur again, because Rip Torn was in it, Keir Dullea was in it. A fantastic group of people, and Lee turned on me like a savage. But I was there year after year, and I think he was so sound. It's just that a lot of people are not on that wavelength, and there's nothing wrong with people who aren't on that wavelength; it's just a different wavelength. And so now, if I go to the theater and I don't see that sense of truth, like Gerry Hiken has, or Marlon Brando had—you know, there's a certain group of actors who just have that kind of truth, detailed truth, they *live* the character, and that of course is what I try to do. And then, Ken Howard, when we were doing *The Norman Conquests*, said, "Estelle, I never know when you're acting and when you're not," and I said, "Just take it from me, Ken; if I'm up here, I'm acting. I'm not ever myself when I'm up here. This is not me; forget it." But people always act as though they're confused about what I do, and then I tend to be aggressive.

When you do a musical, does your voice change from when you are speaking to when you're singing?

I don't think so; 'cause I'm an actor/singer. But you know, when I did *Harold and Maude*, the woman was eighty, and she was going to die in the play, right? Pretty clear, strong images: eighty years old, going to die. So I was perfectly willing to let my voice be raspy, whatever, you know? And then the reviews said, "Well, she should have a clear singing voice." But that's because musicals have changed, and they're not about actor/singers anymore. That musical particularly. I stopped acting it, really; I would act a scene, and then I would sing with as pure a tone as I could possibly sing. The conductors don't follow you and work together for the audience's pleasure anymore; the conductor is playing this music and you fuckin' better well fit into it. It's all different. It used to be called musical comedy, you know, and you were putting on a show for the audience. Everybody in that *Harold and Maude* was a singer. They really couldn't act, except one girl, who had a wonderful scene to act, but they were really singers, not actors, not actor/singers. They tried very hard to act, but they basically had pure tones and they were going to sing it, sustain the tones, not deliver a song. Sing a song, not deliver it.

Can we talk a little about acting versus directing for you? You're doing a lot of both now.

Yeah, I am.

What do you prefer?

They're so completely different. I am an actor, a born actor. And I'm physically very active all the time. So directing, for me, always has to be a secondary thing, even though I'm very interested in creating an atmosphere with the actors. [Laughing] I have this campaign to force actors to do their work, and it's increasingly the case in the theater now, where directors are always going, "Move here, move there, do what I tell you to do, do my vision of things." I don't call what I do directing so much as collaboration. I've maybe learned a lot from Arthur Penn, who, whenever I said anything to him, he would say, "Well, what do you think?" I mean, he would never answer a question. And I think that was part of his technique. You would say, "What is this?" and he would say, "Well, what do you think would be the best thing?" He would never give you an answer, and consequently, you were thrown back on what you really believed should be there.

Directors. I don't know what their training is, but I was excited to work with young directors. I did a reading for a director who's just out of Yale. Everybody said, "Oh, come do this reading, this guy's terrific." Well, I was by that time, I don't know, sixty, but I had a fine reputation. I'd spent my life doing fine work in the theater. This guy never looked at me, never wanted anything I brought in, never paid any attention to the fact that I might be able to contribute a great deal to this reading for him or for whoever he wanted to produce the show. Nothing. I walked in, and he told me exactly what he wanted me to do. And this is the star person who has come out of Yale School of Drama. I mean this is ridiculous. And that's what they come out with. When I've taught directors, they strike me, almost all of them— there's always the few like Arthur or Stephen Porter or something— but almost all of them have learned about the power. They come looking like Kazan used to look, or you know with a hat on, if they're going to be film directors. You can spot them in the hall. And it's all

he, mind you. Women don't have a prayer to have a career as a director. There are very few in theater—and practically none in film.

So you think of it as a collaboration.

That's what I do. Like my group with Al Pacino. He came to me and
said, "Will you do this? 'Cause you have great ideas for this." I said,
"Yes, of course I'll do it, but I will only work *with* you. You're not going to be the actor and I'm not going to be the director, we're going to
do everything together." So that's a good way to deal with Al. He's got
to be dealt with that way, you know, and it's worked fine, since we've
done really wonderful work together, and I hope we'll continue. I
also work with people who—and this is always a source of rumination
and wonder and questioning—I work with people that I have a feeling about. And if I don't have a feeling about them, I can't, I don't
work with them. That's not all fear; it isn't that I don't have good
feelings about people. I've done some Tribeca readings—this Adrienne Kennedy piece—and I just said, "Send me somebody; you
know, just send me somebody," 'cause I think auditions are kind of
silly. If I had to have them, I would, but I think they're silly. And I
didn't have time, so the Tribeca piece was cast with all people I didn't
know. And I loved them! They worked wonderfully for me. They
suited the characters, and this was only a reading; we didn't have to
go too far. I mean, to play Adrienne Kennedy and make it work is just
the hardest thing you can do, and they just came in and did it.

What is it about certain people that draws you?

I need to know they're going to be open to really work. I need to know
they're going to be willing to collaborate, and not be people who
want to wait to be told what to do. Some actors really can't work; I
mean they don't want to, they want to be told. So I have a full group of
actors now that I call on, and I don't know if they're really that great

or not, but I know this Jessica Chastain, who's going to do *Madame Bovary*. She's so brilliant. She's going to do our *Salomé* too. I'm just in awe of her talent. I saw her do *Salomé* in audition; we did the whole play one day with her, and I don't know, everybody was there, I guess, and I thought, Why did I ever go into this profession? This woman is bringing stuff to this, probably the most difficult part in the world . . . I mean, why did I ever go into this profession? This girl is so much more gifted than I am, it's not to be believed. She's incredible. So she's going do my *Madame Bovary* at the Signature Theatre, and I'm hoping that it will find a life.

Well, you've had a long career. Do you see it as—oh, sorry, no. [Laughs.] You are having a long career. But can you see it from a distance, and see where you're going, or where you've been, and where you want to go? I mean hopes and dreams for the next ten years, the next twenty years?

I think I've gotten better. I mean my *aim*, Joe Papp used to say. I'd say to journalists, "I have no technique," and Joe would say, "Estelle, you have a technique. Your technique is that you have no technique." I always wanted to have it just happen. In other words, I don't have a technique. I could never fall back on affective memories of something I have worked subconsciously. I don't know what I do or why I do it; I just do it. So I have no kind of conscious technique, and I always wanted it to be that you would walk out and let the character emerge.

Have you been able to have that happen?

I think so. I think that therapy has been extremely helpful. That's an unconscious thing too. I'm singing much better than I have ever sung, because if I have anxiety about acting, the anxiety about singing is even worse. The anxiety about singing is unbelievable. But because of my therapy and, I don't know, my unconscious . . . you know, I'm from

New England. I'm a totally repressed person. I mean, that's what you learn to be, and I'm from a very very old 1632 New England family, which came from England. My mother was Swedish, but she was a Swedish Baptist from like the Arctic Circle. They're as repressed as New Englanders. So I mean I don't have a good background for self-expression. I think that's why it's mostly unconscious, that I just have always gone out there, and it either works or it doesn't, and in the beginning, it might not. You know, like once Lee said to me when I was trying to do *Medea*, "The moment when you were facedown on the floor was great." You know? Thanks a lot.

But you've always been able to—

All those men, they like the girls. You know that they don't take a woman's part as seriously, which of course is okay. You understand that, and you play into it sometimes, altogether complaining, but one does have to understand that one wasn't getting the kind of interest a pretty girl might.

Did you know that then?

Yeah, you can tell with a man. And of course, you learn with him like you do as an apprentice. You learn from watching. Lois Smith is very articulate about that, how she learned to act from watching people act and Lee critiquing them. So, you know, it's very clear, you have a certain idea about what a woman did up there, and he'll be sort of dallying with her instead of the way he treats me.

Were there actors you watched in your pre–Arthur Penn revelation period that you were inspired by?

Not really, not inspired by. I thought I wanted to be in the theater because I saw James Cagney do the George M. Cohan thing. And when I was a kid, I loved Dan Duryea in the movies. Oh, I loved him, and I loved Lionel Barrymore and Mae West. I just loved them, I loved what they did, because they're always these complicated people, and those are the people I really remember—except for Ginger Rogers and Fred Astaire—those are the three people who I really loved, and I loved their work. I love to create complicated people. I thought I really wanted to be in vaudeville; that kind of musical theater is much more live than a lot of theater. I still remember Jackie Gleason and Gertrude Nieson in *Follow the Girls*. But the theater, the conventional, commercial theater, just meant nothing to me. I did like Kim Stanley a lot. I never saw Marlon Brando in person. I liked John Garfield a lot. I worked with him in summer stock.

You saw Kim Stanley onstage?

I saw her do *A Far Country*, that thing about Freud. And you know, she'd walk on the stage, and she just sparkled. She just sparkled—I mean she lit up, they say that about people. But I had never seen anybody light up the stage. It was like Vince Young plays football. You can't believe it; she just sparkled. And you know I probably didn't see her in her prime. But I didn't finish about my arc.

That's what I want to get back to.

In the beginning, this thing either happened or it didn't. You can see how terribly trying that would be for an impressionable person. It didn't happen in musicals, because that's very easy to act in. But when you have a play, your emotional instrument really has to work. If a part suited me perfectly, like *Mrs. Dally Has a Lover*, which really put me on the map—I was always working after that—but if it didn't suit me absolutely perfectly like that . . . then some nights it would work and sometimes it wouldn't, like this business of auditioning at the Studio. I'd done this thing brilliantly, and then I'd get in a certain situation and freeze up. So you see, that's the trouble with being unconscious about your work. I think I have to credit my therapy with just about everything, actually. It happens that I could produce, and with Arthur's way of doing things I could *always* produce, because he set up this atmosphere for me where I couldn't help but produce. When I look at *Bonnie and Clyde* now, which I did at a tribute for Arthur the other night, and they had these scenes of me, I couldn't believe how every ounce of me was there. I mean it was just like those scenes in *The Miracle Worker*, yeah, just like what he'd done there. And then they put me on, and I thought, My god, there's the same thing. Just every ounce of you, every pore of you is into that. More and more that's happened through my life, so now I can deliver a performance that I don't have to just get through. So now opening nights are all that, because somehow, just because you get older and you do it all the time, I can walk out and I know it will happen, and I don't loll about any longer saying, I hope it happens tonight; I hope it happens tonight; oh, what will I do if it doesn't happen tonight? Oh, tonight it happens, what will I do tomorrow? I don't have any more of that; it just happens. When we were in *Pirates of Penzance*, we had this trio, and there was a laugh at a certain point, and Kevin Kline couldn't figure out what it was. We asked Bill Elliott, the conductor, why was the laugh there, and he said, "Well, Estelle is kicking up her leg." And then, sure enough, I noticed that I was kicking up my leg there. But I mean, I couldn't say to Kevin, Oh, I'm kicking up my leg, maybe that's helping.

Kevin would know why he got a laugh, right?

Oh sure he would. He's a different kind of actor.

So, in a situation like that, with an actor who works differently and who comes up with a really good performance, and you work in a completely different way . . . I guess I don't understand how it would—

It's a musical. I don't know how Kevin and I would do in a play; not that Kevin and I would be in a play, though we could be in *The Importance of Being Earnest*.

So if it isn't Kevin, if it's another actor who also produces a really good performance, as you do, but his journey is so different from yours—

Well, of course, all you have to do is pretend that he's somebody else. I did *Mert and Phil* with Michael Lombard, who was my loving husband. I mean this is not exactly something either he or I could relate to, but it just would happen through the rehearsal period that for my emotional instrument, he would take the form of someone I was very much in love with when I was a teenager or in college or something. He would just become that person in my acting, you see? I didn't say, What will I do? What will I do? No, but once it happened, I thought, Wow, that's The Method working without my trying to make The Method work. And that's what I'm aiming for, for things to just happen. So I often say to actors, "Find out, be aware of what's going on inside you." Even though I'm unconscious about my work, when things come up like that in preparation, then I make note of them in my head. Oh, look what's coming up in me.

Do you analyze your dreams?

I don't have all that many good dreams; I used to have anxiety ones when I was standing by for Annie Bancroft in *Mother Courage*. I had an anxiety dream that they were throwing tomatoes at me because I had to go on one night. [Laughs.] I don't know about dreams; I've never analyzed them.

Do you act for different reasons now than when you started out?

No, I don't think so. If I'm not acting for a while, then I'm liable to take a job I might not take if I was. This might seem a bit dumb but, I like to act, this is looking good to me. I don't have any rhyme or reason. I mean it's changed for me. I don't take a lot of jobs I might have taken in the past.

In terms of your career, can you see something that you've said in your work just by your choice of roles and what you bring to them, your philosophy of life . . . Are you saying something to us in a larger way? And I mean your best work, the things you really had a feeling for.

I don't think so. I think people expect from me a kind of straight-out performance, you know what I mean? I think they expect for my characters to be alive, be a little complicated, be funny, be interesting, have a sense of humor. I think maybe my characters have that, but I'm not even sure of that. What I basically do is, if a person in a play interests me, I don't care so much about the play, but if I would be interested to become that person, then I'm likely to take the part—or I have been in the past. I'm not anymore. But whether it was a big part or a small part, mostly it's a small part, because they're much more interesting. When I did *My Fair Lady*, I was so disappointed because it's a wonderful part, it's a wonderful musical, it's perfect. What more could you want? But it's basically uninteresting; she's not interesting as a person. But if I read a script where the character seems to be there for the purpose of making a point rather than as a full-fledged being, then I don't take it, because I don't know how to do that kind of thing. I probably do now, I probably could, but that's what I call sort of show-up acting—nothing wrong with it, it's just that it's not really interesting. I would read a lot of scripts and say, "I wouldn't know what to do with it, because this playwright is making a point with the play, and he's made these characters fit into his contrivance, and I don't really know how to play that." It means you've got to play something that doesn't have any depth, doesn't have any intricacy. It's okay, it's fine. I might do it now just for the fun of it, or I'm able to do a lot more than I used to do before, and I like to take chances now. You know I do readings, and sometimes I get a big applause when I walk on the stage, and mind you, just because I'm willing to take a lot more chances than I used to. I have no career to build—all those things you're busy doing in the rest of your life, auditioning for the next job, all these things that give you a little tension I suppose get in the way of your freedom. Now I don't care whether I'm right or wrong, or what. I just do, you know? And it pays off. If I could have been doing that all my life—though I may have been, to a large extent.

I think you have been more than you think.

Yeah, probably.

I think so. Are there any classical roles that you're interested in playing that you haven't played, that you would want to do?

Not really. I would like to do them all, but I'm a little too old to do them now. There was a period there where I had worked on *Medea* at the Studio, and I really wanted to do it. I had done Ranevskaya at the Studio, and I called all the people I knew, like Zelda Fichandler, people who ran regional theaters in those days, and said, "Boy, I've been working on these classical roles. I'd really like to do them, and I see them coming up in your season." And it was just the time when those companies turned from really doing good work to serving the community. Poor Joe Papp tried to get me as Gertrude in *Hamlet* so many times, and I never could get hired. Once, I worked on the role of Hamlet, and Lee said, women never do Hamlet, and everybody in the audience went, "Yes they do, Lee. Lee, Sarah Bernhardt. Lee, catch up." 'Cause my father had just died, and I thought, Gosh, maybe I understand this now. So I did something on it.

Do you think today that there's any equivalent to vaudeville for young actors?

I just think it's changed.

Do you think the quality of acting across the board is lower?

It depends on what your standards are. I don't think it's alive. I think you hardly ever go to a production where people are really alive. That's why *Abigail's Party* is so successful; it's not a great play, but they're very alive. In my experience with young actors, what I try to do is be alive. I mean the whole point of our *Salomé* was, you cannot do something tonight, like it, and do it tomorrow if it isn't really there. If the impulse isn't there tomorrow, you can't repeat it. So I wouldn't let anybody do anything but just be there and say their lines and go with an impulse, not that they are not supposed to go with their impulses, but they are not supposed to create something and then repeat it. They're supposed to always be alive.

How did that work out?

It worked great. Fantastic. Every night it was more exciting than the night before, and Marisa Tomei had to make that dance up every night. She could not do some steps and decide she liked them and do them all the time. It had to be an absolute. And everybody agreed to it; it had to be. And when we were rehearsing, if somebody repeated something or it didn't come out of an impulse, I'd say, "Can't do that—if you've got nothing to do, you do nothing. You wait for the impulse to just do the script. Look. That script is as good as Shakespeare." Oscar Wilde's *Salomé*. Extraordinary text. So, if you only hear the text, purely delivered, you've got a great experience. And of course, if you're an actor at all, you're not going to deliver it purely, because things are going to start happening every time you do it. But you can't ever do it, love it, and repeat it. Because then it's dead. And that is what I think of as the vaudeville technique. I mean, every night you had to go out and please that audience, excite that audience, or they would probably walk out.

Well, it seems like it would be thrilling for an actor to act that way.

I think it is. I think that people who work with us get pretty devoted. Marisa said it's the most difficult time she's ever had in her life; she never expects to have that again.

Marcia Gay Harden once said she had to face the same struggle every day, the struggle to allow herself to be.

Well, that's basically what I'm saying, isn't it?

Kevin Kline

The entrance to the Shubert offices is through a small brass
door in Shubert Alley. The manned elevator is barely big
enough for two of us and the elevator operator. What awaits us
on the library floor is a high-ceilinged Victorian atrium with a sky-
light two floors above our heads that was once the apartment of the
legendary theater impresario J. J. Shubert. We're led through a salon
of fringed damask sofas and Oriental carpets to a door flanked by a
white marble statue that might be a muse of the arts or a Ziegfeld girl,
and we walk into the library, where there is more fringed furniture
and a bookcase of leather-bound volumes. It is a fitting place to talk
to the leading Shakespearean actor of his day, Kevin Kline. When
Kevin arrives, he surveys his surroundings with a bemused expression and, without taking notice of the chair we've pulled out for
him—Chinese red, with carved dragons winding around its legs—
starts talking. It has been only two days since he closed in the Public
Theater's Central Park production of *Mother Courage*. He's still
bearded, and his hair, dyed for the role, is still blond. He confesses

his discomfort with this sort of interview and begins speaking before we can even turn on our tape recorder. He's a natural raconteur, good-natured and relaxed, with an implicit desire to entertain his listeners. In trying to explain what sometimes seems elusive to him, he uses his hands expressively, as if to sculpt meaning out of the air.

You started out studying music. Was there a particular time when that changed for you?

When I was at the University of Indiana, I was part of this off-campus company. We had a coffeehouse, and we did our own plays: improvisational theater, satirical political reviews on a weekly basis. How we ever managed to show up at enough classes to stay in school is beyond me. We wrote manifestos about what the theater was—it was very exciting. I was still in the music school at the time; then I switched to drama. Most of the people in the company were grad students, and by our third year they'd moved on to New York. But I and one or two others remained, and we asked Harold Guskin, who was a grad student, to join. We were doing some improv stuff, and Harold said, "You'll have to learn how to act." And he started teaching us. I was also performing on the main stage in *Wingless Victory* by Maxwell Anderson, based on the Jason and the Argonauts story. I asked Harold if he could help me with it, and we took it line by line. Harold said, "What are you doing?" And I said, "Well, I'm thinking if Olivier did it, he'd do it like this, or if Brando did it, it'd be like this." And he said something like, "You're imitating what you think actors who you idolize would do. You're trying to do it 'right.' You think there's a right way to do this. What do *you* feel about that line? What does that line mean to *you*? How can you take responsibility for that line?" I thought that was irrelevant. I mean I'm an actor, I'm playing someone else. What does it mean to *me*? And as we worked on it, I thought it was sort of like being an artist. I could bring my intellect, spirit, soul to bear on this. Harold had a way of going to the essential things, and he knew just what buttons to push for a young college-age actor about who you were, and what being a man was, and what being alive meant. That was the beginning of what has been an ongoing relationship.

Did Juilliard support that point of view or teach you other things?

Oh yeah, other things. It's funny, because I'm frequently cited by the school and the press as a product of The Juilliard School. Actually I went to Juilliard after having had four years of college, where I was acting in university theater and in this company, but I think I learned more doing that than playing Macheath in *Threepenny Opera* or Prometheus. The year I went, I was to join the preexisting, first graduating class. They'd been there two years, and many people had been thrown out or dropped out or had run screaming, so they were down from thirty-five to fifteen people. The idea was to have the fourth year be like a rep company, so they needed to fill out the class. They started this advanced program, and that's where they added me, David Ogden Stiers, and Mary Joan Negro to the class. I missed the first two years at Juilliard, which was, as I heard at that time, the whole structure that Michel Saint-Denis and John Houseman had concocted. The first year, they'd strip you down and tear you apart, and then around the middle of the second year or the third year, they'd start putting back the pieces but in this more informed, educated, inspired, heavily influenced manner.

How did they come to you?

I auditioned, having not been called back at the TCG [Theatre Communications Group] auditions, and thought, Oh I'm a failure. I can't really act. I was getting great parts in college, I was a big shot, and then I was put in my place at the TCG auditions. I opened with a speech of Prometheus', which I had immense success with on the main stage of the university. Out of context, it just *sucked*. So I went to Juilliard for this audition, but of course I thought I didn't have a chance. And in a way, I learned a lesson in that audition about caring and not caring, that strange paradox of trying to do it right, or to be perfect, or imitating some idea in your head about what it should be, or giving them what they want. But at this audition I didn't care. I thought I didn't have a chance. I was freer. I had fun. And I got in.

Did you start working on productions right away?

Right away.

So you didn't have that many classes.

I had an acting class and lots of speech with Edith Skinner. And lots of voice with Liz Smith. And William Burdick came in and taught us all how to bow in every different period, how to take snuff, how to work with a fan, a walking stick, every kind of period movement, and dealing with the accoutrements of those various periods. We were encouraged to read Saint-Denis's book *Theater: the Rediscovery of Style*, which was sort of a textbook about the idea of understanding what style is—you will learn that there is a style that is Shakespearean, a style for Greek tragedy, a style for Noël Coward, a style for David Mamet—and exploring what style is. There was a lot of technical speech, voice, movement. Movement with Anna Sokolow to me was worth the price of admission. Every movement had to have an emotional component. She talked about reaching for the ceiling, reaching with every fiber of your being. She'd pull you by the hair, then get you moving. That and mask class were really good for me because I was very physically and emotionally inhibited. Mask class was wonderful. You put on this mask of a big fat person or other commedia dell'arte—inspired types, and then you look in the mirror and you find something that matches it. It's totally working from the outside in, with a face that's not yours. And then you find a way of moving, a posture, and you find a voice, a way of talking. That's the character mask. The neutral mask is a whole other thing. It's just this neutral mask with no expression. If you hear a horn honking and you have the mask on, it's just using your whole body to hear, to see, to do. I remember one exercise was to wake up, pick up a rock, and throw it in the ocean. And you should be exhausted when it's over, since because you have the mask, you have only your body, your whole physical being, to have the experience.

The purpose is to free you.

Right. And the result is, you are free. You are disinhibited. You get more into your body.

Does this work when you do movies?

When I did *De-Lovely*, where I played Cole Porter, there was this amazing makeup transformation that took five hours. And I thought, All that character-mask work, I can actually use that. It's looking at this face in the mirror and thinking, So what goes with this? Build up the shoulders, give me a little paunch. Not that, had I not had the mask work, I couldn't have done it. It's just that having had it, there was a sense that I was not afraid of the artifice, of working from the outside in. It's not me, it's not my face anymore. So there's a practical, direct application of that work. It's really pushing yourself, pushing the outlook, saying, What if I had this face? The mask is just thinking outside of the personality of the actor. It's not you anymore.

Is it harder for you when you play a role that is like you?

Oh no. I mean, those exercises, to free you, to disinhibit you, get you to think of external as well as internal. Harder? No. I mean I don't work that way. I rarely work from the outside in.

You trained as a musician. Did you sing at Juilliard?

No. There was no singing at all. It was the end of the third year when Gerry Guttierez said, "Let's do a mock Tony Award. We'll call it the Julies" and we started doing songs and things. And Houseman said, "Patti LuPone! You can really sing!" And no one knew. But musicals were not part of the curriculum.

Why haven't you done more musicals?

It was never a priority of mine.

They're offered to you?

Yeah.

And you just don't want to?

I don't now, because they're so expensive. With a Broadway musical they want at least nine months, eight shows a week. Plus an out-of-town tryout. When do you see your family? Your nights are gone; your weekends, when they are not in school, are gone. You catch them a couple hours when they come home from school. I am much happier doing a limited run at the Public, or the Beaumont, where it's a twelve-week maximum. And even that takes its toll. Film is much easier. Shoot a film in New York, you can be home for dinner. If you work with Sidney Lumet, you're home for lunch practically. He prides himself on finishing at five every day. That's the practicality of why I don't do musicals. I was a pianist; my father studied singing and wanted to be an opera singer when he was very young. I grew up with opera in the house. I know what great singing sounds like. I know I'm not a singer. When asked, I'll play a part where the charac-ter sings. When I was doing *Pirates of Penzance*, people asked, "Will you come and do your cabaret act?" I don't have a cabaret act. They assume that if you're in a musical, you have some cabaret act ready to go. Angela Lansbury told me, "I could never get up and sing in a microphone, that's the scariest thing." She said, "My character sings, I don't sing." That's it, isn't it? I played the Pirate King, who not only loves to sing but thinks he's a great singer! That I can do.

Couldn't you play the part of somebody who's a cabaret singer who has a cabaret act?

Yes, I could, though I wouldn't want to see it. Like I did with Cole Porter. My excuse was—and I was the only one who sang live—Porter was not a good singer, so I don't care what it sounds like. It's much better that I wasn't lip-synching, which is what we did for the movie of *Pirates*, which was just insanity. To try to act and listen to a track with clicks to keep you on the beat . . . With Cole Porter I played and sang. I can sing much better if I'm playing the piano, because I'm not thinking that much about the singing. Cole Porter would be thinking about the chords and the thing that he's written, not about putting a song over. So I had all these kinds of rationalizations for why I didn't have to sing well. The same way with the Brecht. Brecht did not want great singing. Good, I don't have to take a singing lesson. I don't even warm up. It's about acting the song.

Let's talk about your work with directors. Your first Hamlet was with Liviu Culei.

With Liviu Culei, I said that I like to explore and really do foolish, crazy things and really push the boundaries and find out, like a sculptor chipping away until what's left is a sculpture. The same way in rehearsals. Some of it is finding out how not to do it by having tried it, by experiencing, by opening doors and going down certain hallways or certain roads and then finding that it was a dead end or that it was a ridiculous idea, but there's something about it that is pertinent. After a week of re-hearsals of *Hamlet*, Liviu said, "Okay, now we've explored. Now we start to set things." I said, "Well, why?" "Because we have to." He's an east-ern European director who has a vision, who's done the play ten other times and has his production in his head in a way. And I said, "The structure is the words. I'll never change any of these words, I promise. But I'd like to still keep exploring it." And he was sort of puzzled by that. I'm sure there are American directors who feel the same way.

Did you have that with George Wolfe in Mother Courage?

Nooo, oh no. Except that he kept talking about "muscularity." We all teased him about it. He said, "Once you step on this stage, you're part of this machine, a bombed-out munitions factory, and you have to go with the machine." I'm the machine. I'm very actor-centric, as you know—eccentric perhaps in my actor-centricity. But I always found that if it comes from the actor, whether it's film or stage—yes, the director says, "More of that, less of that, that was a bad idea and try this,"—but if the director says, "It's gotta be like this," I immediately think, Gotta be? Because of what? Precedence? Con-vention? Some idea you have?

What happens when you say that to a director?

A lot of directors say "great," a lot of directors say nothing. They let the actor do his work and then they catch you when you fall off the high wire, if you've chosen to take the high wire.

But you must somehow come together with the director.

Absolutely. And hopefully you're on the same page before you start, so that you know you're in the same world and that you're doing the play or the film for more or less the same reasons.

Have you ever turned something down because in these preliminary conversations you were just at loggerheads with the director?

I've turned things down because I knew the director worked a certain way. I remember this wonderful Russian man who was the director of the Moscow Art Theater. Was it Efremov?

Oleg Efremov, yes.

He was going to do his production of *Crime and Punishment*, which he had done there, and they wanted me to play Raskolnikov. They had a video of him rehearsing with the actors, and he was literally acting out the parts: "Okay, the hand goes in the pocket on this word, and you can do this on this word." And I've seen brilliant productions done that way. The effect or the result is not necessarily bad; it's just not for me. It's my own personal thing with authority figures or something, some deep psychological peculiarity that I always feel. "Now, okay, you wanted me to do this, you wanted me to do that . . ." It takes you out of the moment. You're a generation removed from the immediacy of it.

So you wouldn't find it a challenge?

It's a very long conversation, how you work with directors. Once you achieve a certain degree of ownership, once you've had enough experience or gone to school, the first thing you learn is, How do I be convincing? When I first started acting, it was, "Did you believe it? Did you believe it?" Offstage or on, "Did you believe I was really upset? I was acting." You know, like "master thespian" on *Saturday Night Live* [very actorly]—"Acting! I fooled you!" So once you know how to be convincing, then there's a whole other array of questions. A prime one is, where is the line between being challenged in a way you want to be challenged, and where do you cross the line where you have suddenly compromised your performance in order to help a director achieve a vision? For years I would hate it when a director said, "I need you to do that while you're walking from stage right to stage left." "Oh, but it feels so much better to be still." Now that I'm directing, I say, "Laertes, you've gotta move on that line because I've got an army coming onstage right," or whatever. And most actors, me included, know they could do it standing on their head, but how many headstands before I've given a performance I don't own anymore? If the director gives a direction and I go, "Oh, yes!" and there's resonance, then it's mine, then I appropriate it. The connection between authorship and authority onstage is if I have had something to do with it. If it's built on instinct, impulses I've had during rehearsal or previously, then I own it. But *if* I am doing it for him, or her, there is this sense of not owning it.

Is it the way a director asks you to do something? Is it the sense that he should back off and let you find it?

I worked with a film director who, after we did the scene and he was happy with it, said, "Okay, now let's do it differently. Just do something else." You have an idea about a scene. If it turns out, in the doing of it, to be exactly as you imagined it, or as the director imagined it or the writer, that's great. But one hopes in the doing of it you'll find something, you'll be surprised by something. Oh, I thought it was about this, and it is . . . but there's this other thing. And sometimes that little revelation of, Oh, I'm learning that there's a part of me that's actually *glad* you're dying. This happened during a deathbed scene, and there was a part of me that was very curious to see what this person looked like dead. If you've never seen someone die, what happens, how kind of fascinating it is to see the life go out of someone's body . . . It doesn't sound like a dramatic choice, like, Oh, I guess I should crumble, or break down in tears. You go through the list of stock conventional responses to any given situation. But as an actor, ideally, you are trying to ask yourself and discover what's really going on. What is the truth of the scene? There are myriad truths. Which is the truth that is most interesting to you? Which is the truth that is the most pertinent one to you? Why do you want to play this part? Why do you want to be in this scene? What is it to you? And it makes the actor less of a puppet doing someone's bidding. If a pianist is playing a Rachmaninoff Third Piano Concerto just exactly the way his teacher wanted him to, you know it's a young player who still has his mentor. But a good mentor is going to tell him, "I want to hear *your* Rachmaninoff Third Piano Concerto. It's gotta be you. So what do you want to do with that phrase?"

When you start working on a role, do you feel that it's already there somewhere in you? That somewhere there's a core of a true response, and you're out to find it?

Yes, but to varying degrees. Sometimes when you read it, it resonates with you. On a very gross level, you read a comedy script and (a) you find it funny and (b) you know how to make it funny. Or you think, Oh yeah, I love the script. Or, I just can't wait to say that line. Or, I want to do that line or play that scene. Because I sort of know how it should go; there's a feeling that you just get it. And it's fresh and original and it's true, and there's something different about it.

Is that why you choose a role?

No. There are always different reasons. Sometimes I think, Yeah, I can do that, and other times I don't know if I can do that, but I really think I need to. There's enough there that I feel the role will push me, but it's scary, and the scariness is part of the charm, not knowing if I can do it. Rarely is there one where you think, There is no way I want to do this or I could do this. Even if I could, I don't understand this world, I don't understand this character. I have no business in this, I have no business at all. But there is a lot that I'm not sure about, that it would be a very interesting exercise to discover. I'm not even sure what I like about this, it just has a good heart, or it's about something, I'm not sure what it is.

What about when you talk to the director? If their vision of—

I'm very leery about directors who have a vision about, say a Shakespeare play: "I have an idea for *Twelfth Night*." "Really, what is it?" "Well, it all takes place in . . ." Or it's really about the husband and wife. Or it's really about sex. Or it's going to be set in this period because it really works. I've seen these productions. The first act works great that way, and maybe the second, but somewhere around the third or fourth act, you're pushing it. And you've lost me. When I met with Liviu, he said his idea for Hamlet was that he's a man who takes responsibility for the age he lives in. That's a big idea, that idea interests me. In other words, he's not just a guy who says, "Oh, whatever." Not all directors have visions. Sometimes they wanna just get it up there and do it well. I remember reading Mike Nichols talking about directing in the theater or film, and he said he'd just try not to fuck it up.

What kind of preparing did you do for Sophie's Choice?

I stayed up all night, I was so prepared! A month into filming, Meryl said, "Are you saying the lines as written? Because no one else is, you know. This isn't Shakespeare." Now I'm giving away all my secrets! Meryl knew I was about to do *The Big Chill* after *Sophie's Choice*, and she said, "Don't prepare. Just roll out of bed and do it." *Sophie's Choice* was my first film, and we didn't have four weeks of rehearsal to learn the lines, which was what I was used to in the theater. I was madly trying to learn the lines. I was blessed with Alan Pakula, who said, "Think of this as rehearsal." He knew I was from the theater, he had seen me in the theater, he cast me from what he had seen me do-ing in the theater. He said, "You know how in rehearsal you just work on one scene, you do it a few times? Just know that the time it all works, that's gonna be the take that I use. And feel free to make a fool of yourself, try anything." I remember him saying that whatever he said before a take, if I got a different impulse, fuck what he said. "You have to find your madness. This has to be your Nathan. Just go with any impulse. We don't have to use it if it's terrible. If it doesn't work, we don't use it."

Did you believe him?

Yeah. I thought, What a cool thing. That's why rehearsals are very pertinent. People don't have open rehearsals, because actors don't want people to see them fail. Same way you have to trust a director. You try something in a take that really didn't work in a major way, and you hope it never gets printed. With Pakula we were invited to watch the dailies, and I realized we totally agreed about what the character was, and it was just so great. So the process and the result was a complete collaboration.

Before you started, did you have a sense of the way you wanted the char-acter to be?

I wanted to somehow marry myself to this character in the book, which was astonishing. Brilliantly written, complex, highly troubled person. I remember meeting Simone Signoret the summer right af-ter I finished the movie, and she had read the book. And she asked if I'd read the book first, and I said, "but of course," and she said often it's good not to read the book, because you try to do the book instead of just looking at the screenplay and serving that. You try to squeeze something from the book that's not there on the page. And I thought that was very interesting. Actually, there were a couple of things that

I did try to squeeze in. I said, "Oh, I'm missing that line, the way he says it," and Alan put it in.

Did it do something to your performance to watch yourself in the dailies?

I remember being told by somebody that if you go to dailies with Meryl, she'll talk not about herself but about *her*, the character. It's like she's not looking at herself. She was able to just look at Sophie. And I had the same thing. At the first dailies, the first thing I saw was how Nestor Almendros had lit me carrying her in the door after she'd fainted in the library. And I said, "That's it, that's him!" I was able to separate myself.

Do you always watch dailies?

Yeah, until I had kids. And then it was a question of, well, I can go to dailies and get home at nine, or I can go home, have dinner maybe, or see my children for a couple of hours before they go to bed. If I'm on location, I'll go to dailies.

And it helps your performance?

Sometimes. I remember seeing this scene I did where the character had sort of an underbite. I have an overbite, but I thought, Yeah. That's him. I should do more of that.

What do you do if, a week into the shooting, you suddenly realize that all that stuff you did last week was wrong?

It's all theory until the camera rolls. Maybe the first scene you shoot—you drive up in a car, you get out of the car, you walk up to the door, you ring the doorbell. As soon as you've done the first take, you think, Oh, I guess that's how he walks. That ship has sailed. And then as soon as you say a line, I guess that's how he talks, because that's how it came out. Unless you've really gotta do an accent or some-thing, you can keep working on that. Well, Oops, the accent went there, it's not there, it's too thick here. You think, I'll fix it in post, or I'll look for another take where it's better. A lot of it is purely techni-cal, external things like that, whether it's the look, the makeup, the clothes. Like, if he wears that jacket, he's not the guy anymore. No more of that jacket. No more ties, whatever. It's like a painter who's painting something: I like this part, I should do more of this. But if I do green here, all the balance is off, the wrong color's down here. In a way I guess you're working from that external place. I've done whole films where I've never gone to the dailies. Maybe I don't like the way he's shooting it or I don't want to care about how it looks or what the result is; I'm just going to work instinctively, internally, and never think about it. Or I do go because I want to see how they're lighting me. How are they making me up? How are they costuming me? What's my palette? Oh, he's using a lot of this kind of light, so it's really making me look healthy. I should be more drawn and sal-low, we have to adjust that with the makeup people, or this color shirt, this is a bad idea. That's why the makeup and hair people go to the first week of dailies, to make sure it's the look that works for the cin-ematographer, for the director, for the actor.

Have you been . . . well, shocked is too strong a word, but surprised at your performance when it's put together? Do you believe that the editor creates the performance?

Most people think that editors do what they used to do in the 1930s and forties where directors made three movies that year, shot them in a certain way so that you could only edit them in a certain way, gave the film to the editor, and he edited it. Today the director is there with the editor, saying that he wants to look at all the other takes again. "I want to start with the close-up, and I want to cut out this."

The editor is there to make suggestions, and it's a dialogue, but the director has the final say.

I mean the director-as-editor, creating the performance to the point that you might have thought, My performance was better than that.

I remember when I thought that the director cut the one line that to me was the key to the character, the best line the character ever said, the most interesting thing that was an underpinning, that suddenly made you understand, as well as sort of making it more mysterious at the same time. "You cut that!?" "Yeah, it didn't move the plot."

An actress we know said that Woody Allen would ask her to do a scene four or five different ways, so that she did not know what her character was going to come out to be. Has that happened to you?

Most notably when I did *Dave* with Ivan Reitman, which is a film I really love and am very proud to be part of. Ivan shot a lot of coverage: "We're gonna do it a little tighter, a little looser; now we're going to do a push in; now we're going to do the scene, move the camera right. Now we're going to do a reverse master." All I know is we did a lot of takes. Also, he'd say, "Okay, now do one different." And we'd try variations. "Try one . . . go crazy." A lot of physical comedy. I fell out of about a dozen chairs. In the movie I fall out of one chair. They showed me the Lincoln Bedroom in the White House, where I'm supposed to spend the night. What Gary Ross had written is, he jumps on the bed and starts going crazy. I said, "When I sit at the foot of the bed, I think of George Washington or Lincoln . . . I think maybe he's in awe, or terrified and vulnerable." He said, "Let's try it both ways." So we shoot one where I just kind of attack it silly and jump on the bed, and we improvised some stuff about trying on the glasses and picking up the phone, just shtick. "We'll just follow you around." He allowed us to improvise. He tried different things. And while he was editing, before I saw it, people would ask me how it went, and I had no idea. It could be really broad, really cheap, really silly, or it could be charming and real.

What did you think when you saw it?

Except for one moment, which we talked about and he said he would change, Ivan always used the take that was the most real, the most not played. It was what I always called the *Dr. Strangelove* tonality. You know how in *Dr. Strangelove* everybody's just really serious: "We're in the war room. There's no fighting in the war room." In *Dave*, there's Frank Langella and me and Kevin Dunn, and Chuck Grodin trying to make it real, as opposed to funny acting. The cinematographer was not doing comedy lighting, where everything's bright and shimmery. There were shadows and depth. It became more of a romantic comedy, more Capra-esque, real. It wasn't just a comedy. And I was thrilled. There's just one take he asked me to do that I questioned, and he used it. It's when I'm taking a shower and Sigourney comes in, I've got my back to her, and she screams, "How dare you! Turn around when I'm talking to you." And I think the jig is up, because I'm gonna expose myself, as it were, to her, and she's going to see something that's different. We did about half a dozen takes, and Reitman says, "Just do one where you look at her, and then you look down, then look back up and look terrified." And I said, "Why would I look?" He just wanted to me to do it, so I did, and that's the one he used.

Did it get a laugh in the movie theater?

Beforehand he said, "See how it plays. It plays great. If you don't like it, I'll change it. But listen to the audience tonight at the screening." And it wasn't just the audience. I was so happy with the movie. Ivan did a beautiful job. But in retrospect I wish I had taken him up on his offer to change it.

Do you prefer the stage because of this lack of final say on the performance?

I know I'm supposed to say yes. You can do things on film that you can't do onstage, and there are things you can do onstage that you can't do on film. But to say I prefer the stage . . . there are fewer mitigating factors that come between your performance and the audience's experience, yes. Theater to me is much more of an aural experience. Maybe because when I come back to the theater, it's to do plays with great language, like Shakespeare or Shaw or Chekhov. And the stories are told through the way the characters speak as well as behave, their particular locution. In the theater, the way they talk is much more of an element to describe who that character is, the way they express themselves. Whereas in film it's the opposite, it's visual. Yes, there's some great dialogue and great language and great characters in film that I've been privileged to play, who speak a certain way and their particular diction is particularly eloquent for the character.

You always come back to the theater. What is the impulse for you to do that?

It's the material. I mean, where am I going to do *Hamlet* and *Lear*, *Measure for Measure* or *Mother Courage*?

What are you doing to prepare for Lear?

Trying to get out of it.

No you're not. Don't.

Mother Courage came along. I had just finished the workshop of *Lear*, just working on it with the idea that if the director and I got along, and we felt like it was something we wanted to pursue and we were both intrigued, excited, and a little terrified . . .

Who was the director?

James Lapine. We'd been working on it for a couple weeks and, in the process, starting to build a company, actors who were not just good for that production, but who were good classical actors to have. And so we worked on it for two weeks, and then *Mother Courage* came up, so I could stop thinking about *Lear*, and now I'm starting to think about it again. But it was so hard to do *Mother Courage*, to step in like that after they'd been rehearsing for three weeks.

It was a very generous act of yours.

Maybe. Foolhardy. I hope I did a service and not a disservice, because it was opening in two weeks and I was still learning these lines and trying to fit in. Whenever I've gone back to the theater in the last fifteen or twenty years, it's not, How can I fit my Hamlet into this production? No, it's all being built around the central character. So here I was playing an ancillary character.

You've never been in that position?

Well yeah, but a long time ago. I've done only major roles for the last twenty years.

But Lear *will be created around you—*

Yeah, and that may be scaring me. I had a terrible bout of lack of self-confidence with *Mother Courage*. I mean I literally told people—

Not to come?

No no, not *not* to come. But . . . I can't know who's there. Even my own family, I cannot know if you are there. I don't want to know who you got the tickets for. No one can come backstage, right through to the closing night party. I didn't go to that. People come backstage and go, "I love your hair!" or, "I love that moment when you do that," and then it's ruined. Or, "Ooh, I loved that scene," and then I think, Oh, and the other scenes sucked, right?

But that's always the problem with coming backstage.

Exactly. Usually I've got a thick enough skin. But this one I was more susceptible, more vulnerable. George wanted it to be assaultive, tough love. He said, "Anytime you get an impulse to touch her face, grab her roughly." And I immediately think, Why does this have to be a rough relationship? I didn't understand. The whole thing changed from what my first impulses were, which were very fresh because I hadn't had the time to work on it at all. It was fairly comic. And some of the speeches are pretty circuitous. The character just sort of loved the sound of his own voice, and he loved giving advice, and he's just bullshitting, trying to get some free brandy and what-ever. And it was funny, but then we have to see this brutal side. Now Brecht's notes said, in that last scene when he tells her she can't bring Kattrin, "at no point must the cook ever seem cruel, it is not about cruelty, it is about the circumstances." I was told that George didn't read any of Brecht's notes, and I understand that, because Wilfred Leach didn't want us to do a D'Oyly Carte production of *Pirates of Penzance*. And even Brecht said, "I have all these notes. I have all these pictures. But if you're an artist, you can't follow exactly what I say. You've gotta do your thing." And I respect that, but I thought, Do I do George's way, or do I do Brecht's way? What's my way? And I kept trying a bunch of different things through the whole run. Some performances I was cruel. I remember Meryl said to me on the first day of *Sophie's Choice*, "Don't ever be afraid to hurt me . . . because you can't." It was kind of a challenge. And I love surprises . . . it was all about surprising each other to elicit a fresh response. So in

Mother Courage one night I would grab her and be really tough, or not even look at her and say, "You can't bring her." You know, just brutal, and that's how it is. And other times it was, "I'm sorry, but look. I know you want to, but you can't."

I remember one night you grabbed her breast.

Closing night I finally got it. I think it was like a closing night present or something. We never spoke about it, but clearly the idea was that sex and the war were purely genital. It's not foreplay, there's no affection, no lovey-dovey. It's fucking and grabbing.

How open and vulnerable are you to what critics say?

I remember Walter Kerr wrote this piece about some moment I had in *Loose Ends*, and that was what killed that moment. It was one of those things I did sometimes, but not always. Then you suddenly become very self-conscious about the moment.

So even if it's a good comment—

It'll make you self-conscious, because no one sees the same movie or the same play. And I've read reviews—never during the run, but at the end of a run of a play or for a movie—and the very thing one critic loves is the same thing another one hates. Did you read some of the reviews for *Mother Courage*? All over the place! And the thing that this guy loves is the *very* thing that this guy hates! Also, whenever you do a classic play, like with Shakespeare, I always say, "Don't read any of the reviews," because Shakespeare especially is every critic's opportunity to air their pet theory about the play and how you've fallen short or achieved, and it's all about how much they know about the play. You've got nothing to do with it.

You don't read anything during the run?

The second time I did *Hamlet*, I waited a year before I read the reviews.

Because you felt that vulnerable?

No. I didn't care. I felt good about it. I could tell that the audience liked it. PBS asked to put it on *Great Performances*, not *Okay Performances*. I thought, I guess it's okay. It's not a failure. Not that it was the definitive *Hamlet* for the ages, but it's all right.

Wasn't there a time when critics and actors actually had a dialogue?

Maybe Kenneth Tynan and the National and his closeness to Olivier. I was talking to Frank Rich a few weeks ago about *Lear*, and he said, "Oh, it's great that you're doing it. The only time I've seen it work is when Paul Scofield did it." I had a conversation with John Simon once, and he said, "Oh, you're being so nice. I know I was very mean to you." I said, "Well, yes you were." But John Simon also gave me some of the best reviews I've ever gotten. When he liked something, he would gush, so I forgive him everything. I remember the night *The New York Times* was at *Mother Courage*: bad performance. Meryl and I both hated that night. The advantage with movies is it's frozen.

And they don't say, "the night I saw it." Theater critics don't acknowledge the ephemeral nature of it.

No. They think that somehow it's frozen. It's different every night! One night we did *Mother Courage* in the pouring rain. Clearly the audience was not going to leave. We were into the show, it started to drizzle, we stopped, we waited ten minutes, it subsided a little, we went on. We were all wearing such shabby clothes, it's not like we had to protect the costumes. And Meryl said, "They sat in line. They want to see this play in whatever form we can give it to them." And we did it in the drizzle, and it was wonderful. Another night, more than a drizzle, pouring rain. We stopped the show twice, waited for it to subside, and we'd start it again. At the intermission, when we announced that we were going to continue, it became this event. And I talked to people, and they forgot it was raining. The same way you forget that there are airplanes, and guns being shot off, or whatever the hell's going on in the park. Meryl actually went out during one of the pauses and started mopping the floor, and they were going, "Mer-yl!" and it became this crazy event about doing Brecht in the rain. Soaked with the mud, and we're all slipping and sliding, and it was great. But that's not the same show that Ben Brantley from the *Times* saw. I remember I was in a terrible depression after I read the one *Hamlet* review that didn't like it. Because I think he was the one who got it. I fooled all the others [laughs]. So that's my sickness. I'm invulnerable and completely vulnerable, so I just avoid critics.

The thing that is so prized about actors is their vulnerability, the ability for us to see you. But it's so difficult to be an actor that—

In college, when I first decided to be an actor, I was reading Camus, and he talked about the absurd, that the actor's life is one of the true absurdist lifestyles, being an actor is really living an absurd life. The more I do it . . . it doesn't get less absurd.

But the more you do it, the more you have, the more experience you have, the more chops you have, the more—

But the continued absurdity of it sometimes is in starker relief than it was in the past. It's also a product, I think, of doing movies and becoming a known quantity. You think, Oh god, I've gotta do an accent, I'm going to grow this beard. But it's just me, it's just that guy again, it's just this schmuck. And you think, Who am I kidding? I'm really not fooling anybody.

But isn't it the same on the stage? I mean it's you playing Falstaff, but it's still you. That's why they're going to see it. Even though you're all made up.

That's why that was such a great experience, because I was scared shitless. Because I had not gone onstage and done anything where I transformed myself. People literally were asking for their money back afterward, because they didn't come to see the understudy, they came to see me. They didn't recognize me! And I was thrilled! But then I thought, What's wrong with the understudy? So I was delighted to hear these reports that people didn't know it was me, because so often, in films especially, it's just me, I look like myself and am pretty much just using my voice and myself. But that Falstaff was real acting: I did a thing with my voice, I did the whole physical thing. And I thought they would just laugh me off the stage . . . in a bad way. Who does he think he is? And people were saying, "Why are you doing Falstaff? You're too young and too thin." Because it's funny! It's the greatest comic role in the Western canon. Which is reason not to do it, because how presumptuous! And then I started thinking—during Falstaff—What about Lear? I mean, it was other actors who suggested it, and I started thinking about it. And then I started thinking, Are you kidding? Ultimately, it can't matter. I have to decide for my own self-destructive reasons.

You are such a Hamlet. Thinking and seeing all sides of the question and what should you do. Do you see what I mean?

That's another part of the absurdity. Because you know what you're going to say, what she's gonna say, how it's all gonna end. It's all pre-destined. And your job is to somehow make it *happen*. I mean, the audience knows the play—it all ends in tears—but still we have to have it happen, we have to have the experience, somehow submit ourselves to that. It's the ability to achieve what Keats called the *negative capability*. Shakespeare did it in an exemplary way: to live with uncertainty. I'm drawn to characters who see both sides. One of my favorite moments from *Mother Courage*—and there were few—was when she comes in and I've just seen Eilif taken off and killed. She says, "Look me in the eye. Tell me what's going on." And I can tell her or not tell her. And what would I lose by telling her, what would I gain, and how much of it is just that I need her? And so to me there's a moment there where I thought, I have to give myself the option of telling her the truth or lying. As you know, he lies. It's a fleeting moment, because that's what life is like, that's the gray area in which we live. And what I hate about most Hollywood movies is they eliminate the gray area. You know from the poster that it has to have a Hollywood ending, it has to have a Hollywood middle, it has to have a Hollywood beginning. And that's a kind of storytelling which is a coddling, sort of "everything's going to be fine." And look, there's a place for that in our culture. We sometimes need to be told fairy tales that are somehow a template that we can measure our own life against.

Are there other things you want to do in the next five or ten years?

Good question. What do you do after *Lear*? I wish I knew. I've always had a list of great Shakespeare parts, like Coriolanus and the Scottish play, and Iago. I've always wanted to do *Othello*. Of course, you could do that in a reading. I almost did it for the radio, just didn't have enough organization. Right now I really don't know what I want to do. I just read a bunch of scripts when the play ended, movie scripts. Nothing interested me. There are times when I think I don't want to act anymore. A lot of that is the level of the scripts. The movies being made just get worse and worse every year. Or I'm not getting good enough scripts. There are only about six or seven a year, and they're going to XYZ. So much of it is just so homogenized, even when there's a ton of money, it's soul deadening. There's no reason to do it. Then sometimes I think I'll just do theater for the next few years.

Have you ever had your own production company to develop properties?

I've been offered that, though not recently, but there was a period in the late eighties, early nineties where every actor had a production company. The friends of mine who were doing it were going through development hell, where you wait for the writer and then you wait for a rewrite, then you wait another year for that, and then . . . By the way, I've never done what I'm doing right now. I've turned down so many "interviews with actor" books.

Why is that?

It's sort of like the magician telling how he does his trick. I hate for anyone to know how truly simplistic my approach is [laughs]. I'd like to keep a bit of mystery or mystique about it. It is a mystery, and I can't explain what it is. And I think that every time out, it's a little bit different, and if it isn't, I try to make it a little bit different, to redefine what acting is. If it's possible.

Mandy Patinkin

M andy Patinkin is looking very fit, fresh from a workout at
the gym, when we accidentally meet him at the service elevator of his building. We ride up with him and enter the
huge, sprawling apartment where he's lived for more than twenty
years with his wife, the actress and writer Kathryn Grody, and their
two sons. The apartment bears the unmistakable evidence of family
life: walls of books, paintings, theater posters, objects brought back
from travels, family photographs, even children's drawings directly
on the wall. Two black Labradors nuzzle us, then go back to what they
were doing. We follow Mandy to his office. One wall of shelves holds
the scripts for plays and films and TV shows he's done. In front of
the shelves is a small piano. We sit on a well-worn sofa, Mandy in a
desk chair on wheels, which suits him, because Mandy cannot be
still. He rolls around as he talks—reaches for scripts to show us an-
notations in the margins, letters for us to read, a photograph of himself with the first teacher who encouraged him to be an actor. Always
in motion, Mandy seems to be looking for something at all times: a

word, a phrase, the right thought; he keeps talking, gesticulating, excited, enthusiastic, and we're carried along with him. And though he's talking *to* us, answering our questions, it seems like what we're feeling must be the effect he has on an audience: he keeps us spellbound, rapt by the energy of his search, his reach in different directions for the thing he's after in life, in art, in performing. It turns out, in fact, that for Mandy, everything is constantly in process.

When did you know that you could sing, and that it was something special?

I began singing at seven years old in the boys choir in the synagogue on the South Side of Chicago, and the cantor's wife asked me if I would come forward and conduct a special number. It was "Dem Bones, Dem Bones, Dem Dry Bones." And while I did it, I turned around and did the twist in front of the whole congregation. That was my first performing moment. I loved it. I got all the attention that I desperately needed. It felt good. My mother thought I should have some singing lessons, because people said, "Oh, he has a nice voice." I hated the lessons. A very nice lady, but I hated them. I had problems in high school, and I ended up at the Kenwood High School on the South Side of Chicago, which was a theater school. There was a woman there named Lena McClin, who was the chorus teacher. She asked me to sing a solo, and I sang it in this high voice because I hated the way opera singers had that booming loud voice. She said, "Child, anybody tell you you can't sing that way, you tell them come talk to Lena." And it stuck in my head that I had permission to sing in this high voice. But I really wanted to be an actor. My mother said, "Why don't you go to the youth center? They're doing a play there." I said, "You don't know me, you don't know me at all. I'm not gonna, that's not for me, forget it." But in freshman year of high school a big football player said, "We're doing this play over at the youth center, why don't you come over with us? It's called *Anything*

Goes, and we need some guys." I said, "Okay." And then I got the lead in the next play. And then we did a couple straight plays, *The Man Who Came to Dinner* and something else, and then we did *West Side Story*. I played Tony. Here I'm a kid, fifteen now maybe, and I'm pasting on sideburns 'cause I didn't have any. And I missed a high note; my voice cracked on "Maria." And I went into the locker room—we'd been performing in the gym—and I couldn't come out. I couldn't face anybody. I was a wreck. I just felt that if I made a mistake, it was horrible. And I'll just jump to years later when I started putting songs together. I put in a lyric that I made up that has to do with allowing myself to make a mistake. It's been my whole struggle. It's why I invented my concerts, to try to be calmer and relaxed. Every day of my life I fight this.

Do you ever fear that your gift is going to vanish?

I'll answer the question this way: I work my ass off. I do everything I can possibly do, so that when I get out there onstage, in front of a microphone, in front of the camera, if I fuck it up, it's not my fault. 'Cause I've done everything I've learned, everything I know. I've practiced everything I've learned, so if it doesn't work, then it's not my fault.

And has that worked for you?

I'm fifty-three. This has been a struggle for my whole life. And my choices, particularly with the songs I choose to sing, are lessons to try to help me with that.

What do you mean?

Take "Anyone Can Whistle," the Stephen Sondheim song. In it he says that the hardest things are simple and the most natural things are hard. I firmly believe people who are artists, actors, writers, have a missing place in them, a hole, something they weren't given enough of. I don't know if it's affection or love or attention, but something's missing. And I believe that to fill that void, they create a make-believe world. People make comments that I always seem to play such strong, powerful people. It's the complete antithesis of who I am. I do it unconsciously to try to be what I'm not.

And after high school?

My girl was going to the University of Kansas in Lawrence, Kansas, so I chased her there. And there was a group of people who were pretty extraordinary, and they cast me as Sancho Panza in *Man of La Mancha*. And right after that they cast me as Tevye in *Fiddler on the Roof*. Now that was the second time I'd played Tevye. The first time was to get out of going to classes at Hebrew-speaking camp when I was eleven.

An eleven-year-old Tevye.

So I was at the University of Kansas for two years in Lawrence, and at some point they said, "You should go to a professional school." I applied to the Goodman School of Drama in Chicago and The Juilliard School in New York, neither of which I thought I'd get in. I go to Chicago to audition for John Houseman and Michael Kahn. And I didn't know who these guys were. I did the piece about being in a box from *Rosencrantz and Guildenstern Are Dead*, and I did Edmund from *King Lear*.

Did you sing for them?

No. It wasn't about singing. And when I was at Juilliard, I never sang a note. It was strictly acting. And I struggled hard. At one point Bill

Hurt was in my class, and we sat around in a semicircle after each piece, and he said, "I would love to do what you do"—meaning I played characters and did voices and things—"but I just wish you would go deeper." What I believe he meant was closer to who you are, with no games, no funny voices, no pyrotechnics. Just what you are, what you feel.

Did the teaching at Juilliard suit you?

I wanted to leave after I was there for six minutes. I just didn't want to be there. But I said to myself, I will not leave until I feel I've learned something. And what that something was I hadn't a clue, but I figured I'll wait. I heard about different teachers. There was Marian Seldes, who gave me the love for it. When I would fall apart, she would remind me why I got into it. "Because you love it," she said. "Because you love it." And she'd hold you and embrace you, and it was wonderful. There were other people there who weren't so kind. They would unzip these young people's souls and play out their own fantasies, and they would do damage. I would see young people have breakdowns and want to kill themselves. And I sat waiting. When are you gonna attack me? I was always worried about being attacked. It was interesting that I chose to be in this business where being attacked is part of the game. It's a war zone! I mean, I'm nuts! But I think most of us are.

Were there other teachers who were useful to you?

It was part of the training that you would get a kind of technique from different teachers—Michael Howard, Marian Seldes, Gerald Friedman—having to do with a process, as opposed to more technical aspects, which I always say that any idiot could do. You must do your speech exercises, your physical exercises, your body, et cetera. That takes no brains. That takes showing up and doing it. But the technique that was the most interesting was with Gerry Friedman. I was ready to quit a million times by the end of the second year. And Gerry Friedman cast me and Bill Hurt in *The Duchess of Malfi* as Bosola and Ferdinand, and we sat around the table talking for three weeks. Finally I got up one day and did a scene, and I thought I was fucking brilliant. I was gonna just sit back, try to put a humble face on, and soak it in, not be too obnoxious, accept the praise, and not make the other students in my class feel bad, because I'm gonna get praised up the wazoo. And Gerry says, "What did you do?" And I said, "What d'you mean? I did the scene." "Well, what were you doing in the scene?" I said, "What d'you mean?" "What were you doing in the scene?" "What the scene was, I was doing the scene." "I understand you were doing the scene. *What were you doing? Write it down.*" Whereupon I wrote like three pages on a legal pad. And he looked at it and crumpled it up and threw it in a pile. He said, "Write down what you were doing, a simple action of what you're doing." This went on for three weeks. Bill got it like that [claps his hands]. My legal pad was enough to fill a landfill for Manhattan. And you know, I couldn't get it, I couldn't get it, and Gerry would say to me, "I understand what you did, and it was—interesting. Could you do it again? You know, in the theater you have to do this sometimes eight times a week. Like, can you do it tonight? Can you do it tomorrow?" I said, "I guess so." "You guess so? I'm gonna hire you because you guess so? You don't know what you were doing!" And I would sit there and write and write and write.

What were you writing?

I was writing long paragraphs about what the three of us are doing here now: I'm sitting with Rosemarie and Barry, and we're going to have a discussion about the ideas of how to talk about acting, or about a process, or about my life. And I'm going to try to get through to them, what it is that . . . And I'd go on and on and on, as opposed to: I'm searching, I'm miming, I'm hunting, I'm giving clues.

So that's how he taught you to play an action.

It was his journey toward action. The simplest word of action. And later, this became my life's work. So if I took the script out from *The Princess Bride*, I'd look for the words I'd written: protect, always be prepared, always stay on the lookout. Sail to insanity. I'm a body-guard, bodyguard. Protection. Lookout. Scout. Security. And I would just search for all the words. Rescue. Save myself. Rescue the girl. Find the knight. Kill the heel!

When you get a script, that's what you do?

That's what I do immediately. But then I hone it down, and down and down, so I'll have lists and lists of words, and I thought, You know, this is crazy. And one day I'm over at Steve Sondheim's house, and I'm looking on his piano, and there's napkins and letters and scraps of paper, and it's nothing but lists of words—rhymed. And rhymes and lists of words, and he's honing it down! He's looking for the rhyme, the one word that matches best. And that's exactly all I do. I'm doing a television series now, which I treat the same way I would treat *Hamlet*. What you learn is your own vocabulary. You learn the triggers for your life that are potent for you, that are your memories, that are your politics, that are your passions, and those triggers be-come your language. There are things that happen to you, moments when Rosemarie yelled at me for calling her a nickname—you know, that's a profound memory. The moment when my child is born, and various other things that I won't say, that I don't want in anyone's book. They're my private business. They're my secrets. They're my food. And they're my actions. Most of the time the material that I'm saying doesn't interest me, but I can put a foundation under it, which is my own story, my own care, my own sensibility of what I want to say, what I wish for the world.

Did you say the material doesn't interest you?

In many cases, it doesn't. Unless you take something like *Sunday in the Park with George*, which is just my life, what those people wrote, which is, you know—white, a blank page of canvas, a challenge, bring order to the whole through design, composition, light, and harmony. And then every word is about it. That's what they do, but it's rare that you have a Shakespeare, or a Sondheim, or a James Lapine.

You're saying that when you don't have great writing, or good writing, this is your way to do it.

That's right, it's my way. When I was a young man, I just somehow knew I wanted to have *Hamlet* in me. So Michael Bennett gave me a studio to work in. I didn't have a production of *Hamlet*, but I wanted to learn those words so they were always in me. I mean, that's probably my favorite play, and I walked around with a copy of it, and I know it, and so a lot of those words are in me, and they're probably the most highly articulated, well-formed ideas ever put to paper.

You worked with Gerry Friedman, years after Juilliard—

An Enemy of the People. And it was so difficult. I wrote everything in pencil: "Fight for the truth. Truth, truth, at all costs." I would personalize everything. I worked for six months on the script by myself. And I was going through some difficult things in my personal life. And so everything was personalized, about people in my life, close, close dear people in my life. And we finally got to Williamstown to rehearse the piece. I fell apart on the floor one day during a scene; I just was crying uncontrollably and had to go in the field. I said, "I've developed a problem in acting. I can't believe in the given circumstances. I'm personalizing everything, and I can't survive it." And we're two weeks into rehearsal, and I knew in that moment I couldn't do it again. I couldn't go over the most painful things in my life every day. They were too horrifying. Gerry said, "Okay, okay," and what happened in rehearsal—and this is where I believe the theater is the righter form for me in the long run, it's scary as hell for me, but righter in the long run—what happened through rehearsal was eventually, the man playing opposite me no longer had to be someone personal in my life, and he could just be that actor. I exhausted myself, and I just accepted it. But there were other things that I couldn't avoid overlaying, and that had to do with the town meeting and the whole fourth act, and that just was . . . the images of the Holocaust, the people, the Jews convincing other Jews to go along with the bad practices. I couldn't avoid it, and I believe in my being that there are some moments when that life still exists. And I would talk to Gerry about this regularly.

Now tell me, this is new? Or this is old?

It's developed over years, and I still struggle. Gerry said to me just in the past year, "This is what you do. This *is* your given circumstances, that you create these truths that are underneath the material." For instance—I will share a simple thing that I use over and over again. It is the defining factor in my life, and I didn't live through it, but it defines me. And that is the Holocaust. As an American Jew—a Disneyland Jew—it's in me. I went there, I experienced these places. And I don't just see horrible images. As I'm singing a song, I see all the children who went with their mothers into the shack, and then I see them come out with beautiful clothing, and I see gorgeous wedding ceremonies, and I see all the others come out of the ground and form into people that've been annihilated. And they're all right there, and that's why I love the theater, because it's all black out there, and it's my movie that I'm watching. And I've learned these scripts. They're things in my dreams, in my imagination, and they become the plays and the books that I've written, that somehow get repeated in various songs or various parts or various plays. Whether I'm doing a scene in a television show or singing a song or whatever, a certain image will repeat itself because it is the song I know.

How do you make this work in a practical way with another actor?

I don't need them to work my way. I need to be present and alive, calm and listening. I need to know who I am, what I'm doing, and what my job is, and to do it. If you are an actor who works in a variety of ways, if you're working, if you're not lazy, then you bring me everything, and it requires me to do almost nothing but be there and listen. Those are the best actors in the world to work with, because they're so full and interesting that you just sit and listen, and you wonder and you search, and you reflect and you learn, and you think, and you debate, and you fight, and you attack, and you heal, and you embrace. They're the basic things I do! What if they're not hitting, what if they're not playing, when they're really terrible—and I don't mean that they're not talented, but that they don't relate to you, that they're audience-directed or they're narcissistic. I use it, I use it a hundred percent. I mean, look around the world. There are people who are doing that all the time, in the name of god, in the name of America, in the name of humanity. They act like they're saving the world and doing it for the greater good, and they're selfish, insane murderers. They're horrible human beings.

If you have a moment where you really need them to, let's say, embrace you, or you need something from them in order to take your next action, do you just assume you're getting it, or what, how would you—

I try like the devil to never ask another actor to do anything other than what they're doing. My work is to create this life underneath whatever it is I'm saying. Including while I'm talking to you right now. I'm babbling. But what's underneath my babble is my struggle to communicate. And I'm *flying* through my mind, I'm searching, I'm doing a rapid scan while I'm talking to you. I have a million different thoughts. And at the same time, we're playing a scene. I'm trying to leave pauses if you interrupt me to ask a question, to put me on track, to rescue me, to help me, and to be open to that. We're on a treasure hunt right now, and that's the scene we're doing.

Let me go back to this moment when you learned about action. Gerry helped you finally get it. And then . . . was it easier, was the rest easier after that?

Well, I got it at that moment. And then thirty years later, when I worked with him again on *Enemy of the People*, it was the clearest work I've probably done in my life. But it's no different. It's the hardest work to do. When you do a television show, the nature of it is often so simple. The ideas aren't that complex, because they're in a race, they're hurrying, they're repetitive, et cetera, but if you do Ibsen or Chekhov or Shakespeare, it's unbelievably rich and complex. It's multilayered beyond imagination. If you think you've found it all, you haven't, no matter how many times you've done it. So I'm constantly doing that search. I'm constantly looking for those keys, for those words, those actions, those triggers, and then I write them down. And the thing is, I do all that work, I make all those lists, I play the scene. That's the gift—why I don't like film and I don't like television, and why I do like the concert stage and recording and singing and the theater, because you can rehearse it. And the process of rehearsing is to practice and invent endless possibilities! The thing that I love in *Sunday in the Park*, the last line in the whole piece, which I think is one of Stephen's greatest works ever, is "So many possibilities." Those are the last three words I say. There are endless possibilities, and if you don't rehearse . . . The beauty of the theater is what you can find tomorrow.

This is your process. You bring your world, your total living in the world to this moment every time.

The student doesn't learn when he acts. The student learns by watching the other person struggle and then having a breakthrough because of a suggestion or a change. I was working with a student once, and she was doing something connecting it to her mother, who had cancer or was dying, and it was just horseshit. It was just all ideas, and just overdone, overdone, overdone. And we went on and on, and I said, "Well, what are you doing? Are you trying to connect what you're trying to say to your mother? All this stuff that's so important, it's too much. I don't know what you're doing." What she was doing was so overdone you couldn't watch it. And finally I just said, "Are you embarrassed? Are you humiliated? Are you uncomfortable in front of the class because I'm talking about something so personal? Well, what do you want to do? If you started right now, what do you mean to do?" And finally we got her to be able to say, "I just want to rest." I said, "Then do that." And she sat there and said the exact same words. She just was trying to escape and rest, and it was riveting. And I relate to that. I'm famous for being over the top and too complicated, and my *worst* work is when I haven't had time to do my work. And when I haven't had time to do my work—because of how my mind works—I have so many ideas, and I must sift through them. I must get through the garbage and the less important ones, and choose one. If I don't have time to do that—when I'm in front of the microphone, or in front of the camera, or in front of the audience—you will watch a train crash. You will watch me talk and see me stand there, but you will see chaos! As opposed to, I'm just doing nothing but listening to what you need to ask me.

Are you saying you're hard to work with?

Yes, because I'm very selfish. I try never to be selfish with other people, but I only have a finite amount of time, and I want every single second to search for every possibility, so I can forget about it and get in front of that audience and see what happens right at that moment.

Do you work differently with directors in film than on the stage?

The process is the same. We just go about the scene. We were doing *Ragtime* with Milos Forman. I'd done all this work, I'd learned this accent, I'd met Russian immigrants, I went with interpreters. That's a fun part of the process. It's not all this emotional crap. I like the technical part too. My favorite thing—and it's a big part of what I love—I love accents. I do some of my best work with accents. I'm trying my whole life to do what Bill Hurt asked me to do in acting class when we were twenty, but I'm freest when I'm singing. And singing, to me, is an accent. Kathryn, my wife, says, "I find you to be the most free when you're singing." I believe it's a mask, 'cause it's one step from the reality we know. And I believe that step gives me a kind of freedom to embrace a word with a feeling or a thought or an extension or an elongation or a little bit of staccato or lightness. The way I go about it is, it's Milos Forman, and I go in and I do an accent for *Ragtime*, and Milos listens to it and he says, "Nah nah no no no, I want immigrant that was here three, six weeks. You are doing a guy who's lived here all his life, he just doesn't lose the accent." So I find a Russian-speaking interpreter and three Russian immigrants. They're all physicists, and they're driving cabs. I sit down with the interpreter one at a time with each immigrant. So for instance, a line that Michael Weller wrote for the script was, "I can do it again. I'll do anything you like." And the immigrant says, "I can do once more. I can do everything what you have desire." That's what he heard the interpreter saying. That's how he put it in his broken English. Well, I taped it, transcribed the tapes, gave them to Michael Weller and Milos Forman, and they put a ton of it in.

How do you maintain a sense of spontaneity when you must sing to the music? If you have an impulse, how do you go with it when you must stay on the note?

That's where I'm a bit of a nightmare to someone like Adam Guettel. Adam likes it very particular. I'm lucky that Richard Rodgers isn't alive, because he liked it very particular too. And I don't do that. Because I backphrase. For example, if it's written exactly on the note, I won't say it exactly on the note. I say the word the way I need to say it in the speed I need to say it in. So I'll let the music play on, and then I'll play catch-up or slow down. I'll do what I need to do. Harold Prince gave me one of my great lessons. We were doing *Evita*, and he came sometime into the run, it wasn't very long, and he says, "What the hell are you saying? I couldn't understand a word you were saying. Don't show up if I can't understand the words. Say the consonants or don't show up."

Well, your diction is impeccable. You seem to take such pleasure in diction.

I have Hal to thank for it. I will not rest unless you know what I'm saying. I tell students, "You're part of an interesting family, but it's not such a gift. You are here because you feel too much, because your sensitivity to the human condition isn't necessarily better than other human beings', it's just greater. It's a heightened sensitivity—to play an instrument and inject into those notes what you feel, to paint with what you feel, to write with what you feel, to sing with what you feel, to act with what you feel. This is part of what is being an artist. And it is costly. So you are a member of a family in which there's a cost for that heightened sensitivity. And the glory of it is, when you connect and you sift it through and you've made good choices, you might affect the condition a little."

When you were a young man, and had much less sense of the world and its problems and what living is really about, how did you approach a character? The role of Che in Evita, *for example.*

I specifically approached Che as "watch the bouncing lady." You remember the phrase, "follow the bouncing ball." In my mind, I had a simple task. I was the schoolteacher with the pointer at the board, and my job was to keep the pointer on the bouncing lady, and there but for the grace of god go you. Keep your eye on the bouncing lady. That was my job for the whole play. And the bouncing lady was Evita. No matter what I did, I said just keep your eye on the bouncing lady.

Would you play it differently now?

No. I like that choice. When I played *The Princess Bride*, I had a personal connection, which was that my father died from cancer, and here I was playing a guy that said, "You killed my father. I want my father back." I made myself believe that if I killed him, it would bring my father back. In Mandy's mind, I believed that if I got that guy, that he symbolized a way that my father would come back for even a second, and that's how I played that. But it wasn't until 1994—twenty-two years after he died—that I had a dream where I saw him, and I had a profound moment of change in my imagination. For a lot of actors, the imagination is a curse and a blessing. My imagination is my mind. It is my life to a fault. And so my struggle is, I can't sometimes know what's imagined and what's real, because I get so confused. Because I spend so many hours of my working day, my sleeping day, my walking day, imagining, imagining what the song will be, imagining how I'll play this scene, this make-believe scene that isn't real. I imagine so much of the time that I lose track of what's real, but that's the world I live in. A lot of guys end up in loony bins for a time. And I think if you're a really great actor, you should be in a loony bin for a little while. You know, here and there. I don't want anything really bad to happen but a little piece. But I saw my dad in this dream, and it was the most incredible dream. I never will forget a moment of it.

Have you ever been as terrified in real life as you have in a nightmare?

I'm a terrified actor. You could put me onstage in front of a thousand people, sing this song, I'm calm as calm, but before I walk out there, you could chill ice with my hands.

What do you think is going to happen? What makes you so scared?

I don't even think. I say prayers before I walk out. I thank god for the privilege that I get to do this. I thank the people who wrote the songs I get to be the mailman for. I'm terrified. I do so much work, I prepare so hard, and I try to forget. I know I work too hard, I know I prepare too much in acting. In singing, I don't prepare as much, I have a greater trust. I've never gotten it in acting. I don't think I'm a very good actor. I've never gotten that trust for myself. I walk out onstage, I know that song, and I'm free to just let it be and let whatever comes into me into that song. I think great actors like Jack Nicholson and Bobby De Niro and Humphrey Bogart have that kind of trust in acting, and I don't. And I'm not a great actor because of it, I'm really not. I worked all my life, but it's not my gift. It's my work. My gift is a voice. The work I do is to keep it in shape. I eat right, I exercise right. That's the work I do. I remember once, we finished doing a scene for *The Doctor*, and Bill Hurt said, "I don't remember what I did, I actually don't remember what I did, I wasn't even paying attention," and he was ecstatic 'cause he wasn't watching himself. And when you experience that, in either acting or singing or performing, you know what it feels like to be free, you know it's an abandonment. It's equal to when you jump out of a plane, you skydive, you give up, you give up literally, you give up in a way that is unexplainable. I don't recommend it to people. It's higher than any drug, it's better than any orgasm. It is what I live for. It's a kind of freedom from myself. It is why I do it. It is to escape from the parts of me that aren't comfortable. And that is why I do it. I'll work at it till I die, but it's a thousandfold harder for me than singing. People say, "Do you consider yourself an actor or a singer?" and I'll say I consider myself an actor who says the words on musical notes because I'm trained as an actor. It's important to me, that training; it's important to me, those words; it's important to me, that craft, those ideas. I love it, and I struggle hard with it. It's a Rubik's Cube I can't solve, and I love the work of trying to figure it out. I love these discussions. I don't have the answers. I'm on a journey. I consider my concerts a purposeful mess. I consider the way I work a purposeful mess.

Would it have been easier to do Chekhov than Chicago Hope?

A trillion times easier. But the difficulty is, let's take Ibsen or Chekhov, that it's so complex. There's so much there, there are so many ideas. I need to work with a great scholar if I'm doing Shakespeare or if I'm doing Ibsen. I need to be with someone who's far more gifted in terms of their intelligence and knowledge of history and literature and cross-referencing religion and stuff like that. My gift wasn't to learn that way, so I learn that way when I'm doing the plays. And so the scholar teaches me or the director teaches me, if it's a gifted director like Gerry Friedman, and then I learn and make choices within it.

What kinds of directors can't you work with?

Television is the most difficult 'cause they're guests. They're not there as really part of the process. They're there to be in charge of the camera. And I have to ask them not to give me any direction whatsoever except geographical direction. Unless the show has a long life, and you're the director and you come and do several shows, then over that time we get to know each other. If we're of the same temperament, or complementary temperament, and we get to learn a language, et cetera . . . It's a very sensitive issue how you talk to an actor. Directors can really derail me. My job is to stay open and sensitive. If you say something stupid, you might derail me for the rest of the day. Or a couple of days. My recovery rate is variable. I'm raw and oversensitive, and I've chosen the right path for that nature. And I'm not easy to work with because of it. A lot of other actors are a lot easier. They let it drop off their shoulders. I don't do that. I'm not like that. I wish I was, believe me. I don't criticize them. I envy them that they can do that.

What do you like about James Lapine as a director?

He'd come to see the show and I would say to him, "Please don't give me notes before the show." And he would write me three or four pages worth of notes after the show. We had a rule: come back in five or six days. I will try every one of the notes, and those that didn't work, you won't see. But it takes me time to osmosize it. Another actor can look at the words, then go right on and say them. I need to osmosize it because I need to go through, you know, "Be rougher, annihilate your wife in that scene. You're not brutal enough with your wife in that scene." Well, there are fifty trillion ways to annihilate someone. I'm gonna look through all of them, you know, before I pick. So I need that time, and then, after I've gone through 'em all and tested some of them in performance, I want to go, "Maybe I don't want to annihilate her. Maybe I disagree."

In the rehearsal process, how do you go forward with a director who is not complementary to your temperament?

As a young actor, with great difficulty. And I cursed. I made my life very difficult. I had no tolerance levels for just what you're saying. I would quit, and I suffered from it, and I regret it. I slaved for years to repair those bridges and repair myself and repair those relationships. And I continue to do that. I think the greatest gift I've been given is getting cancer—that I was able to survive, because that cancer gave me a real wake-up call. It finally allowed me to start practicing meditation. People always said to try to calm down. And it finally allowed me to meditate, religiously, thirty minutes every day. And in that meditation, as corny as it sounds, are the tools I use. These are what Gerry Friedman taught me years ago, and the potent tool right now is CDs put out by a Tibetan Buddhist nun named Pema Chödrön, who runs a monastery in Nova Scotia. And basically she says this phrase that I repeat every day while I'm meditating: "No big deal." Because, really, the big deal is your last breath. The thing is, I know fear, it's my life. And why I do this work is to conquer the fear. It's to infuse in that fear clarity, choices, understanding, and good wishes, for myself, for my audience, for the listeners. People will say this or that about the really great ones like Patti LuPone. She's a genius, she's brilliant, she's wonderful, and any difficult behavior is terror on her part. Fear, fragile terror. And I'm touched by that.

You talked about teaching. Is there more teaching in your future?

I do want to find more time to teach. I think this book would be wonderful for people, because I say to these kids, "Listen, I'm not a teacher. I've been around, I've met a bunch of different people, but all I know is, I've just picked up a bunch of stuff. I'm like a little magnet, and I'll give you what I can in X amount of time. And then take it with a grain of salt, 'cause I'm only giving you one smidgen of an opinion. There are a million ways to go about this out there. And mine just works if it works for you." In terms of process, I would say to kids, "Please be very careful what you say to the other actors on the first day you meet them or as comment or criticism, because it can never be taken away. It's part of the fabric of who you will be together, through the work and for the rest of your lives together forever. It might help it and infuse it and make it good. Some directors, like Kazan, say things to ignite people, to fuel the situation, to set people up, to get what he wants to create on that scene. That's okay, so long as no malice is intended; there's a safety to it, there's a trust. People give in to all kinds of games, people play sexual games at home with their partners they love, and it feels safe. It's a similar kind of game." A great lesson I learned about acting was from Jane Alexander. I was doing a reading at the Public Theater, and on that particular day, this woman I was involved with dumped me. And so right in the scene, I fell apart. I broke down and cried. And Joe Papp came up to me and said, "What a giving, generous performance." But I could never do that again as long as I live. I don't know what I did, but it was a perfect example of what Gerry Friedman was talking about. It just happened, and I let it out. If a camera was running, great, but it was a theater, and there was no camera, and there was no way to capture it. And Jane Alexander said, "All that work your teacher told you to do, that's for when you're lost or confused. When you're not lost or confused, you don't need to worry about that. You just have it. You can just give it." Now, in my opinion, those are the words of a naturally gifted actor, which I'm not. I can't do that, in any acting. And I disagree with her for my kind of acting. My kind of actor needs and must do that work. Otherwise I'm playing a roulette game; if the girl leaves me, and you happen to be in the audience, it might be good, it might not. So this actor always needs to do that work. But if you're one of those students out there that is so available, always and simply available, then that's your gift, and thank your lucky stars. A gifted actress doesn't know how not to, can't not.

When an actor asked Estelle Parsons, "Are you always yourself or are you always a character?" she said, "Whenever I'm onstage, you never see me."

I'm the opposite. You only see me when I'm onstage.

I think she means the opposite too. I think she meant you don't see her problems.

You don't see her personality, but I think she's just so transparent. I think the greatest moment I ever had in the theater was *Fences* with Mary Alice. I sat in the theater, and she had that scene in the kitchen where she smoked, and I just didn't understand how a stranger like me was allowed to be in a theater anywhere and see that. And be witness. That I was allowed to be in the room. I don't know how to do that. I'm thrilled I got to be there that moment. It may not be like that every night with her, but she has been spoken of by several other people as a great actress.

You never had any sense with her that she was pushing her performance out. She was present so deeply, so open. She let you see her soul and her intimate thoughts.

I feel much closer to that possibility when I sing. I feel like there's this hose that just runs through me. And in one end of the hose goes all these geniuses who wrote down on paper what they wished for themselves. And so I'm the mailman, and it goes right through me and cleanly comes out, and I can give it to them. But there's no holes in the hose—like in a good garden hose, so you get to water yourself—and I don't often get watered myself. It doesn't get in me. I find sometimes when I'm doing my best work, I'm just happy it gets to them. I wish the hose had some holes so it would seep in.

You said you find television the least rewarding—

The part that I enjoy about it is the crew and the cast members, the family aspect of it, and that you're there all the time. The part that's a nightmare for me is this: I learned a while ago that if I don't learn out loud, I can't learn. I was struggling with the script, and I never said it out loud. And I said, "I really don't understand. When I work on Shakespeare, I learn it; when I work on music, I learn it." And my wife said, "Well, you're doing it aloud." And I said, "No I haven't. I've just been reading it." And she said, "Why don't you do it out loud?" And I had only four days. Because that's how my brain works. In television I gotta do the work. I can't shoot without the words in my head; otherwise I'm completely self-conscious. These other guys, like Brando and Pacino, they can wrap the words all over the room and put them on things. I've tried it. I can't do it. It takes me out of the scene. I can't concentrate. I feel like I'm lying. And I have a tremendous problem with the truth. My need to tell the truth is off the fucking charts. If a lie comes from me, if I hear it in my head or I hear it out of my mouth, if it's not truthful, it's not connected, I'm finished. I melt down, I can't recover, I can't do another take. I'll lose a scene. It's just a nightmare. It's gotten easier, through medi- tation, through saying, "No big deal, lighten up." Joe Papp said on his deathbed, "I see life everywhere in everything." And years later I realized I forgot to ask him what it was about life that he understood. And then I got cancer and I survived it, and I was walking around the hospital with my eldest son, Isaac, and I said, "I think I know what Joe meant. I think he meant that you just show up and live it. You roll the dice, you make some choices, you do the best you can." And I think that's what acting is, and that's what I'll practice from now till, hopefully, the next fifty years. And see if, before I die, I can be a bet- ter actor. I know I'll never quit trying. My friend Bob Hurwitz always loves to analogize everything to baseball because of the fragility of the game—and I think it's very similar to acting—one minute it's just right there and you have it, and then the slightest thing happens, and the team unravels. Their confidence flies, the greatest players in the world. They can't hold the ball, they can't get a pitch, they lose one run after another, and they lose. It happens all the time, and it happens to actors, great actors. One of the thrills for me is to see Stephen Sondheim or Jack Nicholson be *bad*. It's the greatest gift they can give people like me. You wanna just run up to them and say, "Thanks!" And they're terrified, and you give them some horseshit about, "I thought it was a very interesting piece and I saw what you were struggling with." But the fact is, you couldn't understand a fucking thing they were doing, and you were so grateful that they had a faltering moment, you can't thank them enough. Meryl can screw up. Oh, my god, thank you! There's hope for the rest of us.

Frances Conroy

I t's a cold, cloudy day in November as we wait for Frances Conroy in front of the Apthorp, a square block of a prewar building on Manhattan's Upper West Side. In New York for only a few days—she lives full-time in Los Angeles now, though she maintains an apartment here—she has been seeing as many plays as she can squeeze in and has been at a matinee of *Light in the Piazza* at Lincoln Center this afternoon. It's five-thirty, and the last of the day's light is gone as she emerges from the subway, carrying packages, swathed in a floor-length saffron-colored down coat. If one has not seen her onstage, one is surprised initially by how tall she is. Her brother, a husky, bearded fellow significantly taller than she, accompanies her. We go into the building, to the office of a psychotherapist we know who has been kind enough to lend it to us for the interview. It's small and cozy, perfect for the exchange of intimacies. We pull a few chairs together and sit in a small circle. Our psychotherapist friend has left us soft drinks and health nut bars. If one has only seen Frances as the mother on *Six Feet Under*, her youth and beauty—white skin, blue eyes, red hair—are the next surprise. During the interview she is lively and animated, but she rarely smiles fully. On the few occasions when she does, she is strikingly beautiful. We turn on the tape recorder, ask the first question, and Frances takes off, fully committed and in charge. She warms immediately to the topic of an actor's work life. Her attention is first on one of us, then on the other, reaching out to touch us to affirm a point. She guides the interview, seemingly intuiting our questions. Her answers are thoughtful but not hesitant, full of specificity and detailed incident. Her feelings, her experiences, her memories, and her analyses of their significance are readily available to her.

What was the moment—whether it was something that you felt or that you thought—where you realized that what those people on the screen or on the stage were doing was acting and that you wanted to do it?

My sister was in a ballet in Boston, and I remember going to see that. There was a flower that they used—one side was green, one side was red—and they turned it, and that moment . . . that was magical. We had two half sisters from my father's first marriage. They were photographed by Scavullo, these young women, very beautiful and very theatrical. One was an aspiring actor. She was just a sort of fantastic presence.

When did you know that you could act?

My older sister Helen was a wonderful actress, and she's six years older than I am. So while I was ten, she was going to play Helen Keller. And I remember her talking about it with me, how she was going to do it, and her asking me questions and I said some things, and she said, "Oh, that's very helpful." And then I saw her do *Joan of Arc*, *The Skin of Our Teeth*, *The Madwoman of Chaillot*, and I just *sat* there, just taking it all in. And I think that something in me saw Helen doing it, and I wanted to do it.

Did you go to the theater, I mean the formal theater?

A wonderful woman named Kitty Hirs had a Saturday workshop for children in the basement of the Episcopal church that my sister and I went to. And we did little acting things. She took us to see *Man of La Mancha*, and we went backstage. And then my Latin teacher, Vincent Sucato, whom I'm friends with now, he took us in to see *Iphigenia in Aulis*. And I watched a lot of movies on television. And I liked watching Imogene Coca and Sid Caesar. When I reached high school, I auditioned for Anna in *The King and I*, and I got the part. I know one girl hated my guts for getting this part. And I was wonderful. I had the most wonderful time, and I loved singing. I loved every minute of it. I loved the orchestra. And then my friend Peter Harris directed *Our Town* when we were in high school. I was Emily. There was no drama department. He just wanted to direct a play, and he was the Stage Manager, and we put everything together, with costumes, and the next year he directed *The Diary of Anne Frank*.

And you went to regular university?

I got out of high school a year early. My father died just around that time. So a lot of extreme and complicated things were going on. I was living by myself in the house. They were taking my brother to college. I was terrified of being in the house, even in the daytime. But I did get out of high school a year early, and I went to a liberal arts school that was good in languages, Dickinson College. I didn't even think, Could I, would I go to drama school? It wasn't really in my vocabulary. So I went to Dickinson for one year, and I was very mixed up. I thought, What am I doing in this college? So halfway through the first year I talked with this wonderful woman, and she said, "Why don't you stay in school for another year." I think if she'd insisted, I would have quit school. And so I went for another year and was just as equally confused.

Did you think to try to get into a drama school?

I auditioned for Juilliard once and didn't get in. I did the maid's speech in *The Bald Soprano* because we had done that at Dickinson. John Houseman was so sweet to me, but I didn't get in. Lisa Pelikan was the redhead that year. That was Peter's class; he got in. I got a job at Avis, but I was so confused. I was out at the Macarthur Airport working at the Avis counter, and at one point my boss, a young woman, almost fired me because I was so "in" myself. Then I got a job at the MOMA gift shop and moved to Delancey Street.

What did Juilliard mean to you?

Peter Harris was there, and I had met all his classmates, Mandy Patinkin, Bill Hurt, and I felt such jealousy, like why are you here and not me? I want this, I want this. I felt real hunger. I remember going in and demanding to speak to John Houseman.

You?

Oh, I can be very pushy! My monster comes out. I never got to talk with John that day. A year later, I auditioned again for Michael Kahn at Juilliard, and this time I got in. I was there for four years, and it almost drove me crazy, because I'd been on my own for a year in this wacky existence of working for the Museum of Modern Art and going to all the parties. And then suddenly I was in this conservatory. And I had no money, totally broke. I worked at the movie theater up on Broadway and Seventy-second. It's no longer there anymore. The Regency.

What was the first thing you did at Juilliard?

They give you a part of a Shakespeare play—we did *Romeo and Juliet*—and you go rehearse it for a while, and then they, sort of, let you do it, which we did, and then they sat us down in this room and started critiquing us. One of the faculty was eating a sandwich . . . and it infuriated me. Because we had just been put on the line and I said, "Excuse me"—and I wasn't just out of high school, I was twenty—I said, "Excuse me, we're very hungry too. How can you eat a sandwich when we're very hungry?" And she stopped eating the sandwich.

What did you learn there? What did they teach you that you didn't know? Or how did they funnel what you were feeling into something that was manageable and usable?

It's a place where they teach you so many things. And in one way it's kind of a nurturing ground for four years, where you're in a continuing laboratory with various people directing you or teaching you. Jane Kozminski was a brilliant modern dance teacher. She was incredible. She had been with Paul Taylor and had an injury. And then we had Anna Sokolow. And then John Stix, who was with the Actors Studio, would come in and teach and direct. He was a very good acting teacher. I think he liked young students. Marian Seldes taught. She was a brilliant acting teacher, not just nurturing, but incredibly perceptive. I mean she had her "mannerisms," but she could *see* things. Here's an example. Lisa McMillan and I were doing a scene from *Mary Stuart*. Marian put her fur coat on my shoulder. And suddenly, just having that fur coat on, I decimated Lisa in the scene. Marian was very good at just giving a little key and then letting you go.

Was that a kind of technique that you could carry with you?

I would think that's more elemental than a technique. It was somebody who had the insight to help you become somebody who was written on a page. How to step into that person for that moment in that scene. Michael Kahn was a great acting teacher. He made it seem so simple. We would do a scene, and he'd just say two things, and I'd say, "Oh, my god! Okay." So the acting teachers helped us to become characters, to accomplish what the scene requires, to take what you have and invest it with the information of the character and the demands of the scene. To make it come alive. To make you breathe and live within that scene. You have a lot of things coming at you, a lot of people coming at you.

Having seen you on Six Feet Under, *I'm struck by how young you are!*

A lot of people say that when they meet me.

My assumption now is that you put her on, but how did you do that? How did you decide that this woman walked this way? You have a different voice in this conversation we're in now. Her voice seems pitched higher, more nasal.

Well, I can't speak of the nasal quality, but this is a character you're talking about from *Six Feet Under*, the mother of three children, two of whom are grown men, and a high school daughter. So what does the script tell you? It begins with her husband being killed in a car crash, and it also begins with their having an argument, and it's Christmas Eve, she's making dinner. And there's tension in the air. And so the story started with a tragedy. Her having an argument with her husband, him walking out, calling her from his car on the cell phone—and we're having an argument about smoking in the new car, and then we hang up and then he's killed. So the information that you get about her is that the bottom has dropped out from underneath her feet. She's got these kids; she has had an affair, which she confesses to in the first episode. She feels horrible that there's no love in the marriage. So all these different things come out about her, and she's got these grown children, and so it puts you in a certain place, and you just go with the scene and it takes you where you've got to go.

Were you in on the physical creation of the character, the makeup, hair, costume—

No, not at all. And that's an interesting thing because in the theater you do your own hair and makeup. Unless they have a wig, and they make some amazing wig for you. But by and large you do your own makeup. In television or film, you don't do any of that stuff. There are union people who do your makeup and your hair. And in fact, I made a big mistake. The first thing I got in L.A. when I went out in 1985 was an episode of *The Twilight Zone*, with Uta Hagen. And I made a big mistake. I didn't know I'd done anything wrong, but I was punished severely for it without anyone explaining what I'd done. This young hairdresser put my hair in a French braid. It felt funny, and it looked funny to me, so I redid it. And she said to me, "Did you just redo your hair?" And I said, "Yeah, I did." She never did my hair again. So every day I walked in to do the TV show—I was really naïve—I just did my hair again. And the other hairdressers were there looking at me, feeling horrible about the whole thing, and that bitch never did my hair again and never explained why she wasn't doing it.

But in Six Feet Under?

The producer had a certain idea for my character. I auditioned for him twice. Then they flew me to L.A. for the network, where you audition for all the producers, and there were doubts as to whether I would look old enough. When I read that script, I said to my agent, "I'm too young for this. She has a thirty-five-year-old son, this is ridiculous." And in fact Peter Krause and I were saying I was fourteen when I gave birth, but they of course hired me. I found out later that Alan Ball wanted me for the part. I put a French braid in for the audition, but the hair crew and Alan—you know, they tell all the characters how they would look—and the hair person said that my hair would make more sense in a bun, and so that's how Ruth had a bun. And then they had all these discussions about Ruth's various buns. It was a riot. Ruth's dress-up bun, Ruth's cooking bun. I would sit there thinking, Please, just do my hair and let me get out of here. Because they're so great, and they take such care. But sometimes I just want to run screaming from the chair and just act. The one thing I've noticed, having just seen two musicals on Broadway: when you're in a play, it's yours. It's your space. You get out there onstage, nobody's coming anywhere near you with a powder puff. You have that audience, you own that stage. Sure, you may have to go off for quick changes or for intermission, but you don't have eighteen set-ups where you wait fifteen minutes while they adjust the lenses, the light. And it's an interesting thing; it's a different rhythm.

How do you work with a director in TV or in film as opposed to a director in the theater?

They're totally different relationships, because in a play you have at least three weeks in rehearsal, so you're all creating a bond together. And you're all sort of conceiving the entire world of the play and the part, and everybody is threading together into this tapestry, so that it's all a piece. And then you go into tech, and that's the most wonderful experience in the world. You live at the theater. Twelve hours a day. And you just sort of fall asleep when you're not on. You can sit back and put your feet over the stage and watch what's going on onstage and go eat a sandwich, and you're in costume, and then the audience comes. And they haven't been told what to think. It's a spontaneous reaction to what's going on onstage. And so it's just growing, and they may be changing, rewriting, or redirecting. And the director's always there. It's fantastic. And you're exhausted. Half the time you think, Oh my god! I'm getting sick. And you don't want to get sick. And then you open. Big party. If the reviews are bad, everyone's incredibly depressed. If they're great, then that's wonderful. And then, of course, you go on the next night, and the audience is totally different because they've just been told what to think about the play. And so then you're filtered for the next month or so. You're filtered by the reviews.

All of this doesn't apply in films?

Not at all. For television you get a different director for every episode. For the pilot episode of *Six Feet Under* we had fourteen days to shoot. For the last episode of the last season we had sixteen days. But the first, second, third season I think we had eight days, maybe it was nine days, maybe ten. You meet a different person each cycle. Some of the directors come back. Some are just new. So it's a very quick sort of trust exercise. On a television shoot, the director doesn't have the power. The producers and the writers have the power. And the actors. The director is stepping into something that's already established. He or she can give their voice, but they have to stay true to the show. And that's determined by the writing that's set up, with the characters having been delineated. I think on every show it must be the case—that it's a marriage of the characters and the actors. It's just got to be, because the writers are watching you, and they're watching what you're giving, and eventually it starts to be molded to you. I think that's what happens.

What I was curious about was, in a play, you start out at the beginning of the experience and you know the arc. I mean, you might not know on the first day of rehearsal, but at a certain point you know the arc of the entire character and the entire play, but in a series like this, you can't.

Of course not, because the writers don't know, and Alan, the creator, didn't know. You have in your mind that, well, you think you know the arc of the characters in a play, but you don't really know it until you've gone through the rehearsal. And you don't really know it until you start performing it. You need the audience to inform you, ultimately. And then the character itself starts informing, and you learn things from the other characters. So you are informed to a degree going into a play, but it's theoretical in a sense. And then you learn. It goes on. But on a television show, you just know the arc of the episode handed to you. They would give us the episode to come midway through the episode we were shooting. So we'd get it about a week in advance. I would not read the next episode until the last second, until my scenes were shot. And sometimes that meant I was literally reading them during the read-through. Because then—I mean, as in life—I don't know what's going to happen when I walk out the door. It would tell me too much about the character. It would tell me things that I shouldn't know.

But on the stage you would read the whole play—

But that's different because from the start you'd be rehearsing the whole thing. Well, for example, I didn't know that the character of Nate was going to die. And everybody knew that they couldn't tell me things. They knew that I didn't read anything until the last second. I said, "Stop," in the makeup and hair trailer, so they wouldn't talk about the next script. They said, "Oh, do you know what Ruth is . . ." I said, "No, I don't want to know. I didn't want to know the last episode." And people griped; I got really angry because somebody said something about the fact that I die. I said, "Stop right there. I've said many times, I don't read the episodes to come. Hello!" And then somebody else made the big mistake of saying something, and I said, "Excuse me, I do not want to know!" And then I knew that everybody died, but I didn't know how. But I was really pissed off about it. It's not their place.

You made the acting choice of not knowing what would happen next. Most people just read the next episode.

I would ask the assistant directors, "Am I working tomorrow? How many scenes am I doing tomorrow?" So that as I read it, I would know what scenes I had to memorize, so that I wouldn't go, Oh my god, I've got that scene that's all dialogue. How can I memorize that? So I'd make sure I knew that. 'Cause sometimes you wouldn't work for three days. If there were five scenes in the kitchen, they'd all be shot the same day. Because it was the most expeditious that way, right? It wouldn't be putting the camera in different places. In that sense, you'd shoot out of sequence. And that's an interesting thing. People say, "Oh, how can you do that?" I say, "Well, it's very interesting, because it's like taking your life and going, mmm, taking that slice and putting it under the microscope, and thinking, This happened before this? And it happened after that: jump in. And it might be a scene where you were screaming, furious about something, and you just had to go there; you had to take that within yourself and just go. So that was a very interesting exercise. It was like doing your scene in scene study class—informing yourself of what came before and after, and thinking about it, and doing the scene.

Many of the actors that I've observed will play somebody rather unlikable, but they'll put in just that little thing that makes you like them. And I was very aware, watching you do this part, that I often just didn't like her. You must have been aware of that.

Oh, yeah. I remember I had an interview with someone from *Newsweek* magazine. And he said to me that he hadn't liked me from the first, and then he liked her. And I said, "Well, she was in a terrible state of mind at the beginning of this story. Her children appeared like monsters to her, like total strangers. You realize that her marriage was nonexistent; it was a terrible marriage; it was dead. And how do you go forward when you're walking in quicksand? You sometimes say things that are totally out of line. You don't necessarily have a good relationship with your children. Especially when they're not making your life very easy to begin with. And so you may not be the nicest . . . well, it's not even a matter of being the nicest. You may not have the easiest time in the house that day. You may feel awkward beyond measure in a lot of situations." And so it was coming out of something that affected her life at that moment. I can't say, because I wasn't the audience, what would turn somebody off about her at any given moment. I just know that they wrote difficult things for her and she really was going through a lot. Her children were a pain in the ass a lot of the time, and really kind of snappy at her, and she was very needy at times.

I think that we're not used to seeing a mother on television like that . . . I think it was shocking.

And she gave as good as she got. When they write something like that, I'll do it. Fine with me. If somebody's gonna give that, I'll give it back a hundred percent. When they did the episode when she took Ecstasy by mistake and was on a camping trip with her boyfriend . . . With her boyfriend—I mean, this woman had how many lovers? Whoa, look at her! And suddenly she was released from her chains. She returned to a state of innocence in a way. She was able to go above all of this crap she had been in for such a long time, and there she was in a nightgown, in a state of total innocence and joy, running through the woods after a bear. And then seeing her dead husband in the woods, and that being sort of a total reunion without the stress, without the tension. And they talked about love and eroticism together, and it was a real release, and it let her go on to the next phase of her life in a way. It let her laugh at the end of that episode when she came out of it.

Is working with a film director different from working with a director on television?

Working with a director in film is a whole other entity because the director ultimately has the power, and that's different from a television show. The director owns the film because he or she is not coming in and out. The whole time the film is being made, it is that person's project, and that person ultimately says what's going to happen in that film experience. They have more say as to who the character is. When they discuss it, they're not stepping in to carry on a character. They are shaping with you who the character is. And so there's a difference there. They are more autonomous.

I just saw Broken Flowers. *Tell me about that scene. What did the director say to you?*

The whole experience took place over an eight- or nine-day period. Each of the scenes of the women took three days. Tilda Swinton's took half a day. But I was in on the very start of it because they were using a new saturated color from Kodak, and the director, Jim Jarmusch, wanted to test it, and he was testing it very carefully. The costume designer had one thing put on me, and another, and I stood with Bill Murray and he had all these new suits he tried on to see how the color came out. And the women were each going to have a different hair color. Jessica Lange was going to have red hair; I was going to have brown. But Jim said my red hair was so beautiful in film and Jessica looked better as a blonde. That took a few days, and the actual shooting was about a three-day period.

It was very stark—I mean each one of them was very different. Yours was frighteningly stark.

Well, it was shot in a new house, huge, very expensive, in a neighborhood of these very expensive houses in a community in New Jersey. It was supposed to be the house of a real estate couple. It almost could have looked like a showroom, something that was not lived in—perfect—so that you could show somebody around, show what the house looked like.

Was that the thing that you took for the character? That it was all new?

Jim told me that's what it was going to be like, and then they showed the photographs of the house, and then the wardrobe, which was beautiful. It was from Brooks Brothers or something, and it was that kind of very beautiful, tailored, very perfect. I thought, God, how do you keep all that this clean? So right there—somebody wears this kind of thing every day. That was an interesting thing, and how do you sit in that? In fact, a real estate person's very public; you have to deal in a seductive way with the public to get them to buy a house. So those little things informed me about who the person is, but it also says in the script that this woman was constantly startled by Bill Murray's character, and constantly at a loss for words. Because he'd walked in on her after so many years, sort of appeared in her life again. So it was almost like I felt like, Oh, what do I say to him? Who is he? Why is he here? And that was sort of the rhythm of it, like, "Would you like some tea?"

There was a scene they didn't use. Jim wrote it, thinking that he might use it. In the scene, I'm showing Bill around the house when he first comes in, and then I say, "Oh, oh I feel like I'm trying to sell you the house, I'm sorry." They didn't end up using it, but it was so brief. And part of the process was a trust exercise, as it is with any actor working with another actor they don't know. Who is the person, and how are you going to relate to them on an animal level as another actor? And I was dealing with a huge star, Bill Murray, and I had no idea how he would relate to me, another actor, in a scene, what his process is, how he thinks of the work of another actor he doesn't know, of himself. Does he think of himself as Bill Murray? I didn't know, so that was kind of an animal feeling, an unspoken thing that went on of, How is this going to happen? Because there was no dinner party or anything beforehand, I met him at the screen test trying on the clothes. On the day of the shoot we talked for a little bit, and we worked. So that was a very interesting thing.

That happens a lot in film.

Oh, in plays too. But film is just a briefer period. So that was part of the process.

Did you rehearse with him?

You don't rehearse very much for television and film. The director feels the casting is the most important thing. So it was interesting to see it after having done it, because it was such a brief period of time and Jim Jarmusch doesn't talk a lot. He sort of loves watching actors. He'll say, "Oh, that was great; let's do it again." And we'd say, "Should we try anything else?" "Let's just do it again." And so it wasn't like a graduate study class dissecting the characters. You know, there was not much said. And that scene had interesting pauses in it that the other scenes didn't have. And those pauses were saying a lot. And they're also close-ups of me that he put in a different spot. When you're watching, usually you can remember the sequence of things you do, and I thought, Do you remember how these all fit together? He told me afterward, "That was such a beautiful close-up, and it told an emotional truth. I put it here." I said, "Oh, that's interesting!"

So he helped shape the performance?

The editor shapes the performance. The editor creates a movie and creates a performance.

How do you survive if you get into a situation when you don't like the director's vision, or you don't respect the director's vision, or you don't think the director's smart?

I think there's a continuing dialogue, and if you're in something, there was something to begin with between the two of you that worked. And so that person wanted you to be in it. And it would stand to reason that you would want to be in it as well. The audition process is a very telling process for both of you. And again, it's an animal thing. You're both doing some unspoken thing while you're talking or while you're reading. What's going on, who that person is. So by the time you start working, you've learned more about one another. But still there's that base of things happening at the beginning. And this just has to be an ongoing dialogue. I mean, if you hear in the gossip trades or whatever that there's trouble on the set—if it's not being concocted for publicity—it might mean that the dialogue was somewhat broken somehow, that it's harder for people to come to one mind about something. But ultimately, you have to reach some consensus to keep creating—either that or somebody gets fired, bottom line.

Somehow, you make it work.

You make it work. Simple, you make it work.

When you act on the stage, what happens? You get the script, you like it, you like the director. Then—

This whole process of being in a piece and creating is rather mysterious. This thing called acting. Vanessa Redgrave says it's reacting as well as acting. You're reacting to what you're given. And of course that's absolutely true. I feel that stage work has nothing to do with camera work in some ways, nothing whatsoever. But in other ways it does, because your imagination has been at play doing plays over certain periods of time, you've created over and over and over again. And I believe that helps you do twenty takes of the scene, where there's a master, a two-shot, a single, a close-up, another close-up. That becomes mentally exhausting, and you have to sustain the same reality each take because you don't know what they're going to use in the editing process. I do believe that doing plays over and over, eight times a week for however many months, makes you able to go to that spot, because your muscles know how to do it. I don't know what it's like for somebody who never did a play to jump in front of a camera, but I know that's a tool that gives me a very nice reservoir to draw upon. And that's from doing plays over and over eight times a week for six months. So that when you've got to do something, whether it be an emotionally heightened moment or just the simplest moment, you can go there even though you've got everybody in your face. You've got the powder puff, the wardrobe, these people on crew that don't know anything about acting. They're setting up these lights and stuff, and all you are is somebody in the way. And then they say, "Okay, talent to the set. The first team." They call the actors the first team, and the people standing in are the second team. You have people standing in because the regular actors are getting a nervous breakdown at the end of the day because the scenes take so long to light. So they say, "First team to the set." And then the powder puff comes and the makeup, and you know, they're making you look right. And then they'll rehearse once to make sure the lights are right. And then they'll do slate, speed, rolling, action. And you do it again, and you do it again.

So the stage is the first work you have to do for sustaining a performance.

I can say that's true . . . And also, it lets you lose yourself. Onstage, you have the dark in front of you. You're in a dream state—you can see the audience, but it's a dream state. Everybody is sharing it for however many hours the play goes on. And with a camera—a camera can be this close to your face. And you've got to forget about the gaffer, the focus puller, the camera operator, everybody in that room who is within ten feet of you, and it's not dark, and they can't be an audience and applaud or respond; it has to be absolutely silent. In the first season of *Six Feet Under*, my eye kept wanting to jerk to the camera, because it was like, What is that thing? And I'd have to just say, Read it along; it's okay. I mean, I'd done other work for the camera, but doing it day after day . . . And so, in a way, having done theater, you can sort of remember this dream state and go into it and forget that the camera is now this close to you and you're supposed to look at a red tape mark that's supposed to be Lauren Ambrose, who can't stand close enough to you to be in the correct eyeline. And you're having a scene with somebody, but between you and the person you're having the scene with is a big camera. And you can't even see the person. And so if you can forget that it's a red X made out of tape and just remember that person you are supposed to be laughing at or yelling at . . . that's the kind of dream state you have to be able to enter. 'Cause there's all this machinery and people in the way. You're not doing this onstage, where the lights are on you. You're right next to the camera. They're constantly saying, "Let's check the eyeline. Is that the right eyeline?" "No, they're not close enough. Can you come here? Here, sit on this apple box"—if you were sitting on a couch before. "Get the couch out of the way for the camera. Put her on an apple box. It's too high. Put her on a . . . turn the apple box over." And then you're sitting there right next to the camera. "Not close enough yet—don't move, don't move. That's a good eyeline."

And then you're supposed to have the same emotional truth with this actor. You can't touch them; you've got all these crew around you, and you're supposed to be in the scene. And it's very instinctual; you can go up on your lines that way. You can go totally blank, because you're having to give them what they need, but you are so distracted by the fact that you can't move your head and you're perched on an apple box. I've gone up several times, gone totally blank. And other people have gone totally blank, and it's like, Oh, fuck. Because you're doing the scene, but you're also not doing the scene at all. So that's another weird thing. So again, if you can remember the bond that you've got with that person and just try to forget this stuff that's around you . . . that comes I think from doing plays eight times a week as well. Going to the moment. And also, you can do a take where everything is lined up, you and whoever else. But something happened with the sound, or something fell in the background, or there was something on the table that shouldn't have been there, and they have to do it over again. And you think, Okay, okay, I'm just going to do it again. And you have to go into that moment again, instead of saying, Fuck, or whatever, or just getting depressed thinking, How are we going to do this again? You have to drop it, drop it, do it again, enter it again. Because there're so many technical things you are totally vulnerable to. A light can go out. They'll say, "Cut. That light just went out. Did you see?" And then they have to put the light back in, and you're like, Okay, just be quiet. So I would just go off to the side, and I was constantly just being quiet. Just sitting, finding some place away from everybody, waiting to go back to when they say, "First team on set." Because in the theater you can be backstage most of the whole play, just listening to it, or in your dressing room listening to it, and you're in this state, this circle, and you're just part of it, and nobody is between you and them. The stage manager is running the show. You know how many minutes you have to get downstairs. It's like a ballet going on backstage, and then you go on. So, it's yours.

What does it take you to get from the script to that moment when you go on?

In the play?

Yeah.

Well, just rehearsing each scene. You've got an eight-hour rehearsal day.

But how do you do it? I mean, you've got the part, you've got the first day of rehearsal. Do you read the play a lot before the first day of rehearsal? Do you—

I think about it. I don't read it a million times. Some people memorize their lines all at once. I don't, because I know I'm going to memorize them; we're rehearsing eight hours a day.

Your preparation for the first rehearsal is—

You think about the script. You might dress something like the character, just so that it'll sort of feel true to your body, and so you can sort of exist in your body, kind of like what the person would be like. For *The Little Foxes* we did at Lincoln Center, I found this dress that was mid-calf length, with long sleeves. It had a collar. I think I probably still have it in the closet. And it just seemed like a nice dress to put on in rehearsal for Birdie. And so I would wear it, go home, wash it, take it with me to the theater, change into it, and just put it on. 'Cause it just kind of felt like her. And then you do the first read-through, when everybody's there—the director, producers. And that's a wonderful thing because it's a happy day. Everybody wants it to begin; everybody wants it to succeed. And then everybody hears the words together; you meet actors that were hired that you may or may not know. You may see somebody you've worked with. And as Marian says, you leave your personal life at the door. More wise words from her. Because you're just there to do the play. You're not there to talk about fifteen things that happened before you walked in the door. And so then you start rehearsing, and you rehearse one scene over and over and over again, or a few scenes, because an eight-hour day is a long time. So over that process of eight-hour days, six days a week for three weeks, you know why you say, "I'd like that, please," after you took that step and turned around because you heard somebody. It all makes logical sense. Just as in life—I'm thirsty; I'm going to pick up this glass and take a sip, and meanwhile, I know that I'm talking to you, so I'll put it down and ask you another question. And so it's all part and parcel of the logic and the sense of it, of the life that's being created in these rehearsals of the scenes. It's not just lines you're remembering. It's, I want to shake his hand, and I want to ask him this, and I've got this dress on, and I want to talk to him this way. And so it's all built up into a character, into the needs of the scene. So if you happen to go up on a line, you can usually fall back, because it's all grounded in the reality that's built up in rehearsal. So it's not like you've forgotten a line; you've sort of gotten lost in space for a moment. Unless you're having real problems, if you just take a breath, the life sustains you when you go on. Or somebody else may say a line, and you go on.

I was going to ask you about your system, your craft, your technique, and the technique you're able to use in each role, but what I'm hearing is that you're so open to the events of the scene and what is happening that it feels like your body and your imagination and your body's memory just—

It's being informed. It's constantly being given these countless things from everybody. The other actors that you may or may not know. The things that start popping out in rehearsal. The rhythms in the scene, the way somebody talks, the way you react to the sound of their voice. Again, animal things, the way you're relating as actors doing this. They're unspoken things that start growing from just working together. When an understudy goes on, it affects the experience, because you have to keep the same life of the play going, but there's another person inhabiting the soul of the character, and it can change a performance completely. It's really quite exciting. The understudy is really thrilled to be doing it and also stepping into a situation. Whether it be one performance or more, it's a very interesting thing because you are very alert. You are being given things from a different person within the same character. And so you've got to be awake. It's an interesting experience and an interesting trust exercise.

Do you ever doubt yourself?

In what way?

"I'm not up to this. I can't do it. I'm not right for it." This is once you're already within the rehearsal period. Has it ever happened to you?

Oh, I think there are questions that can form in your mind when you're trying to find the character. I remember during rehearsals of *Ivanov* at Yale with Austin Pendleton and Lee Richardson—it was directed by the head of the Moscow Art Theater, who spoke no English, this brilliant man, and the translator was a Russian American actor—and Austin said, "I don't know what I'm doing!" He trusted everything so much that he could literally stand in rehearsal and say, "I'm completely lost," which Austin is very good at doing. He can say, "I'm lost. I'm looking, but I'm lost." And I think any actor can feel that at a point. You can be tired after a rehearsal, or discouraged. I remember doing Steve Tesich's *Arts and Leisure*, directed by JoAnne Akalaitis, and it was hard to find things in that play. It was such a brilliant play, but a lot of it was very elusive. So you do go through different things, and it also depends on the world of the play you're in. The world of the play can totally inform your moods going in and out of rehearsals. If it's a dark play, if there's a lot of tension in it, you're having to go in and inhabit that for eight hours. And so that can inform you; you can be sleeping on it every night. If it's a comedy, making the lines work in your head—it's a kind of mental geometry of making the lines fit in the right way. So there are a lot of stages that you go through in your mind. But you just take the next step and go into rehearsal just having had breakfast or whatever and see what the day is going to bring. And your mind is so ready to jump in again that it eats up more things and then feeds on it. I stepped into *Three Tall Women* when Marian took over Myra Carter's role. And I believe we had, oh god, was it ten days to step into those roles? Maybe two weeks at the most, and it was hot as hell that summer in New York—1995. I could chart my life by the years I've done plays. I could chart things in my personal life. It's a nice way of remembering things. But I remember Marian was rehearsing one role in the day and performing the other at night. And I thought, Oh my god. And I remember when I saw *Three Tall Women*, before I did it, saying to my husband, "How do they do this play eight times a week? How do I do this? This is such a beautifully complex play. How do these women do that?" And then I found out that they wanted me to take over, and I said to Larry Sacharow, the director, "Aren't I too young for this part?" Edward Albee knew me from *The Lady from Dubuque*, and I said, "Well, whatever, I guess I'm doing this." And I remember in rehearsals just listening very carefully because Marian and Christina Rouner had been in it. And so I was taking them in, and it was funny too because I felt kind of short around Christina. I usually feel kind of tall, but this was a real kick. And there was so much to learn. The first act doesn't have a sequential sense to it. It's more like a piece by Bach, a three-part invention or something. So it's musical notes you have to remember in the form of the words to take off from a word.

But how do you do that? Step into a piece that has a life already?

Jump off the diving board, honey. Let's go. Edward's play, part of it didn't have a story line and part of it did. And again you just trusted the stage manager. An actor who's stepping in for someone works with the stage manager for a certain part of time. The stage manager takes you in, works you into the play, and when you're ready to work with the other actors, then they come in, because they have to perform tonight. They're exhausted. The last thing they want to do is to rehearse during the day. Because it means they're doing a matinee an extra time a week. It's the worst thing imaginable. So they come in when you're ready. And then you've got to really be on your toes, because they're not going to give you ten days of rehearsal. You're going to get a couple days of rehearsal, and then you're goin' on. They've fitted the costume to you, you're goin' on. And you better know what you're doing, because the lights are going to come up. Then you have to trust everything that you've just gone through for the days that you've been given to remember that part, and then be very aware of what's going on on the stage around you with these people that already know the dance. And you're doing your dance, but you're doing the dance that's been done, and then you're making it your dance. So that's a very interesting process. And you remember that poor Marian was working fifteen hours a day. I remember a few times she went up completely, and it was such a great test for me, because your brain's doing so many games on you it's unbelievable. It'll do synonyms on you. It'll dare to you to go up; it'll dare you to forget your words. And all this while you're talking and the audience is responding, and your brain is going, You're going to forget it; you don't know the line. And then you're saying it, and you're going on, thinking, I'm having a nervous breakdown. And when somebody goes off, all that falls away, and you have to step in and give them a line. And suddenly you're sort of given this wonderful active role of stepping in. And I remember that happened a few times, and I just stepped in. And she got on the track, and we kept going. So that's an interesting process in itself. In *Ride Down Mt. Morgan*, where I replaced, there was a time constraint. The Public Theater canceled the week of previews. Blythe Danner, who had the role, had to leave because her husband was sick, and I had to come to meet Patrick Stewart, who didn't know me. Arthur Miller knew me from doing other pieces, and the Public Theater knew me from doing other pieces. And so that was wonderful, to see you, Rosemarie, and see Arthur, and then I remember saying to Patrick, "If I can help out, if you think I can step into this and be okay, that's fine with me, but if you don't, it was very nice to meet you." Because I thought, This man wants to do this play. I don't know what he has in mind, and he knows what he has in mind. And so, I guess, he decided that it was okay.

You just take it for granted, but that was an extraordinary, simple, generous statement that moved him a great deal.

Well, maybe—

I want to talk about roles that you want to play, if you have any. Things you want to do.

I would love to sing a role in *The Light in the Piazza*. I have a great singing voice. One of my singing teachers, Kurt Peterson, who was in *Follies*, said, "You have an amazing range." Kurt said, "Oh, you should go and do *Gypsy* in summer stock. You could easily do that part."

Do you feel in any way that you've missed something? Is there somewhere along the line in your career when there was something you wanted and it just didn't happen?

I don't put anything in the past tense. I mean, I'm not twenty-seven; I'm fifty-two. But I still don't put anything in the past tense, because

I don't think anything is over. I mean, I didn't play Ophelia in *Hamlet*, but that doesn't matter; there are characters who go through the same thing Ophelia goes through in another story.

Do you read reviews?

I don't. I did a little bit. But I just don't see the point in reading absent words, because those words determine your fate in the project you're working on, and they stick in your mind. You automatically know that the audience has been told something and they're seeing it through a filter. And you either have to wonder, Why do I do that like that? or Oh! This is really a kick. The time that I read reviews was the opening of *The Lady from Dubuque*. I was twenty-six; it was 1979. We had a brief preview period, because it was different then: plays opened after two nights of previews, and all the critics came on one night. Opening night was either the guillotine or a lovely send-off into a run. We all went to Tony Musante's town house for a party. Andy Warhol came up to me. It was all very heady. Then someone made a big mistake and turned on the TV, and Pia Lindstrom came on. We all watched it. It was quite a moment. She viciously vivisected my performance. Finally someone turned it off. I remember later Edward saying to me, "Thank you for doing the part the way I wanted it to be done." I don't know if it's true that the *Times*' junior critic, Mel Gussow, had written a rave, but Walter Kerr was the senior critic. His wife had dealt with cancer, as my character in the play did. His review went into the paper and closed the show. I remember reading that review on opening night.

One thing I've observed is how, on the one hand, an actor must maintain the vulnerability and the access to your emotional life that is completely prized on the stage, yet at the same time, there's so much viciousness coming at you.

From which quarters—you mean backstage?

Whatever quarters they may be. The review, the director.

Well, that's the external thing, and whether you read the reviews or not, you're still doing the play. You have to do the part, you've got a contract. Bottom line, you've got to do the play.

Is there anything, any role or kind of role, you absolutely won't do?

There was a movie that I went up for last month, and I hated the character to the nth degree, and I thought that it was a black-and-white, simplistic character. There's an updated movie coming out where there's an idealistic teacher played by Hilary Swank—called *Freedom Writers*. And it's about a teacher in an L.A. school where lots of kids are remedial, a lot of kids come from Latino or African American backgrounds. They come in; there're gangs, things going on. And she loves these kids, and she kind of brings a miracle about. Sort of the same story as *Up the Down Staircase*. And the role that I was supposed to read for was the doubting Thomas, the boss who says no in five hundred different ways—the one you hate, the villain. And I read it and I said, I hate this person so much, and it's written so simplistically. I called my agent in L.A. I said, "I don't want to go in on this, because I don't want to play this person. It's too black-and-white." And he said, "Oh, that's why they wanted you to go in; you'll make it interesting." I said, "You can't; it's ironclad. The writing is telling you what you're going to ultimately be and what the director's going to make you do, and I don't want to do it." It's just a despicable person, and very much a certain kind of white take. And so they got back to me, and there was a little beehive buzzing. And I said, "I don't care. I don't need a job right now; I'm fine. I just finished working." And then my New York agent, Paul Martino, called and, after all this discussion, said, "You want to go in on it?" He talked about it, and he said Mary Beth Hurt went in on this movie and said exactly what she had in mind, and she got the part right there because she told him exactly what she thought.

So you felt—

I said, "All right, I'll go in on it. It would be nice to meet the director." And so I went in on it, and he had heard all this stuff second-
hand. And he said, "She's a villain right now; I'm doing rewrites on
her, and—" I didn't quite get so passionate, but I said, "Well, she's
just, she's fuller than this. She's more of a person than this. And it
would be a more interesting movie if she's more complex than this.
Because it's a complex situation. People have responses to different
things, and everybody has a validity in their response. So you can't
make one person totally wrong and another person totally right. It's
just like things are so complicated in life. It's much more; it's why
truces are hard to come by." So, you know, we read the scenes, and I
said, "Well, it must be interesting for you to have people come in and
read this," and he said, "I'm hearing it for the first time." This was
fascinating. And I said, "Well, look, thank you for letting me come
in." I said to my agent, "It's very easy to go in on some new movie.
It's a thrill to be asked to go in. But to have an opinion and to talk
about it is a good exercise to do."

Are things being offered to you now as a result of Six Feet Under?

I've been doing a movie in Canada for a couple months, but that's
because I went in and auditioned for it. I mean, I think maybe I got
the audition because I got a Golden Globe and was nominated for
Emmys. You don't know why, you just go in. I mean, I feel like actors
know one percent of what's going on in the audition process. And I
think that's fine, that's all I need to know. All I need to know is, I
have to go in and do the material and leave. I don't want to know anything else. So I worked on one thing, and then I'm working on something else that they called and asked me if I'd do. I said, "Are you
kiddin' me? I'd love to do this. This is such a funny role. It's a wonderful movie." So things just come up. It's funny; you do all these in-

terviews when you do a long-running TV show that's a hit. When the TV show's all over the world, you suddenly get people interviewing you from all over the world, and they say, "How do you turn down things?" And I say, "Don't you understand? Actors are so thrilled to get a part!" I don't say that, but I say, "Honey, I mean, you don't un-derstand. It's really great when somebody calls to say they want you."

Patti LuPone

It's a little before eleven in the evening. We're sitting at a corner table in a restaurant a few blocks from the theater where Patti LuPone is starring in the much-praised revival of *Sweeney Todd*. We were hesitant to meet so late in the day, fearful that Patti might be exhausted after the show, that she might prefer to go home to a warm bed, that we would have to drag the interview out of her. She insisted, however, that postshow was perfect for her. The maître d' has assured us that he will keep the few tables near us free of customers so that Ms. LuPone might have some privacy. A few minutes later, Patti makes an entrance, arms outstretched, calling our names. Any hesitations we had about her being up for the interview are instantly dispelled. She's been onstage for two and a half hours and is still ready to go. A quick embrace, a minute deciding who sits where; then she tosses down her bag, shrugs off her coat, flicks her hair out of her eyes, and starts talking. We immediately switch on the tape recorder. Patti's energy is so high, the interview feels like a continuation of the performance; it's we who have to keep up with her. The waiter arrives at the table, and Patti orders red wine, a shrimp cock-tail, and a wedge of iceberg lettuce with blue cheese dressing. When it arrives, she manages to eat without missing a beat of conversation. She's smaller than she looks onstage, her face more delicate than it appears on the screen. It's not difficult to imagine how this woman sitting at the table, eating and drinking, laughing, remembering, entertaining us while informing us, is also the dynamo, the diva, the theatrical force she is on the stage.

You've just come offstage in this terrific revival of Sweeney Todd. *How did you come to do this role?*

The thing that I'm all about in this production is that I'm so free. I haven't been free like that since . . . I don't know. And I don't know whether it's because I haven't had the creative directors or they didn't know how to direct.

But didn't John Doyle do this production elsewhere?

He did it in Newbury in the U.K., where he has a theater company, the Watermill Theatre—and that's where they started. Necessity is the mother of invention, and they didn't have any money, and so they did it this way, with the actors also playing instruments, because this is the only way they could do it.

Did you have the sense that he was going to fit you into this concept?

Yes! Of course! But that's great. I mean, I'm a trained ensemble player. The thing that I liked so much about studying at Juilliard was it gave me the opportunity to work with eastern European directors and French directors that have very strong concepts. We don't have that in America. We have directors that talk a lot, but they're not conceptual the way they are in Europe and in eastern Europe. And

having gone to Juilliard allowed me the freedom to go with this concept, to understand and go with the director's vision. John Doyle
showed me the costume sketch. I remember the costume they put on
Angela Lansbury in the original production. How could you possibly
find sex in that, with those silly baubles and that sort of painted
makeup? You'd have to fight against that costume if there was going
to be any kind of sexuality in it. The costume they did for me . . . it's
a miniskirt, torn mesh hose, high heels. And I went, wow, that's
great. In the original Watermill Theatre production, the character of
Mrs. Lovett played the trumpet, so the fact that I play the tuba wasn't
that different. And John was open to who I was as a person and what
I was bringing to the role. But he didn't want it to be musical comedy,
or what he had assumed Broadway would be, or what he thought I
would be if I was a product of Broadway. I don't think he ever would
have wanted a star in the role, because he wasn't sure whether a
quote-unquote star would be able to give herself over to his concept.
And I told him, "I'm an ensemble player." Yes, I'm a star because I
have charisma, and I love to be on a stage, and I can command a
stage, but that doesn't mean I don't want to be a part of an event!
You're a star for other reasons, not because you don't want to participate. Maybe some stars don't want to participate, but I had a different kind of training.

*How do you see this production as different from the original on Broad-
way?*

I thought I'd never seen a production quite like the original on the
stage. You know, we were used to a musical comedy, and then all
of a sudden they're not singing musical comedy anymore; they're
singing something dark. But the overall vision of that production
was not as clear as I think John has made this production. John did
the costumes and the set. John's vision was total on this.

Were there conflicts about fitting you into his vision of the production?

He said to me that I'm the most directable actor that he's ever worked with.

What does that mean?

Well, I think it means I'm completely stupid, is what I think it means. I go, "Okay, whatever you want." You look at a production and it's like a theatrical totem pole, and the one on the bottom is the actor. But once the curtain goes up, it's actor and audience. The actor's a storyteller, and it's my job to fit into a vision. The actor's job is to tell a story, so I don't—how do I say this?—I think it's dangerous for an actor to comment, or dangerous to have an opinion about the parts of the play that don't involve you. You can, but you can't let that come onto the stage. You can't. I've seen too many performances where actors didn't like the play.

And they wanted to let the audience know this?

Not exactly, not consciously, but if it's in your body and you bring that onto the stage, subliminally, the audience is gonna know.

What do you do during times when you haven't liked where a director has led you? How did you cope?

When I got *Evita*, I was sitting in my friend's apartment in Los Angeles, and I went, "Holy shit, I'm gonna go on a roller-coaster ride." And I got this big grin on my face, and I said, "You know what? Evita must have gone on a roller-coaster ride as well." And I thought, She must have smiled too. So I thought the whole thing was gonna be a—wheee!—ride. First day of rehearsal, Hal Prince said, "I don't want any smiles and gnarled hands . . ." And I went, "Oh my god, this is so different from what I want to do with her."

What did he mean by that?

Whatever he meant, I didn't succeed in giving him what he thought he wanted from me. I changed my performance to what I thought I should be playing, because it was how I related to her journey. The hairdresser who put my wig on thought I was gonna get fired because what I was doing seemed so different from what Hal directed, but when he showed up, he said, "That's exactly what I wanted."

How did you do that?

You have to be appealing even as a villain. You have to seduce the audience and take them with you. You have to find a way to let the audience in and take them on a journey. So many actors don't want to let the audience in. But what else are we onstage for?

There was something you did that I remember very vividly in Anything Goes *at Lincoln Center. At the end of the first act, you turned and you winked at me. How did you make me think you winked at me?*

Well, it's possible that I actually did wink at you. If you're going to be onstage, you have to be able to connect with an audience, because you have to tell a story. And I love the audience. They can also be really hideous. But getting on the stage and playing with them is fantastic. I look at them and they're looking at me, and I'm gonna take them someplace. It's like I'm saying, Come with me. I love you. I'm so unprofessional; I look at them every night in between my songs. Or I'll find a place to peek out of the curtains to see the audience and know who I'm playing to. I put that wink in because of the poster of *Anything Goes*. She's leaning on the railing, she's looking over her shoulder, so I thought, I've got to some way relate to that poster. If it's on the poster, then I'm going to put it at the end of a part of the play. As a button. And it worked! It's all about taking in the audience. Involve the audience. Involve the audience.

When did you know that you could do this sort of thing and that it would work?

Four years old.

How did you know?

It chose me. I was tap-dancing, downstage right. Capezio tap shoes, Capezio leotard . . . and I looked at the audience, and they were all looking at me. They were all smiling. And I went, Hey! They're all smiling at me. I can't get in trouble up here. I can do whatever I want and they'll still smile at me. I fell in love with the stage by falling in love with the audience. And so that's always been the way for me. I'm always onstage for the audience. And I think if you're gonna be a stage actor, that's what you need to do. They need to be your best friend; you need to be their best friend. Spin the tale. So many actors drop a wall in front of an audience. I mean, I've seen some theater lately and I've been totally disengaged, and I try to figure out why I'm sick and tired of going to the theater. I think, first of all, the musicals are so damn loud, and performances aren't coming across the footlights. There's a disembodied voice coming from someplace in the theater. The actors do not have to reach across the footlights, and they are forgetting that you have to reach the back row with your eyes and voice and body.

How do you do this—how can you—on film?

It's always the same thing.

You can do this on film?

I think you can in film because you can use the crew. The litmus test is the silence during the shooting, when you sense a stillness in the room. And yes, they're trying to make sure that the lights are right, bada-bing, bada-boom, but if you've got the crew, man, you've got the audience. I use the crew for my audience, and you can tell whether I acted it well, whether they were involved. It's just a question of involving an audience.

I want to talk about the play, David Mamet's The Old Neighborhood, *in terms of acting with an audience. I remember your scene with Peter Riegert was stunning, in the moment-to-moment detail and the listening. How did that have to do with an audience's involvement?*

Yes, I remember that. That particular part of the play was about David's sister and a story that is so familiar to all of us, where the family falls apart and a family member's wailing that somebody got more than she did and she can't get a grasp on anything. A very familiar story. David's language is stylized, and Peter and I found it as a song we both sang. It was one melody and it was one voice—I mean, it was a duet, but it was really one voice. It was that idea of throwing the ball back and forth, and it was not difficult to commit to. I was able to get a laugh out of a line that was also shocking: "Who gets the mink coat and who gets the armoire?" I didn't shy away from those words, even though I knew the effect was shocking to the audience. I let them know right off that this was going to be the temperature of the piece; then they could relax and listen to the story of a woman in incredible pain, incredible rejection, who can't let it go. And that's a story we all have. It was a difficult play to do, because the language is so stylized, but I think I have an affinity for the stylization, the musicality of his language. I love doing his stuff, and I love to work hard . . . I've never shied away from that. My life is either crawling into or crawling out of an abyss. I like to walk the edge, and I think we all do. And I think there is a voyeuristic or a vicarious pleasure out of taking that chance with an audience watching.

What would you have done if the actor you were playing this scene with was just not there? How do you cope with an actor who isn't giving back?

Well, you can't leave the play, so you gotta find ways to stay. You don't manipulate, but if it comes to that, you have to find a way to still get the story out. I've been onstage with actors who either didn't comprehend or didn't want to go in that direction or didn't commit. And it's like: Why are you onstage? A lot of people bring their own issues into it. David Mamet wants to see this dark place. And he is so right, but it's hard. There are a lot of actors insensitive to the need to serve the playwright and serve the audience.

In that kind of situation, can a director help?

John Doyle found a way to fill in each and every actor. Sort of a self-important but mad entitlement. So the actors honored the most noble instincts they had, because he honored them. It was rehearsed so well, and the ensemble is so tight that we can actually talk to each other onstage without thinking, Uh-oh, I'm going to break concentration . . , And everybody's doing the best that they possibly can. That's an incredible gift.

Let's start now with your childhood.

My dad was principal of the only elementary school in Northport, Long Island, and he needed to create an extracurricular activity, so dance was one of them. There was Ms. Marguerite, who was a hoot. She had a cane to whip you. So Mom enrolled me in dance because the children of the principal of the school needed to go. I went, and there was no looking back. My brother, Bobby, fell in love with the hula skirt I was wearing, and he started dancing. We both fell in love with the stage. We both went, "Okay this is what we're doing." And there was no question. There was so much sacrifice, and there were so many people making fun of me. Bobby was the one that really committed. He used to take the Long Island Rail Road at three o'clock after high school to the Martha Graham dance school— Martha Graham was grooming him for her company—and then come back on the ten o'clock train.

And how did you get to Juilliard?

Well, Bobby went to Juilliard, Dance Division.

But you were no longer a dancer by then.

No. I went to class choir. I wasn't gonna be a dancer. I knew I could sing. I knew very young that I had a Broadway voice too. I knew a lot of things; it's just instinct. And that's divine. I knew that my career should be in Europe, not America. I knew that I was more European than I was American. At fifteen years, I knew I'd be on the Broadway stage. I knew I had a place on the Broadway stage.

Were you into a lot of musicals?

No. I was into rock and roll. Mom loved opera and my father loved jazz. And, you know, in those days, at the A&P they'd sell Ed Sullivan condensed versions of musicals and you'd get them for a dollar: *Ed Sullivan presents Kiss Me Kate.* I always reacted strongly to male roles because they had the balls. It's the difference between [sings lyrically] "When I Marry Mr. Snow" [and gustily] "My Boy Bill" . . . So I would go to visit Martha Graham's dance studio, and I started singing at fifteen and somebody thought I had an opera voice. I auditioned for Juilliard Preparatory and got in. I didn't want to be an opera singer; I just wanted to move to New York City and party. Mother was horrified that I wasn't going to have a proper college education.

You went to Juilliard at eighteen?

Bobby had graduated from the Dance Division and told me they were starting a Drama Division. I auditioned doing Dolly Levi and Kate's last speech from *Taming of the Shrew*. They gave me an improvisation to do—that I had just received a rejection letter from the Drama Division of Juilliard. Then they asked me if I could sing, and I did a Carol Burnett imitation of Shirley Temple's song from *Fade Out Fade In*. They asked me if I could play an instrument. I said yes, the tuba from the high school marching band.

That must have been a thrill—to get into the first class.

But they hated me. They tried to throw me out. Michael Kahn and John Houseman didn't like my personality. So they threw all these different roles in my direction, and I played them, so I stayed. By default.

What did you get out of Juilliard?

Oh my god—technique! And pain. I don't think anything was as tough as Juilliard. I thought a lot of it was not necessary. Some of the professionals they hired I guess didn't want to teach, and they took out their frustrations on young students. But I stayed and joined the first-ever Acting Company and got beat up there too, but it was an amazing experience. After being together at Juilliard for four years, we went on the road touring the country for four years. (When I saw what I had to do in *Sweeney Todd*, I said, "Yeah, I can do it.") It was really a crucible by fire. It formed me. I thought I could do anything because I had done everything. Because I was exposed to so much. We played *Measure for Measure* on the altar of a Baptist church. We played *School for Scandal* in barns with no mikes. So we had tremendous experience. The Acting Company still goes out on tour, but it's not all Juilliard, and a lot of recent graduates of the acting program don't want to act on the stage. They want to be famous in the movies. But audiences are starving for an emotional experience of seeing live theater. We don't pay a hundred bucks and walk into that theater to be disengaged. And this particular production of *Sweeney Todd* by John Doyle is full of audience participation. It forces you to come to the stage, and that's something that hasn't happened in years. I look out there and I want to weep because I see people so engaged. It's why they come to the theater. Even if they walk out on the street and go, "All, right, let's eat . . ." they're still in that thrall. And that's what we're supposed to do. As an audience member, that's what I want to go to the theater for.

What does your life as a performer feel like when you're doing a play that's been directed like a television show and the audience regards it as if there's a wall of glass between you and them.

I won't let that happen; I'll stare them down.

Tell me, you did four years with the Acting Company. Why did you leave? What did you want?

The new artistic director came in and said that the senior members of the company might not be getting the leads. And we went, "Excuse me, you're gonna have somebody that's just spent six months in the company play the lead, and I'm gonna play the footman? I don't think so." One actor quit, and then thirteen of us quit. And then everybody quit. And that company broke up. This is my favorite story about the Acting Company. We did a musical, *The Robber Bridegroom*, a spectacular production, and the writer, Alfred Uhry, and I got Tony nominations. The Acting Company was then going to remount our production for Broadway, but we all had to reaudition for our roles. And I went, "You want me to reaudition for my role?" I said, "I sure as hell will not!" . . . They said, "You'll be playing opposite Barry Bostwick . . ." And I said, "I've got the Tony nomination!!"

What happened?

I auditioned for *The Baker's Wife* and I wanted it so badly and I didn't get it. And the actress who did get it didn't work out, so they called me to come out to L.A. to replace her. This is during the time when the producers were saying, "You've gotta come in and stand next to Barry Bostwick, you gotta come in." I called John Houseman and said, "I've been called out to Los Angeles to do *The Baker's Wife*." He said, "Don't accept anything until you talk to me." I went, "Oh, so now I'm a hot property . . ." And I signed on for *The Baker's Wife*, which turned out to be a disaster. And then I had a nine-month depression. I gained so much weight. I was in a blue robe for nine months. I was on Valium.

When you're in a state like that, as an actor who needs to be hired, how do you get out of it?

Well, I worked. I worked with Jack Hofsiss at the Public Theater. I did *The Woods*. I did *The Water Engine* in Chicago, which moved to Broadway. The shows weren't successful, but I kept working.

When you get a part, whatever it is, what do you do? How does it start for you? You get the script, then what?

I read it. Ultimately the only thing we're responsible for is the text. It may take me a long time to learn it, though. Pierre Lefevre, the mask teacher at Juilliard, told me a really good lesson. He said just pick three adjectives for your character. You don't need anything more than that. So you read the script and you try to come up with three adjectives.

Like what? Give me three for Mrs. Lovett.

Greedy. Horny. Pragmatic.

Yeah, that would do it.

And you try to incorporate those into the director's vision. If you have a good director, and the director spins a yarn for you, you're covered.

You come to a first rehearsal having read it several times. And with music, how do you—

With musicals, it depends on who's involved. Thank god I did a production of *Sweeney Todd* before this one, because this time we didn't have a lot of music rehearsals separate from play rehearsals. It was all incorporated into that one thing. But the music is really complicated. All the notes that Steve wrote . . . it takes a lot of work. But I had played it before, so it was easier for me.

Did you have to throw away anything that you had used previously?

Yes.

Like what?

It was a different interpretation. It was a different director. And every time the old interpretation came up, it would be glaring; it was wrong. And I love to explore. I love to walk the edge, so I'm willing to go wherever. I blow with the prevailing wind. That may not be an attractive quality in life, but it's what I do.

But would you ever shed those three adjectives? Were they the same throughout different interpretations?

Yeah, sure. But I would be able to shed them.

Did you?

Well, things change. I'm taking different information from a different leading man. Michael Cerveris is very threatening. George Hearn was threatening too, but he never laid a hand on me. He was threatening in a different way. And I was directed in a different way. I had a blond wig, very Victorian. I think it depends on the actor's ability to let go and go with what's new. In America we have a tendency to hold on to some ideal or idea of what we're responsible for as actors. And, in fact, we should be empty vessels. We fill up with the information provided by the playwright, the composer, the lyricist if there is one, the director. And then that all sort of just bubbles up into a performance.

Do you ever, when you've done plays by David Mamet for example, question the writer?

Yeah, but see, David is his best editor. I really like when David directs me. He's not a great blocker, he would not get in my way if I wanted to change blocking, but he is there to eliminate a line. He's the best person that I've seen who can edit his own work. A problem with a lot of American directors is that they really don't know what they're doing. I don't know how they got into the position they got into. But they don't know what they're doing. During a rehearsal at the Public Theater, David looked at us all sitting in the house while he was on the stage. It was the middle of giving notes, and he said, "Leave actors alone, and they make the perfect stage picture." John Doyle said the exact same thing thirty years later. For example, there is an aesthetic distance here, between the three of us, that we are experiencing right now. I'm not in your face like this, right? And the same thing happens with actors on a stage. We know how to give the space and to take the space. And so you want to have a director who acknowledges that actors pretty much can do anything they tell us to do or not tell us to do—who has that trust that you know what you're doing.

Do you feel that directors don't trust actors?

Here is one of my favorite examples of that. Cameron Mackintosh saw that I was coming to London with *The Cradle Will Rock*, so he asked me if I wanted to stay and play Fantine in *Les Miz*. In a minute! I knew it was gonna be a hit. So I'm rehearsing with Trevor Nunn and John Caird, and these two British guys are telling me how to deliver a song. I'm looking at them, like, You guys, I'm from Broadway, and you asked me to do this because I'm from Broadway and you needed somebody . . . All I said was, "I know how to deliver a song." They said, "You must look at the audience." I know that. I didn't know whether to laugh at them or tell them to shut up. They were not used to directing musicals and had no trust in me because they couldn't trust themselves. So I just looked at them, and I let them talk, and I went, "When you're done, I'll continue my thing. Whatever." They were also dealing with Royal Shakespeare Company actors who had never done a musical before.

Were you a threat to them? Or did they enjoy your American-ness?

The thing that I admired so much in London about theater acting, directors, and actors was that there was such a connection. The actor makes his place on the stage. There was no obsequious subservience on the part of the actor to the director. There was sort of a "This is what I do. That is what you do. And I understand what you're trying to get me to do." There was this equal dialogue between actor and director. And it wasn't who was going to win the argument. It simply evolved. And so Trevor and John I think realized what they were saying to me, because I got nominated for an Olivier for the role. I mean, excuse me, but you brought me over to do a musical. Teach me Shakespeare, I thought; don't teach me Broadway.

But it wasn't out of disrespect; it was out of ignorance.

No. It was out of their desire to dominate.

What about Shakespeare? Why don't people offer it to you?

When I was at Juilliard, Liviu Culei offered me Rosalind in *As You Like It*, and I did it at the Guthrie. I could have been better. It had Val Kilmer as Orlando, and I don't know whether he was very good in that, but it was an internationally famous production. It was so wonderful to work with Liviu. That man was unbelievable. To work with Peter Sellars . . . These gentlemen were put in the wrong theaters. Minneapolis is a corporate town, and you have one of those visionaries, an eastern European, a Romanian director there. And you have Peter Sellars, who is a genius, working in a national theater in Washington, D.C. I was in his production of *The Count of Monte Cristo*—three hours and forty-five minutes. On matinee day we had just enough time between shows to shove down a piece of lettuce. And there would be symposiums, and there were heated arguments. It was a very controversial production. He took the script of *The Count of Monte Cristo* and interpolated Alexander Pope, the Bible, and the original novel. The casting was brilliant. Zakes Mokae was the villain, and Roscoe Lee Browne the good guy. That sort of skewered the casting. He gutted the Eisenhower Theater. I cannot think of a more spectacular scenic change. But the production failed because people were not able to accept his visionary ideas.

You also do one-woman shows. Would you rather be in a play or in a musical?

You have to generate your own work. And the thing about generating your own work is, you pay the bills, but there's nobody yelling at you; there's nobody bossing you around; there's nobody diminishing you; there's nobody hurting you. I remember saying to my production supervisor at Lincoln Center when I did my show, "This is so much fun; it's just a bunch of friends creating. There's nobody hurting us. There's a lot of not wiping your feet at the door." You know, people go into this business for reasons other than storytelling.

What do you substitute for that when you do an evening of song? Or are you telling a story through the lyrics?

I have a director who does that. He's the lyricist for *Hairspray*. He's brilliant at what he does. And we tell stories, because I can't do it any other way. So we devised a couple of different shows, and the songs themselves are stories. Really really wonderful little vignettes.

Do you miss having another actor?

No, not really. I mean, I've got a band, so they're gonna be another actor.

Your reputation is as a star, a singular thing that exists by herself on the stage.

Well, I've played those kinds of roles. I mean, Evita was singular.

Do you think it's marked you?

Totally. Killed my career. No, it didn't kill my career, but I was a comedian up to that point.

You were a versatile character leading actress. And then you became Evita. Afterward, were you offered dramatic, non-singing roles?

They offered me Lady Macbeth. Sarah Caldwell was directing at Lincoln Center. That's the only offer I got. *Evita* was such an icky-icky experience, people couldn't get a bead on me. I wasn't, you know, Mary Sunshine. So, don't bring her out to California and put her in a sitcom, because she was, you know, Evita.

What did you do?

Right after *Evita*, I got a call to go back to Chicago into a Mamet play, *Edmond*, and I said yes, and my agent said, "You can't do that . . ." But if I was waiting around for something to top *Evita*, I'd be sitting around for the rest of my career. I mean, it would be great if there were roles out there that were as powerful as that.

But another role wouldn't mark you in the same way.

No. You know, Evita was a villainess . . . with a sense of humor. I wrung laughs out of the first act, and I got tears out of the second half. I said, They're not gonna hate me all night. They're gonna feel sorry for me in the second act.

How difficult was the rehearsal period?

When I got the role, they said they wanted a white sound. I said, "What's a white sound?" A white sound is for the high notes, and there were *high* notes in that. I was fucked; I was gone. I mean, I got the role and I was in over my head, and there was nobody helping me. Nobody. It was sink or swim. I was like a deer caught in the headlights. And you know my rider is a reflection of every mistake in my career. It will never happen again.

Your what?

My rider. You know, my "requirements."

I don't understand.

What happened in *Evita* was this: we had a rehearsal. We flew to L.A. We never worked a full rehearsal without microphones. And then we had a ten-out-of-twelve day, you know: a full-out day. An orchestra rehearsal. I said to Hal, "Let me concentrate on the blocking and the technical stuff and let my understudy sing." And he said no. As punishment. By the end of that night, people were saying, "Why didn't they supply us with microphones?" And why didn't somebody instruct me? They knew that I'd never done this before. Why didn't the conductor say, "Don't sing out"? Because after it I had no voice. I went to this famous doctor in L.A., and he said, "Your vocal chords are like raw hamburger meat. You cannot sing for five days." And I'm opening in five days! This had never happened to me! I'd never been in a show like this before!

There was worse to come. Should we talk about Sunset Boulevard?

We did it at Sydmonton in the U.K., where Andrew Lloyd Webber has a house. Kevin Anderson played Joe. That's where Webber offered me the role. He said to me, "What do you want?" I said, "Kevin Anderson." I should have seen how bad it was gonna be, right from the very beginning. You can't ignore how tedious the negotiations were.

I should have known. Then I heard Meryl Streep wanted the part. Andrew wanted to do dual productions because of his greed. Well, that isn't fair to the actor, because it sets up a competition, and somebody'll lose. I'll never be part of a dual production; you can count me out. They said to me, "Well, we're gonna have a dual production." I said, "I'm gonna be in London, and there's also gonna be an American premiere? And I'm not doing the New York production?" I mean, if I'm premiering it in London, I should be premiering it in America. I'm not even in rehearsal yet, and I'm thinking, What the fuck? It was very painful. They gave it to Glenn Close. That was rough.

You're not yet in rehearsal in London and they announced the L.A. production?

Yes, which was ten months down the line. I was like . . . aaargh! They had to negotiate to get me on a plane to London. I got there, and I said to Andrew and Trevor, "You're setting up a competition." "No, no. You're our most important." Then Andrew didn't get the reviews he wanted in London, and Vincent Canby buried me. He said I was miscast. When he saw Glenn in L.A., he said *Sunset Boulevard* found its superstar in Glenn Close.

No one had seen you in London yet?

All of it was going on in the U.S., and nothing was going on in London, because I was getting standing ovations in London. There was nothing in the press in London, but it was all over New York! Andrew blamed all of us. My friends kept saying, "Stay, don't walk. They'll have to pay you off." And in the meantime I got handed a 35,000-pound bill from Really Useful company for my trip to Sydmonton. It was unbelievable. So I went through something in my career that affected my life, and that isn't what you have to do ever, ever, ever,

ever. I'm not the perfect casting for the role, but I delivered what I was directed to do. Kevin was fired too, and nobody ever talked about that.

Who were your idols when you were coming up? Not just people you looked up to with awe, but who made you think that you could do certain things.

Bette Davis. That's my all-time favorite.

What is it that she has?

Balls. She was just out there. And Edith Piaf. That voice just rips your heart out. I have no idea what it was about Bette Davis, and when it happened, you know . . . I want my heart ripped out. I want to sit there and go, "Aahhh." I want those experiences. And why? Why do we want those experiences? It's part of the human condition, and it's hard to have them. Critics like it clean and ordered. And I think those two women were raw. I think it's why people love them passionately and sometimes critics don't.

The same thing could be said about you.

I've always felt that critics are Anglophiles. It's why they love Kate Nelligan, why they love Meryl. It's white girls. I'm serious. White girls. And the Latin women, the Mediterranean women are a different breed in this country. I'm an organic actor, not an intellectual actor. That's why years ago, when I was a kid, I thought my career would be in Europe. I wasn't an ingenue. If I *was*, I would be an Italian ingenue, not an American. If you could see Chekhov done by an Italian company, what you would get is an Italian ingenue in the role of Irina, and there would be a different kind of emotional thrust than you get with a British actor or a white American actor.

(As circumstances would have it, during this interview our tape recorder picked up the sound of every dropped fork, clattering dish, and murmured conversation from the far reaches of the restaurant, necessitating a second visit with Patti. This one is in her dressing room suite after an evening performance of Sweeney Todd *. . . Patti is very different from the first time we spoke, her manner more subdued; she's fighting off a flu. She's warm and relaxed, though, eager to know about how our book is going. During the interview, a fierce thunderstorm breaks out, pounding rain on the window air conditioner. As we leave, Patti, despite not feeling well, prepares to spend a few hours studying lines for an upcoming concert version of* Gypsy.*)*

What do you do before you go on?

I prepare for it all day long. I sleep as late as I can. I work out if I can, if there's time. I eat correctly so that I'm not too full before I have to perform. I vocalize for about forty-five minutes. I stretch. Then I come to the theater. The key for me is to not do anything during the day. I play in these fantastic cities, and I've never seen one of them. I'm in my apartment or my hotel room preparing for the evening show. The thing I can't stand is going onstage tired.

Is it in your mind all day too?

The part, no. The preparation for the part, yes.

Could you read? Could you get involved in a book?

I can't do anything that's going to take energy away. And reading . . . unless I was lying down and could take a nap . . . yeah, I could read. But I'm here two hours before the show. This is where I vocalize, this is where I stretch. Look at the fan mail. Check the dressing room. Everything has to be neat. This has been created as part of the character. I look at my makeup table, and I look at the stuff on my mirror. All of that is a way of preparing. That is all a mind-set. It's all recognizable. You start to put your makeup on after you've stretched. I have the same warm-up clothes, the same makeup shirt and makeup pants I've had for eighteen, nineteen, twenty years.

Oh, I love that.

It's a shirt David Mamet gave me that says TWELFTH NIGHT. DAVID. People say, "What did you play in *Twelfth Night*?" and I say, "David."

What about preparation for a television show? When you did your series?

Oh my god. Well, you just have to wake up; you use the makeup chair. I don't know how you prepare for that. I love the discipline of the stage, because you know the curtain's going up at eight. And the television show that I was on . . . I'm sure there are better-organized shows—but we got later and later each day. We would start at 6 a.m. on Monday and finish at 6 a.m. Saturday. It was a disaster for me. My eating was off. When I was on *Law & Order*, I saw Sam Waterston, and it didn't matter where he was, he ate at twelve o'clock. If he was in the middle of a scene, they brought him food and he ate. Twelve o'clock every day. Because by that point he understood: if they go overtime, your lunch is pushed by an hour. If your lunch is pushed by an hour, your body is thrown off. I think it's really unhealthy if there's not an organized set. And I have not been on an organized set on TV. The situation comedies, yes. There was food ad nauseum. On the hour-long episodic, it was an hour later every day. So dinner was an hour later. I was on that show four years. Four years!

What kind of different approach did you have to take to it?

I didn't. I've done enough performing in my career so I was able to look at the crew and go: if I can get them quiet, I know it'll work for the audience. And they're crusty old people, and they're also not an audience sitting down watching a play; they're shooting it. They're at work too. So I could tell that if we could sense a silence on the set, the same silence you sense in a theater . . .

We've talked to other actors. We know that if you're shooting a scene, you might be standing on a box. You don't see the other actor . . . How do you compensate or cope with that?

I've always seen the actor. If it's your close-up, they usually have the actor stand by the camera. If the actor you're playing opposite is selfish and he's not there . . . but I've always worked with good actors and they're right there. I think you distill it to the dialogue of the scene. I've seen actors telling people to get out of their eyeline. What are you talking about? Getting out of their eyeline? It's life! What do you do, tell people you're talking to on the street to get out of your eyeline? I'm having a conversation here: get out of my eyeline! It's ridiculous. So you have to be able to understand how to encompass that whole thing. If somebody is talking and you're in the middle of a scene and they're at work, that's another story. I use everything that's given to me in the environment in television the same way I use everything that's given to me on the stage. Maybe not in this play, because it's so intimate. I'm onstage, and I'm thinking, I can stop this show. And I can tell that person to turn that telephone off. If anybody said to me, You're wrecking my experience, I'm going to say, What are you talking about? I'm on the stage; this is part of theater. Anything I do onstage is part of the theater environment.

*In a show like this, in which all the elements are so interdependent . . . or
with* Evita, *which was sung-through . . . how do you maintain a sense of
spontaneity?*

By being prepared. You prepare your character, and then you forget it.
Then you are available to everything that's happening. You're able to
open your eyes onstage. You can step onstage and say, Okay, I know I'm
Mrs. Lovett in this particular play. I know that. So what else is going on
that's interesting? I think for the most part actors don't release that
character, don't trust that it's going to be there, so we don't look out. It's
interesting in this play: everybody's looking out because everybody's
got to watch one another's back! We're all playing instruments, there's
no conductor, so everyone has to be as one: eyes open and *out*. There are
a couple of actors who I'm working with now in this production that are
not out, but for the most part, the actors are out. They're looking out.
They see what's going on in the audience. They see what's going on in
the scene. They're commented on. It gives them confidence. We were
very well rehearsed. We have a good director who directed us well.
Something spontaneous can happen if you're well rehearsed by a good
director. And if you trust that you are good at what you do.

*What do you do if you're working with someone who isn't spontaneous or
isn't there? If you're acting with someone who can't look at you? How do
you save yourself?*

You try to assure them that you are on their side, so that there's trust
and safety with each other. But if there isn't, you act the best scene
you can in that environment.

Do you assume that they're giving it to you and act accordingly?

But that's a dangerous assumption, because then you're acting independent of the scene, of the play, of the other actors.

Can you think of an example, without giving names, where there was a problem?

Sometimes it's a problem on this one. It's a problem on all shows. If you're looking for a great acting partner . . . that's rare. It's rare that actors step up to the plate and go, Here we go. It can be a problem, especially in a long run. I had problems with *Evita*. Not with Mandy, never with Mandy. It's an unhappy thing, but you can work around it and be successful. Not by acting independent of the individual you're acting with, but by accepting what you're getting and not compromising your own performance. It takes negotiation.

Is there a way to negotiate it during the rehearsal?

It depends on your director. You can complain to the director. Actors shouldn't give each other notes backstage when you're in a run. It should all go through the director or the stage manager. You can absolutely attempt it, but if it doesn't work, because they're on their own plane, then you simply have to say okay, this is what I'm getting, and this how I'm going to deliver my performance within it. It's hard.

How do you keep it fresh for yourself in a long run?

The audience keeps it fresh for me. I always think that the audience that sees it that night has never seen it. I love the audience. It's real easy for me. I also know that when I'm bored is when I do my best work, 'cause I'm not acting anymore.

Say it again?

When I'm bored, I do my best work, because I stop acting quote unquote. Three, four, five months into the run, you're bored, and then moments start to happen. You stop acting. You stop putting more effort into it than it needs. And I look at the audience. I'm a famous peeper. You know in the theater they used to have peepholes in the fire curtain so you could look at the audience. You have to know who you're playing to.

Mandy says he loves it because it's dark out there and he can imagine what's there. He can have a whole story going on.

I'm happy there.

He said that in Evita *his action was to remind the audience to watch the dancing lady.*

[Big laugh] That's great. You have to convince an audience, and however you can tell that story and take the audience with you is what you have to do.

Since you're doing this, how are you also preparing for Gypsy*?*

I learn my lines. I *drill* them. And I've read the original biographies of Gypsy and June. The mother was not a calliope, she was a music box. They talk about how small and vulnerable she was. Our image is a tough lioness, Ethel Merman. She was a manipulator, she was a mantrap. She got what she needed, but she was a charmer. I got the strength. I keep saying remember the charm, remember the charm. The more I read the script, look at the interpretation of lines, the more secrets are revealed, the more I get what the point of it is, because it's a great script. Jonathan Pryce told me a great thing. Get to the end of the line, make the point. So now I look at what that arc, that line, is. It's brilliant. I must have been talking like this onstage [she speaks very very slowly]. I have no doubt I can play this role. I doubt if I will be able to realize it in this amount of time, two and a half weeks' rehearsal, staging the entire play, and then three performances.

You keep coming back to the theater. What's the ultimate draw about it for you?

There is no wall that separates the play from the audience. That's the thing for me that ultimately you ought to achieve in a musical, in a play . . . a collective experience. I've had this a couple of times in the theater as an audience member, those moments where it's galvanized, where I know who's to my right and to my left and there's an electricity in the audience directed to the stage. Your audience partners can mean everything in a play. You didn't pick your seat, and look how close these strangers are to each other. They're touching—they don't even know they're touching; their eyes are focusing on the stage. They're about to finish their individual experience, collectively, together. And to me, that kind of energy, that kind of silence, that kind of focus could raise the roof. I want to cry every night. I do. I'm having that experience with the audience.

Well, then you're the luckiest woman in New York.

I am. The lights go out, and the music starts, and I just want to burst into tears. Because they came in the door, they want the experience, and they can have it with this production. They can if they let themselves go.

How perfect, then, that the critics also love you now as Mrs. Lovett. What's changed?

I'm older. I think that helps. A young woman who was that out is much scarier. And I didn't go away. I think, paradoxically, it's made people more comfortable with me. It's not, "What's this?" Now it's, "Oh, it's Patti!"

John Lithgow

★

John Lithgow has lived in Los Angeles for more than twenty years, so while he's starring on Broadway in the musical version of *Dirty Rotten Scoundrels*, his producers have rented for him the thirty-first floor of a furnished apartment between Lincoln Center and Central Park. We arrive in the late afternoon, a few hours before he's due at the theater. John answers the door and welcomes us in, takes our coats and hangs them in a hall closet. He is dressed all in brown, a very large man, tall and well built. He has the physique and square jaw of a leading man, with a small nose and delicate mouth that keep him just this side of handsome. It is a face and body that have allowed him a wide variety of roles over a thirty-year career: graceful, unself-conscious, and zany in comedy; warm and sympathetic in drama; surprising and darkly unsettling in villainy. The apartment is handsomely, if impersonally, furnished, the living room dominated by a large, red-velvet fringed sofa. The room is composed of odd angles, dominated by windows that give out onto views of Central Park that would no doubt be spectacular if the fog were not so dense. Leaning against one of the windows is a realistic painting of a highway patrol woman. "My son was stopped by her for speeding, and she let him take a picture of her," he tells us. John has turned the photograph into a painting as a gift for his son. He offers us tea. We decline. He makes some for himself, informing us while he does that he has been asked, though he doesn't know why, to be the cohost with Barbara Walters of Michael Bloomberg's second inauguration as mayor of New York City. Even without knowing the reason, he is obviously pleased. He sets down his tea—and glasses of ice water for us—on a round marble dining table in an alcove bordered by windows. The fog makes the physical arrangement cozy, and the conversation flows naturally into the interview.

You come from a theatrical family. Your father was a director. Did you know early on that you wanted to be an actor?

I didn't intend to be an actor. I wasn't ambitious to be an actor. I certainly enjoyed it and was drawn to it. My dad did outdoor Shakespeare in Ohio at Antioch College. Summers were about hanging around rehearsals and being in the plays. It was a lark. I loved actors. I lived in this adult world as a little boy, because actors are very welcoming people. I had many adored aunts and uncles among the acting company. And among them, Bill Ball and Ellis Rabb were splendid people of American regional LORT [League of Resident Theatres] theater. But it was always just a lark, and mainly I had a very specific ambition other than that, which was to be a painter, an artist, a printmaker. By the time I got to be a junior and senior in high school, I was living in Princeton, New Jersey, and traveling into New York on Saturday mornings to the Art Students League. I was quite serious about it, but then I got into Harvard, and Harvard is just no place for a painter to go to college, nor an actor either, for that matter. But I did fall into the theater gang immediately, and I was already a very experienced actor. I never consciously thought I would end up being an actor, but there I was at Harvard, and within weeks of starting, I was a campus star, hired in a major role right out of the gate, and for four years I acted and directed and designed.

And then did it stop becoming a lark?

Well, no, it's still a lark [laughs]. I mean, it was extracurricular. I did not study acting at Harvard, and I always thought that was a wonderful thing. It was four years, and it was just pure fun. In fact, we rejected any pedagogy. We didn't want to be told anything. We were obnoxious, actually. And then I did have the good sense to go to London and study in earnest, get some really solid training once Harvard was over.

Was that the time when there weren't that many choices in this country?

That's right. That was pre-Juilliard. There was the Yale Drama School, I guess, but I also wanted to travel, and I wanted to go to England. I'd never been there before. At that time my big heroes were Olivier, Gielgud, Ralph Richardson, and Alec Guinness, all English knights. And so I ended up spending two years in England, and it was a fantastic time in London, just an explosion of energy. It was 1967 to 1969. The Beatles were still together—they broke up while I was in London. Peter Brook was doing fabulous things. Trevor Nunn became the youngest artistic director of the Royal Shakespeare Company. I would go to see three productions a week, generally.

How did studying change your ways of working?

Within that very very rigorous and tough dramatic British training was the D group at LAMDA [the London Academy of Music and Dramatic Art], which was almost entirely Americans overseas. The presumption was that you were not being turned into an Englishman, although you were, by osmosis. It was a full day of work—breaking down speech and diction, fighting and historical dance, and Shakespeare training—and then you would rehearse various projects all afternoon. It was very tough, also lots of stage movement.

Did you find that it was sort of codifying what you'd taught yourself over the years?

In a way. Codified is a good word. My main problem was that I was very tense. Voice lessons would begin with half an hour in which we'd give each other back rubs. The whole thing was about relaxing the voice. In fact the whole scheme about the course of that year was to develop this forty-minute warm-up that you were supposed to do before every audition, rehearsal, or performance during the rest of your career, which I've never done since. But it was certainly very codified. By the end of that year, different people would lead the class in that warm-up, and it included body and voice and diction and exercises. It was very rigorous, and I was a glutton for it. I just loved it. It was terrific training.

At that point, you were in your early twenties. What kind of actor did you want to be? Your father had come from a resident theater tradition . . .

I was there on a Fulbright scholarship, and the Fulbright application asked, "How do you intend to use your studies?" And I remember writing down three words: "American repertory theater." That was the world I came from. I had done a lot of student directing by the time I went to London. I even directed a Shakespeare workshop in my dad's company, Great Lakes Shakespeare, so I thought if anything, I might end up a sort of actor/manager, the way my dad was. My dad was pretty much a role model. I never thought I'd be on Broadway. I certainly never dreamed I'd be in a movie or a television series. All my heroes were repertory actors. Donald Moffat was my great mentor; I just adored Don. And so that was the context, that was where it comes from. My dad is the one who hired me first; that's where I got my Equity card. I worked for him for one year at the Mc-Carter in Princeton, doing everything—designing, directing, and acting. I played Higgins in *Pygmalion*. It was a huge role. My part was so big I lost my voice and they canceled opening night. That was my Equity debut. They canceled opening night.

You started off just getting these great roles, but what did you see yourself as? A leading man? A character actor?

Oh, certainly a character actor. I like the idea of being a leading character actor, but certainly not a leading man. A chameleon. I mean I had already done twenty Shakespeare plays at the age of twenty, and Shakespeare, when you think about it, wrote for character actors.

At age twenty you did twenty Shakespeare plays? That's kind of amazing. Did you play the young leading man?

No, no. I had worked for my dad up at Great Lakes, and I played Nym and Pinch and Hortensio and the Second Musician and all these dreary little parts. I mean I had great fun, but it was using a pound of makeup every night. That was back in the days when actors had putty noses and crepe hair and they actually thought they looked different from one role to another. And that's been a template for my whole career, to be as different as possible every time out.

When did that change in terms of your being a rep actor?

Well, I worked for my dad for a year, and at the end of that year I decided to go to New York. He wanted me to continue working with him; in fact he wanted me to be his associate artistic director. I just felt . . . two things happened. First, I wanted to go off and see if I could do this without my dad hiring me. I just felt I needed to prove myself. And second . . . I mean I adore my dad and I revere my dad, but I did find out he wasn't quite as good a theater manager as I thought he was. He settled for too little, I think. He wasn't enough of a son of a bitch. You worked for Joe Papp. You know what I mean. Joe was a tough cookie, and you have to be to get really high quality these days. My dad loved hiring married couples for spousal appointments, you know. He did not like hiring prima donnas, and you know the best players are prima donnas. That was a failing. It's a very virtuous failing. He surrounded himself with nice people, but at the end of that first year—it was a sort of oedipal thing too—I felt I had to test myself in the toughest marketplace. So I went to New York and had a terrible time there for a couple of years. My dad's company was right there waiting for me, but I just didn't go back.

Have you found yourself to be a tough cookie?

No. I'm certainly like my dad in that way, which is why I'm not directing. I was actually doing better as a director in those couple of difficult years when I couldn't get any acting work. I directed at the Long Wharf in New Haven and at Center Stage in Baltimore. In fact, on the strength of a production of *Beaux Stratagem*, which was a huge success, they invited me to be their associate artistic director, under John Stix. I accepted the job in Baltimore because I had gotten nowhere as an actor, but about two weeks later I was finally offered a season at Long Wharf as an actor, and that's kind of what I had wanted all along. And so I pulled out of the Baltimore job with great recriminations. It was really quite nasty. I felt awful about it, very guilty, but I went to Long Wharf with a contract to do six roles over the whole season. I moved up to New Haven with my wife and my baby, and my second role was *The Changing Room*. And that was such a stunning production. It was brought intact to New York, and it was probably arguably the most successful transfer that came from Long Wharf. It opened in early March 1973, and in late March I won the Tony Award for the supporting role. And that was the end of my acting worries. I really have been an employed actor—I mean I've had my share of anxieties and bad choices—since 1973.

Is it difficult for an actor to stay in New York and have a career that could support his family?

I did go to Los Angeles in 1982, but I went out there for love, not to make my fortune. And within four months of moving out there, *The World According to Garp* came out, which is a film that was cast and shot in New York. It was a big hit, and I was an Oscar nominee. It was just like *The Changing Room*. Within two years I had done *The World According to Garp*, *The Twilight Zone* movie, *Terms of Endearment*, *Footloose*, and *Buckaroo Banzai*. Five wild, flashy roles, and about half of them were big, big films, and suddenly I was a movie actor who sometimes did theater, instead of a theater actor who sometimes did movies. And you look at my cachet now, coming back to New York theater.

Does it change the way you act, knowing that the career is sort of taken care of?

Well, I think it's only in the last few years that I have felt that secure.

After thirty years?

Yeah. You know what I mean. You've been talking to actors; you know how you never feel safe. I do now, I do feel sort of like a confident old man, but it's that worry of what's next. Starting in spring of 1973, I really would go from one show to another. I think I'd done a dozen Broadway shows by the end of the seventies, including working for Joe Papp, to the point where I did very few films.

You didn't really start films till 1979, right?

I was in *All that Jazz* and *Obsession*, a De Palma film, in the early seventies.

How did that sense of insecurity affect your acting or how you approached a role?

I did learn early on that insecurity is a part of the process. Every time you start another job, you're sort of starting all over again in lots of ways. Moss Hart wrote that about writing in *Act One*, that you're starting all over again every time. It's not quite the same with acting; you do have a backlog of experience, but you're starting every job working with a new set of people and a new director. Now I feel downright venerable. People are thrilled that I'm in *Dirty Rotten Scoundrels*, and I can relax, and I feel that in everything I do, I'm quite confident and almost arrogant. But that was a long time coming, and I always felt that you should be a little off-balance; you should be a little frightened. I say glibly that a few years ago I made the decision that I would only do work that I'm afraid to do. That's just another way of saying you have to keep challenging yourself somehow, and that gets harder the longer you work, because you've done so many different things. It just occurred to me that doing a musical for the first time on Broadway with *Sweet Smell of Success*, I was terrified, and I felt how great that at age fifty-seven, fifty-eight, I can be scared of a project, I can feel, Oh my god, am I capable of doing this?

Were you not a singer?

No! I mean I had done Gilbert and Sullivan and lightweight stuff as a college kid, but I'd never been in a musical and I'd never taken voice lessons regularly. I still don't think I'm a terrific singer, but I have spent an entire year in an extremely demanding vocal role, and I haven't missed a single performance!

You said you haven't taken voice lessons?

No. I took some, but ultimately there's this feeling—well, this is what you got [laughs].

Did there come a time when you went from simply being in front of the audience to saying, "Here I am!" It sounds as if this arrogance, the confidence you talked about, comes from the fact that you know they like you, that they are there because they want to see you.

It may be that the biggest transition was really becoming a celebrity; I mean that's a curious new dimension. I remember when I was a college kid coming down to New York and seeing Alec Guinness in *Dylan* on Broadway. It was incredibly exciting, actually seeing him look at you from the stage, and thinking, Boy I'll use that. If I'm ever that well-known, I'm going to play on that. There's a thrill to that, to seeing somebody who you came to see, who you paid your good money to see. Doing comedy on the stage, after having done *3rd Rock from the Sun* on television, is a terrific asset. But you also have to work against it. You have to go out there and do a role that has no laughs at all, just to get people out of the habit of laughing at you.

But you feel that they're there in the theater and they're excited because you have made them laugh?

Yes, and you can feel that excitement. The other interesting thing is, you know, having said what I said before about playing so many roles in Shakespeare, I have played a range of characters. I've been a creature of horror, and the bad guy, and sadistic psychopathic killers, and really scary people in one thing, and very funny and silly and lightweight in another, and quite genuine and moving in *Terms of Endearment*. But people know that what I'm known for is being unknowable, not knowing what to expect. The most exciting thing about acting is surprising people, setting up some expectations and then defying them. That's why playing a scary part is so much fun. When you jump out of your character and scare the daylights out of someone.

How do you use this celebrity? What is it exactly?

In a way, it's how other people use it, how producers use it. The loudest round of applause in the first half hour of *Dirty Rotten Scoundrels* is when I have my back to the audience and then turn around and look at them, and their response is, Oh good, he's in it tonight. There's just that feeling of—oh, this sounds so self-congratulatory— but there's a sort of, Oh boy. You don't consciously use it, but you're glad it's there, and it just makes you settle into a role.

It doesn't let you off the hook?

No. You still have to do it, or you disappoint people. In fact, it's all the more important for you to be somehow extraordinary, because that's what they want from you. It's funny—I have this other career over the last few years, which is entertaining little children, and one of the great things about performing for little children is, they have no idea who I am. Even if they know every syllable of *Shrek*, they can't put it together that I am the voice of Lord Farquaad. They may have seen *3rd Rock from the Sun* with their family, because it is a show that appealed to little children too, but they don't make that connection. Therefore, you come out and you are trying to win them, and you don't have what you have with adults and it makes you feel that the challenge is all the greater. You have to captivate them with the magic you bring on the stage. And to me, it's very good for me to have that as a constant counterpoint.

Has being a celebrity trapped you or freed you?

I don't feel trapped; I find it fun. People ask if it's a drag to go walking down the street and have everybody stop you. I think it's wonderful. Generally the instinct to stop and say something is because
they've enjoyed something you've done, and to get that kind of feedback, you feel very lucky. My wife doesn't get that kind of attention
teaching history at UCLA.

*Your celebrity has freed you to say, "I'm going to do Broadway." That's a
big freedom.*

There's another thing that is great for this small group of us who do
film and theater and television. The whole trick to sustaining a career is reimagining yourself, giving some brand-new version of
yourself as often as you can, not letting anyone get tired of the one
thing you do or are capable of doing or intend to do. It's very very
hard to sustain a film career over decades at a very high level.
Whereas I just jump from stone to stone.

In Sweet Smell of Success, *your first musical, you played a dark character, not appealing to an audience. How did you work with Nicholas Hyt-
ner on it? How did you approach it?*

It was like doing a scary character: just how far are you going to push
this man, who's evil, who can be very charming—but then there are
these heart-stopping moments, and you realize, oh my god, just how
dangerous this character is and how he uses his charm. That's sort of
how we talked about it. What people found fault with in the show was
its adventurousness in the way it used music. You didn't step forward
and deliver a song, which was good for me, because I didn't have the
courage to get out there and deliver a song anyway. They went easy on
me too. They fitted the role so comfortably to what I was capable of

doing. They didn't raise the bar. If I couldn't quite hit a note, then they would lower the song rather than the other way around. In fact, in *Dirty Rotten Scoundrels*, I'm constantly amazed at what I'm capable of doing just because they kept making it so difficult for me.

But they must have wanted you rather than somebody who could hit those big notes.

Yes. It was a tricky part because it had to be more acted than sung, for sure. It would have been great if I had those notes.

But no matter what role you've played, I think you carry a sort of native sweetness that's very useful for a role like that.

That's what I meant about surprising people. Bonnie Turner is a good friend of mine—she and her husband are the creators of *3rd Rock from the Sun*—and she said about me that my great asset is my kind of neutrality. She used the word blandness. There's a sort of or- dinariness about my face—this is her speaking—that it could go any- where, that it could be scary, be silly, it can go any which way. The curse of the dazzlingly handsome man or staggeringly beautiful woman is that it's very hard to break out of that.

Kevin Kline is always cast as the leading man because he's romantic- looking, and yet his gifts in comedy and character work have really not been explored as much as they could be.

It was great to see him play Falstaff, for that very reason. I remember auditioning for Stephen Porter for *School for Wives* before I had a sin- gle New York job. He cast David Dukes, who was very handsome, and not me. Bless his soul, he's a very good friend of mine, and we always invoke this. Stephen in his wisdom, that dear man, said, "You know, you're going to have trouble for a while because you are a character man"—and here I was auditioning for the earnest young lover—"and you're not going to be cast in that role. Because you already have all the attributes of a character guy, you're going to grow into your career." And this is before I had a single job in New York. And it's true.

What do you do or what have you done when you have a director who turns out to have a completely different idea about what the character is, or the way your character's supposed to go?

It's a very interesting process, and I love the process. I'm rarely combative about it. I take a sort of analytical approach, talking and talking and talking, breaking things down until things make sense to me, working it through. I would say the only times I really have been frustrated with a director and his approach was when he—I just say he because I hardly ever work with a woman director—when it's an idea that is artificially imposed, and it brooks no discussion: "This is the way we're going to do it." I try to reason and get my way, or not even get my way, get a way that makes sense to me. There have been very few instances of that, but when it's happened, it's exhausting and upsetting, and it usually ends up in some sort of explosion.

Have you ever quit?

No, I've never quit, but I have chosen not to work with that person again.

What about the same sort of situation with another actor? I mean, another actor who works in a way that is destructive or hogs the rehearsal or just doesn't give you anything back?

That has happened so rarely in theater.

What about film?

I think it's more frequent in film, though it's not the same process. I've been in television a few times when it was just impossible.

What's different about the process?

Well, I think I said earlier on that insecurity is part of the process of building a role. In movies, the air is charged with insecurity. Everybody's afraid of how they're going to come off, and it manifests itself in all sorts of ways, and one of those ways can be just unbearable behavior. People are frightened, and that's what turns people into prima donnas—refusing to come out of your trailer and having everything your way, accumulating so much power that nobody can overrule you, and surrounding yourself with "yes" people. That all comes from insecurity and fear of how you're going to come off. On the other hand, there are a lot of absolute requisites to conducting yourself onstage. You have to be able to stand in front of a thousand people and do it, or else you wouldn't be there; you won't be hired. You have to have experience. People have to be able to count on that before you get a role. And therefore there's a kind of egalitarianism about acting onstage—people can either cut it or they can't. That's not true in a movie. There are people playing huge roles in important, fifty-million-dollar movies who would be terrified to act in a play, because they're afraid they can't act. And yet they're the stars, and they can be very threatened by a supporting actor from the theater. They can be made very nervous by it.

How do you approach a role in a movie that's different from the way you approach it in a play?

You get better at that the more theater you do, because there's an awful lot of mechanics that you have at your disposal as a theater actor.

Movies are such fragments in so many ways. You're hired for a very specific quality, you deliver up a whole bunch of stuff that the filmmaker covers in many angles and takes. It's a matter of capturing happy accidents. You often play a role having barely rehearsed it. There are a lot of film directors who don't believe in rehearsals, don't even know how to rehearse. I walked on one set where the director said, "I don't know how to rehearse." So you get in the habit of sort of saving your ass, or very often you come on and just knowing your lines is an impressive feat. It's really amazing. Good lord, one of the nicest jobs I had in the movies was *Terms of Endearment*, and I was replacing another actor in the role then. I know he was let go; he had the wrong quality. And they brought me in with no warning at all, and they were literally hearing me say these lines for the first time when the cameras were rolling. There's a line—"You must be from New York"—that broke everybody up because they had not even heard me rehearse it. And the take was no good because everybody laughed; they didn't know it was a funny line. That's one of the best scenes I've ever been in on film. It's capturing happy accidents. Whereas on the stage, you can't afford any accidents. You have to be absolutely solid. In that sense, sitcom is more similar to theater than to film because you're delivering a very good performance to an audience, having rehearsed it and perfected it as much as you can in the space of five days.

You do rehearse? I've heard that the writers give you the script at the last minute.

Yes, but the rehearsal process is all tied up with the writing process. It's a very exciting process on a sitcom actually. It's the best of both worlds.

Tell me why.

Because you're working very directly with the writers, you're acting full out all the time, to make sure the writers know what's working and what isn't. And *3rd Rock* was a wonderful instance of a bunch of really sharp actors just giving it all they had all the time. And the writers loved it because they could immediately find out what worked and what didn't. In the theater, you're rehearsing a minimum of four weeks before performing; this is rehearsing for four days, but it's certainly rehearsing.

And then if the series works, and stays on, you become a company.

Yeah, it's an ensemble.

How do you use the response of an audience? I mean, you do a performance and you get a great laugh there and another one there, and then the next night nothing happens. Do you feel a physical response from the audience, like something's going wrong?

You know, if somebody just sniffles on a certain syllable, then there's no laugh there. If somebody crackles a candy wrapper. The tiniest little thing can totally eliminate a laugh. You're listening for that, so you just say, not tonight, baby, and you move right on. Doing comedy and working from laughter—especially if you do a long-running comedy like I'm doing right now—it reminds me of perfecting a circus act. If you see a really great circus act, one that lasts seven minutes or something, like a clown act, like David Shiner did in the Cirque du Soleil, or Bill Irwin, it's like polishing a jewel. When you've refined it to such a degree, that's its own satisfaction: the perfection of that jewel. Well, people always ask, how do you keep it fresh, and how do you make it still exciting after a year? Well, what that process is, is this: I can't wait to get my laughs tonight. I can't wait for these scenes to work, and I've been at it for a year and a half.

Is it the possibility of it getting better every single time?

Mmmm . . .

Or has this been polished to perfection?

Very often it's overworked. I mean you polish it too much, and fabulous moments get way, way attenuated, and they have to be repaired. That's a danger. The actor doesn't necessarily know, doesn't necessarily have his own best interests at heart.

He thinks he does!

He thinks he does. All actors need to be watched.

But who watches?

Well, you let the stage manager watch. In the best of worlds, your director drops in once a month and has a look. I still get notes now and then from stage management and certainly from the dance captain and the conductor on *Scoundrels.*

Do you like that?

Oh yeah, I don't mind it at all.

Has Michael Caine come to see you?

No, neither Michael nor Steve Martin, and I know them both. I've invited them both. But I understand. I never went to see *Footloose.*

Do you have any roles that you are looking forward to playing? I remember we had a conversation—

I remember. It's nice that we have that history, because I called you, Rosemarie, and said, "What about me playing King Lear?" And you said, "Aren't you a little young?" Which I was; it was a very smart thing to say.

How old were you when you asked?

I was fifty. I had been asked to do it by Robert Brustein the year before, and I turned it down because I was unavailable. But it certainly made me think, Whoa, I was asked to play King Lear; I'll call Rosemarie.

As I was getting dressed today, I was thinking, I'm going to call Oskar Eustis and say, Call John Lithgow.

Oh, I actually had a wonderful lunch with Oskar. And we had a wonderful time. We talked about big roles. We talked about Lear and other things. He said, "There's a bit of a queue, as you may know." [Laughs.] I tend to think that I may not make the best choices. All my best work has come at me by surprise, people thinking of me for something that I have either never heard of or never thought of. And I must say my favorite roles to work on are new material. I've done about nineteen or twenty jobs on Broadway or in major productions in New York, and at least seventy-five percent of them have been brand-new work, very few revivals, and only one replacement. I did *Once in a Lifetime* and *The Front Page*, and I replaced in *Bedroom Farce*. Apart from that, virtually all of them were world premieres or New York reviews of brand-new pieces or musical theater. I find that so exciting. The appalling thing is, after all that Shakespeare and that Shakespeare background—and I say in all modesty, I'm one of the best Shakespearean actors out there—I have only done two professional Shakespeare productions, and neither of them were great experiences. I did a poor production of *Troilus and Cressida* at the McCarter when I was just starting out, and *Hamlet*, playing Laertes, which is simply the most thankless role in Shakespeare. God knows I'm asked to do Shakespeare all the time. But you have to have a minimum of ten really good actors to have a production where there are no potholes.

You could get that.

Well, I'd love to be in a great production of Shakespeare, and I certainly will be. That's why I was having lunch with Oskar. I know perfectly well that I have to do this. I'm over sixty now.

But you don't think about roles?

I do sometimes. I executive produced myself in a TNT production of *Don Quixote*. That was also a role that somebody had asked me to do years before, on film, and it was a very nice kind of conventional rendering of *Don Quixote*, but it wasn't the most exciting thing I've done. I've just come to realize that other people's brainstorms are better for me than my own because they introduce me to ideas that I'd never thought of myself, and that's where you expand your sense of yourself.

Do you ever regret not directing?

Not really. I was a very good director, and I sometimes think it would have been interesting, but acting, on the face of it, is much more fun than directing. I vividly remember directing shows and feeling a great sense of achievement and triumph on opening night and then sinking into this terrible depression and envying all the actors because they got the fun of actually running the show. And you come back two weeks later and they have no use for you anymore.

Have you directed yourself?

Yes. I've been in productions that I've directed. Never a good idea. One of the big reasons why I went over to acting—and pretty much stopped directing—was that there's a very clear line between them. It's like labor and management. You can't go back and forth between directing and acting very easily. Some people can, but I find it screws up my social relations. That was very complicated when I was working for my dad, and it screwed up my oedipal relations too. I've also come to the point where I feel that acting is an incredibly creative thing. Especially in working the material, I have a huge amount to offer, just in terms of pulling at the threads and saying, This can look much better, where is the moment in this scene? It's constantly asking questions.

Are there directorial skills that you have to sit on?

Yeah, yeah. I don't believe in directing the actors that I'm working with. In fact, I'm adamant about that. I think it really is a serious no-no.

Do actors ever ask you because they trust you?

Sometimes. More often understudies. Or sometimes you get a great relationship. I'll give you an example. One costar and I talked all the time—what about this, what about that—and things would happen without even talking about it, and we both felt the thrill of that. But then something happened. A third actor was out for a couple of weeks on vacation, and an interesting little moment happened with the understudy, and I said to my costar, "Should we talk to the original actor about this moment when he comes back from vacation?" So we did, and to make a long story short, it ended up a catastrophe. The actor was so injured that we would urge him to do something he didn't feel was right, simply because it worked so well with the understudy. And it was breaking a cardinal rule of mine, and I only broke it because I was so accustomed to things being so loose among us. That's why the director's there.

In the circumstance, would you have told the director?

Yeah, if he'd been around. In fact, the problem was so serious that the director had to come back and deal with it, and he dealt beautifully, I have to say. The fact is, the actor was right and we were wrong. The director said, "That is not a place for a laugh—we cannot stop the show there." So not only was I inappropriate, I was wrong. And I'm sensitive enough to know this will happen. I said it before, I'll say it again: actors are not the authority on their best performance.

How about when you're working on a new play? Do you make suggestions about the script?

Good writers want to hear an actor's input. I worked with Jerry Zaks on *The Front Page*. Jerry is very meticulous, and he really orchestrates and conducts. I was using my usual manner—you know, what about this, what about that, which is the way you survive on a movie set—and Jerry took me aside after rehearsal. We're very good friends, by the way. He said, "John, I just have to ask you, if you have anything, take it up with me afterward." And I realized, well, that's theater as opposed to film. On film sets, all bets are off. Very often there is no director, so everybody's got to direct or there's no directing going on. I certainly make plenty of suggestions in theater too. I try to be as decorous as I can. I usually say, "Can I just make a little suggestion?" I usually get my own way because I'm usually right and I know what it needs. But I'm wrong often enough to say please overrule me.

Jerry choreographs every moment. Does that feel intrusive to you?

Not really. Every director is like a musician working for lots of different conductors. They've all got different manners. One of my favorite directors in movies certainly was Bob Fosse. If you watch *All That Jazz*, you'll see me drum my fingers once. Well, that was Bob's direction and I loved it. You can be a fascist if you know what you want. The worst directors are the ones who have no talent and are defensive about it, and that is a nightmare, because all their suggestions are wrong. And if you try to suggest something else, it's, "Do you think I'm stupid?" You know? And you just think, Life is too short, the rehearsal period is too short. And yet some directors just create the most amazing atmosphere. Jack O'Brian is so open to the creative activity of other people. He'd be perfectly happy to sit back and do a crossword, look up now and then, and say, "Oooh." And yet he's as sharp as a tack, and when you're actually in previews, his note session is just amazing.

In a film, do you feel that you as the actor are more in the position of lending yourself to the vision of the director?

If you're going to do movies, then you have to accept that. You're offering him a whole bunch of stuff to work with. You're generating raw materials for this movie.

So you can't hope to shape your performance.

You can try. My whole philosophy of film acting is to try to act so well in a master that the editor will use that as his guide for cutting the scene, so that if there was a moment of great power, that's what he'll cut to. If you deliver a really good master, then you're more likely to have your performance actually presented. But you know, you can carefully calculate pauses, and they'll just cut them down. Sentences will be removed that to you made the whole scene make sense—that's all in the cutting room. They're not going to call you and consult you about that.

Explain what the master is versus—

Any given scene in a movie is covered from four or five different angles. The master is generally the first thing that's shot: a sort of big room in which a bunch of stuff goes on, that's like the proscenium stage version of the scene. And then you go in and cover it in two-shots, a close-up here, a close-up there, maybe a shot that will carry you out of the room, another shot that will bring somebody in, a lot of different shots. But that master is the best version the editor will have of the rhythms of the scene and where the important moments are, and he'll use the "stubs" to make that connect. It's the old stage actor in me: what I want is for the scene to work just great before we start doing all the coverage.

When you look at the arc of your career . . . or do you even think it has an arc?

Well, it sort of has an arc. Yes it does.

Okay, what is it?

It breaks down into major acts of a five-act play, and I'm sort of in act four. The theater was the first. In the 1980s I became a major supporting actor in films, and the nineties were dominated by *3rd Rock from the Sun*, television. And in each case there was a major event that sort of kicked them off. *Changing Room* in the seventies, *The World According to Garp* in the early eighties, and *3rd Rock from the Sun*. And as soon as *3rd Rock* ended, I made a conscious decision to come back to the theater, because sitcom makes you so extremely well-known. I felt it was important to stay active and keep doing important work, but for a smaller audience, and just get forgotten for a while. Besides which, I missed New York and I missed the theater, and along came these wonderful jobs. I thought, Don't try to get back into movies desperately after doing a sitcom, because it ain't gonna work, you're too well-known as a goofball. So after I do *Sweet Smell of Success* and *Retreat from Moscow*, then I can be a goofball again and it's okay.

What do you hope for in the fifth act?

I certainly intend to be acting as long as I can remember the lines. Things get very interesting in all sorts of ways when you're over sixty. I've started all these other things. When you ask me what I want to do in the fifth act, I just want to stay creative and experimental. Life has given me all these fabulous opportunities to do things. I've nursed the fantasy of taking a year off and just painting. I will probably never do that. A new sitcom has been proposed to me, and it's got a wonderful notion, involving linking me with another person, I will not tell you who, an even better actor than I am. It's a wonderful notion, so we shall see, we shall see.

How many years did 3rd Rock *run?*

Technically it was five and a half seasons, 138 episodes.

Is it more fun to do a sitcom than Raising Cain?

Sitcom is more fun than movies, by definition. The most interesting thing about movies is this little nugget: you can be on set for twelve hours and do a half an hour's work, and that's so draining and so slow. You can spend your entire day doing a scene, just because of all that coverage I was telling you about. And it's exhausting. Sitcom is roaring, it's racing, you feel so creative, you can't waste a minute of time or a minute of creative energy, and bam! You perform it for this wildly hopped-up audience, just being whipped into a frenzy with the warm-up man, where they'll laugh at anything.

I think I meant, is doing comedy more fun than doing something serious?

Not really. I mean you think when you're getting big laughs that nothing could be better than that, but I would say, at the end of it, *M. Butterfly*, which was the most stunningly theatrical thing I've ever been a part of, was just as much fun as the wildest comedy. Basically, you're after impact. You want to throttle that audience somehow. Who knows what that urge is all about, but you're just trying to thrill them. You want to give them an amazing experience.

S. Epatha Merkerson

We're rushing along the labyrinthine corridors of the Drama Division of The Juilliard School, heading for the office of the school's director, Michael Kahn, who has graciously lent us its use for our interview with S. Epatha Merkerson. We arrive finally, a bit breathless, ten minutes before the interview is to begin, only to find Epatha already there, comfortably ensconced on a sofa, amiably chatting with the staff. "I'm always early!" she says, laughing as she hauls herself up off the sofa, and we go into Michael Kahn's office to begin. Epatha is small and compact, wearing a vivid crimson blouse and architecturally dramatic earrings. Expectations that her apparently effortless, naturalistic portrayal of the no-nonsense sergeant on *Law & Order* is what she's really like are dashed in short order. Though her manner is straightforward—she often leans toward us or touches us to stress a point, as if to say, This is just between you and me, honey—it is lightened by frequent bursts of hearty, sensual laughter. As the interview proceeds, it feels more and more like a conversation. Epatha gives us the feeling that she'll say anything as long as it's true, felt, and doesn't hurt anybody.

Was there an event that started you off on acting?

It actually started in the dance world for me. My older sister Linda was a dancer in high school. She was at the performing arts school back in Detroit. I remember seeing her dance and thinking, Omigod, this is something I would really love to do. Through junior high and high school I did a lot of acting, but I always focused on the dance. I had this desire to be one of Alvin Ailey's dancers. It wasn't until my second year of college at Indiana University that I knew I didn't want to dance anymore. A friend of mine—Sharon de Bonzo, I remember her name—was taking an acting class as an elective, and she asked me to take the class with her. I found myself taking these classes every semester, until after a second year of doing this, I realized I was heading toward a major in theater. Then I left Indiana, moved back to Detroit, and finished at Wayne State with a bachelor of fine arts.

So you acted in high school, but you didn't really get the bug for it till college?

Well, I did it all through high school, but it never occurred to me that it was what I wanted to do. I had an incident in high school that was really quite painful, and it made an impression on me and stays with me to this day. I was cast in *Anthony and Cleopatra*, and I just happened to see this beautiful new black girl in school. And two days later the director for the drama club came and got me out of my English class and told me she was giving my part, Cleopatra, to this girl I had seen in the hall. It broke my heart. To make up for it, she decided to give me all the smaller parts and have me choreograph all the little dances. But I just thought that was an awful thing to do.

There was also still a lot of racism within all the departments. This was the late 1960s and early seventies. At Wayne State they actually did two black productions a year, and I was the only black undergraduate student, and they would cast them from the community. I was too good for a small part but too young for the lead. Yet I was the only one paying the tuition. So in retrospect, coming to New York, I came more prepared than any student that I graduated with, because I came here with no expectations. I came to New York to see if I actually had a viable talent and they came here seeking fame, because they had gotten all the roles in college. *Dark of the Moon* and *The Count of Monte Cristo* and Shakespeare parts.

You came from Detroit right to New York?

I didn't come right to New York. I got a gig at this children's theater up in Albany that actually got me to the state. I was a little nervous about coming to New York, because you know, if you can make it there, you can make it anywhere, that whole thought of it. But it was probably the worst job I've ever had, up in Albany. And so the only logical move was to come here, because I knew I didn't want to try Hollywood. It was something about the stage that I really wanted to try, and then when I came to New York, there were a lot of CETA [Comprehensive Employment Training Act] programs going on. So literally, I could start rehearsals for a show, open that show, and while that show was running, I could start rehearsals for another show.

And your family, were they supportive of that?

My mother always thought that theater should be my minor and I should take English and history so that I could teach, or take a typing class so that I could work in an office. And I never did. I just felt that if I did, it would push me further away from a personal goal and that any obstacle I would have to cross on my own. It was the way I was raised, first of all. So she was talking contrary to the way she raised me, but I just felt that the only way to do it was to step in it with both feet. And then if it didn't work . . . and I still say to this day, I think I'm a smart cookie, and if I needed to find something else to do, it would break my heart, but I would do it.

When you first came to New York, did you get work right away or—

Literally, I was here for two months and then I met you and Oz Scott on the street, and you said to come in and audition. And I went out on the road with *For Colored Girls*. While we were on the road, Yvette Hawkins said to me—she was one of the ladies in the company and we shared a dressing room—she said, "Here's the deal. No one knows you but us and your mother. So while you're out here, save some money, join Actors' Equity, take a loan, pay it off, get some credit, and when you get back to New York, do anything and everything, and let people learn what you can do and your work ethic."

That's great advice.

That's what I'm telling you. That is how I was able to exist. I borrowed five hundred dollars from the credit union, paid it off, and when I got back, I had a line of credit because I had paid it off so quickly, and I started working *immediately*. Literally, there were all these small theaters.

Off-off-Broadway, you mean?

Yeah, hundred-seaters. And I would invite my friends: Barbara Montgomery, Mary Alice, Yvette Hawkins, all these actors who had been around for a while. And they were willing to critique me along with the directors that I worked with. Constructive criticism. I remember having a meeting with Sidney Lumet, and he asked me who

I studied with. I started naming actors: Adolph Caesar, Barbara Montgomery, Mary Alice. And he goes, "No, no, no, no, those are actors. I want to know who you studied with." And I said, "Well, you wouldn't know them. Professors at a university you wouldn't know. But these are the people that I've learned from." He was totally unimpressed with what I said. But it was very important, because that's how I learned: on-my-feet practical experience.

Are you still in touch with these actresses?

I see Barbara Montgomery at least two or three times a month. I thought about Mary Alice the other day. I was her understudy once, and I was sitting in the Colonnades having a little glass of wine, and she came up to me and said, "Do you know your words?" And I said, "Yeah." She said, "I think I'm gonna be sick tomorrow." And when I walked into the theater the next day, Mary Alice was not there, so I had to go on. And the next day she said to me, "How'd it go?" And I was like, "Mary, I wish you had told me." She said, "I did. I did! When I came into the bar. I said I'm gonna be sick tomorrow. How'd it go, that's what I wanna know." And I was telling her about where I had difficulty, and we talked about it! It was just amazing.

Are you saying she did that on purpose?

Yes! Yes! And yet I've had other people that I understudied—'cause I did that for a long while—say to me, "You'll never go on for me. I love you to death, but it'll never happen." But she did it on purpose.

And then you did Tintypes *on Broadway.*

Actually, we were doing *Tintypes* off-Broadway. I was understudy for Lynne Thigpen. And I was a little outspoken during rehearsals. A lot of full voice, you know? We were about to close the show, and there were three understudies having dinner, but I didn't know it was a celebratory dinner, I thought we were just having dinner. And Marie King opened the door, and she goes, "Aren't you excited?" And I was like, "For dinner, yeah, I'm starving." And she goes, "We're bringing the show to Broadway!" And they hadn't called me!

Oh, my gosh.

It was the hardest dinner I've ever swallowed. And it was the longest night I ever had, because I was absolutely broke. Eventually, they did offer it to me.

And so you understudied Lynne Thigpen?

I used to say to her all the time, "As long as you're working, I know I have a job."

Did you understudy her in An American Daughter?

I almost did. But when they auditioned me for that, it was an awful audition. I didn't know what I was doing. *Tintypes* and *Balm in Gilead* were where I understudied her, and the only reason why I ever went onstage for her—when I had my little what I call undercover Broadway debut—was because she was doing a soap and she had to do the soap, and I got one show of *Tintypes* [laughing]. But, yeah, I used to say that to her all the time, "Sister, continue to work and be healthy." 'Cause I knew if Lynne was working, there was a job out there for me somewhere.

When you look back on it, do you think you weren't asked to do the part because you were too outspoken during rehearsals?

Yeah. I mean, I understand it now, because, even going through *Law & Order* when we have these script meetings, the writers have spent their time writing, and the musicians have spent their time, and the composers are writing, and here you come saying, "This shit is wrong." I understand why people get upset, and I wasn't being tactful. There's a way to explain yourself, I've learned over these years, being tactful and being very clear in what you have to say. Then people listen to you. No one wants to hear you when you're screaming.

That's something that you know as an actor on the stage, as the character.

It took me a long time to learn that personally. Onstage, though, yeah. But you know, all lessons are well learned whenever they're learned.

You went from acting job to acting job right off.

One of the things I'm most proud of is that in my thirty years here, I have—for all but two months—made my living as an actor. I did two weeks at Hill & Knowlton as a receptionist. And I worked for an answering service called Metroliner. I worked the graveyard shift, which was all hookers and escorts, so I used to get these wild calls. I'd work through Sunday morning, then I'd wake up, watch Abbot and Costello, and get home by two, three o'clock in the afternoon. But those are the only two jobs that I've had. Because when I first came to New York, there were all these little theaters. So, literally, you could get your unemployment and do theater, because they were only giving you sixty bucks for transportation. It never hurt your unemployment, but it gave you weeks of work.

Were you satisfied with where you were going, or where you were with your career, when Law & Order *came along?*

Oh, absolutely.

Could you have been fine just staying on the stage?

Absolutely. I mean, it certainly doesn't pay as much, as we all know. But absolutely—and you know, it's interesting because one of the things that happened with *Law & Order* was that it allowed me to do theater. I ran into Seret Scott once on the subway, and she said, "What are you doing?" And I said, "Nothing. What do you have?" And she said, "I have this play." And that's how things can happen. One of the things I do appreciate about Dick Wolf is that my voice is important to the run of the show. For so many years I've been not heard, and it is *truly* one of the reasons why I'm still on the show. Here's the deal about *Law & Order* that I think is so cool. When we sit down at script meetings, there's black and white, male and female, Jew and gentile, young and old. It is a microcosm of the world. We can do a lot with that. I don't know everything about you as a man, as a Jew, as a writer, but you don't know everything about me as a middle-aged black woman. There's things that we can learn, if we listen. And lots of times, people don't want to hear that. But I think the opportunity we have at that table can make television not only entertaining but educational. 'Cause there's no reason to sit in front of that fuckin' thing if you don't get up with something in your head. And it's one of the reasons why I think people *really* love the show. There's always watercooler conversation. People learn things about the law. They learn things about procedure. And in the midst of that, they're being entertained. And so when we sit down at those script meetings, I take them very seriously. And when you give me a script and there's a character that says "nigger" six times, I think it's gratuitous. You say nigger once, and I know how you feel about me. You don't have to say it six times. So we've had fights. I remember Steven Hill used to have major conversations when there were issues about Jews. What I appreciate the most is that the texture of the show grew with Ed Sherin coming in and saying, "Script meeting." And we could do it! Because the shows have two sides: law and order. We can sit and read and discuss. Certainly the writers have difficulty with that, and I understand. Because they're closed up in a room, they're writing something, and then you get a bunch of people coming in saying, "That's not gonna work."

Are the writers a mixed bag as well?

The writers are all white men. Every now and then there's a white woman. I think since I've been there, there've been five. I've been there thirteen years. That's not good. And there've only been maybe that many female directors. And the only director who was ever fired was a black female.

They must have enormous respect for you to let you do so much theater.

Right [laughing].

They want to keep you happy.

Yeah. Yeah.

How do you manage that?

Because out of our eight-day schedules, they can shoot my character lots of times in one day. And usually, when I do theater, rehearsals start toward the end of the season, and then the play ends before the shooting season starts. I'm really the only one on the show who has that kind of schedule, outside of the D.A., so it's easy for them to shoot me out—not so easy with the other guys. Even so, at one point I was thinking, Why the hell are you staying here so long?

Why are you?

First of all, it's a really good show. Secondly, it's shot in New York, so I get to stay in New York. And then, with the schedule, I can do film and theater. So it's one of those opportunities where you *literally* can have your cake and eat it too [laughing]. I love it. There is nothing like being able to live in New York and having some money to live here. I love this city, and now I can actually live here in a very different way. I can spend some money and go hear some music. And then there's that little name recognition: "Can you tell them Epatha Merkerson wants to come?" These are the perks that come with it. So it's been fun.

Did new opportunities present themselves after Lackawanna Blues?

Yes, but not in terms of acting parts. I've been getting more calls from friends of mine who are trying to do film than I have from any studios or anything. One of the things that I'm really trying to do is change my focus. I'd like to produce. And so after *Lackawanna*, I was able to get a two-picture deal from HBO. And *Law & Order* helped me do that too.

You mean you're going to produce two pictures?

And be in both.

And you're going to bring them the scripts?

I'll bring them one, and they'll bring me the other. In that sense, the clout has changed. I remember a few years ago there was a book that I was trying to purchase. I'm an avid reader, and there are just so many incredible stories about black women and existence and families that I'd really like to see on film. So I've been reading voraciously for the past eight years, and I found this book—*Sugar*, by Bernice McFadden—that I thought was just extraordinary. And it'd be a great story for me. So we did our presentation to the writer's agent about how we would love to purchase the book. The guy wanted $350,000 for the option, which is way too much. And then he suggested that I purchase it for Angela Bassett. Which I thought was just the rudest thing anyone could say to me. Why don't I purchase it for Angela Bassett! [Laughing.] And I'm like, "Angela Bassett's doing okay. Let her buy it herself if she wants to!" But it's that kind of treatment that is so unnecessary. I mean, if he didn't want to sell me the book, that's one thing. But that was just rude.

I think they might be more interested now.

Yeah. Maybe. I know the author's got four books, and I like every one of them. But I think those things have changed. Now my name has a little more cachet, so the opportunities for me to move into this other direction are ripe.

How did you come to see yourself as a producer?

I think there is something behind the camera that I could be very good at, though I don't think I'd be quite good as a director. I think that's also a personality trait, because there is always somebody above the director, and I really am a control freak. I'd be lying if I said I wasn't. I do like to have control of things. It's why I love the stage. While you're onstage, it is all in your control. And there are all these stories that now African Americans have the opportunity to present, and I think I really want to be a part of that. I don't think I ever want to stop acting, because there is something in it that is really who I am. But I think as a producer, being able to bring onto film all these stories that I'm reading and this history that I know, it's very exciting for me. I thank Dick Wolf for a lot of things, I really do, because Dick gave me the opportunity on *Law & Order* to be able to see more things than I normally would have seen. Every now and then during the seasons, I follow a director from the beginning to the end of a show. And once people knew I was doing this, everybody sort of told me what they were doing: the comptroller, the payroll person, the scenic designer, the set dressers. Everyone involved saw me sitting there on a day I wasn't working, and they said, "What the fuck are you doing here?" And I told them. And so little by little I started getting paperwork from people: "You wanna see how we do so-and-so, and here's how it goes. These are the locations we chose for them, for this part of the scene." I sat through the auditions. I sat through the production meetings with the costume designer and hair and makeup. The whole nine yards. So Dick Wolf may not want to produce with me, but he's given me an opportunity to learn many many many things. I have a lot of respect for Dick, and admiration, and I love his loyalty to people. Being on the show all these years has given me the opportunity to learn.

You were the lead in Lackawanna Blues, *which is different from the way most of America knows you.*

Absolutely. You know, it's funny, because usually I'll walk out on the street and hear a lot of: "Oh, it's *Law & Order*, I love it." Now, it's funny how people say to me, "*Lackawanna Blues*." You know, they'll see me and they'll immediately talk about *Lackawanna Blues*.

We haven't talked about working with directors. On Law & Order, *do you get different ones every week?*

Yeah. There's a group of maybe eight, and out of that eight there's probably just two that I don't like working with.

What is it that you don't like?

They just don't know what they're doing. They may have come from some other discipline in the film business, and they don't know how to talk to actors. They see pictures instead of moments. They don't see the meat of the story, they see pictures, and you can't do a story like that.

How do you cope?

I just sort of ignore them, really. I mean, you get a direction like "Could you just speak louder?" What does that mean? So you just do what you do, and they go, "Yeah, that's exactly what I was talking about." Then there are some directors that will shoot a scene until the horse has been beaten and died and buried six times. "The horse is dead." That's something I say on set a lot when we've done ten takes of this scene. Usually you get it on the first two, so I might get out and say, "Whoo, this horse is fucking dead! Can we kill it any more?" I know it's awful [laughter.] See, I can be a bitch too, sometimes.

Are there directors that actually help?

Oh, my god! I used to love when Ed Sherin would come on the set, because Ed trusts the actors.

It must have been a great pleasure to work with a director like George Wolfe.

Don't get me wrong, 'cause there are some incredible directors on *Law & Order*, like Michael Pressman and Ed Sherin and Don Scardino. These are the kind of directors that come on the set, and we just know we're gonna not only sail through, but the story will be uplifted. It's another thing with George. I've known George for a long time, though I had never worked for him. And the only reason we could come up with was that every time he was doing something, I was working. The funny thing is, *Law & Order* allowed me to say no to *Lackawanna*—three times.

What do you mean?

Well, because after a while, you can't do things for free.

Oh, they weren't offering you—

Nothing. HBO doesn't pay any money. Now I know this about myself: I know this is a part I can do. And I really want to do it. But I also know that I'm gonna give you two hundred fifty percent, and I gotta be compensated for that in some way. So I sort of stuck to my guns.

What were your guns?

That, no, I'm not going to work for free. And I was willing to back off from the offer and be disappointed. I could do that, and I could do that comfortably because of *Law & Order*.

But what else could they give you besides money?

They gave me a two-picture deal.

Ah. Everybody should have a series.

And that's why I don't take it for granted, because it has afforded me opportunities I never could have gotten so quickly. Who's to say where my career would've gone in theater—but it's a slower process. There's less visibility.

What about film? You've done some, but do you think you could have had more? I'm thinking of the film work for middle-aged women, black or white.

How many do you see? I always say that Meryl Streep, Jessica Lange, these are our greatest actresses, and how often do you see these girls working? So the chances of my working any more than them is slim. I got the most incredible e-mail from Gary Sinise after he saw *Lackawanna*. We had done some theater together, and one of the lines in the e-mail was something like, "We're not doing bad for a couple of old folk." You know? That there are roles that come along once in a lifetime, that you have the opportunity to put your teeth in. And he said, "You really have the opportunity with this one." And there's so much truth in that because by and large my work in this business, other than the theater, has been in a supporting capacity or as a character actress. I think you have more longevity that way. Ingenues are not gonna stay ingenues forever, but a character actor will always be a character actor.

Let's talk about your method. How you act. You get a script. Now what do you do?

I just read it and read it and read it. Who, what, when, where, why. Those very simple words really tell you everything you need to know. You start with: Who is this woman? Where does she come from? How is she living? What is her age? Those things that make us a who. And why are we here? Why is this moment happening? Why are these people talking to her this way? What are they saying? What is she doing? What is gonna happen next? Do you know what I mean? Where did this happen? Where is it going? Where are they coming from? As I read, I find myself answering those questions, and then once we get into rehearsal, I just sort of try to figure them out: Oh, yeah, this is where she's coming from. Oh, this is where she's going! I really love the process of rehearsal. I think it's the most fun you have. Discovering the through line. And what is true. And then there's more discovery after that initial discovery that's so exciting. And also the discovery of words coming out of your mouth and hearing them. And hearing someone else say something, and going, "Oh, my god! I never heard that!" It's what I love about the theater. It's constant discovery.

There isn't a sense of, Oh, I have to do this again tonight.

No, no. And I think especially so now because I'm so greedy for theater. No, it's not that at all. Physically, I may be a little more tired than I was when I was younger. My knees aren't the same. Those things I'm noticing too, just being older.

I missed one of your great performances at the Public Theater in Fuckin' A.

That was because of my knees.

I didn't know that.

Yeah. They wanted to extend it, but my knees were this big because most everything I did was on my knees, and the way they designed the set, there were really deep drops. And even though I had gotten a couple of cortisone shots . . .

Did you love working on that?

Oh my god! It was extraordinary because there were no boundaries. And then there was this language that the women had to learn. It was, like, mystery. You know, only women speak it. It's that. That's what I'm talking about. Suzan-Lori Parks created this entire language that only the women spoke. And every night it made more sense to me, the language. And I don't know, it's just . . . there's something so fascinating about leaving yourself open to discovering and also staying a course and discovering within a course. One person I've been working with lately quite a bit is Seret Scott. And Seret has an understanding of my instrument like no other director I've worked with. She knows that I like to be fearless, so she allows me to really go far out and then come all the way back, just to find out what it is that we need to do, how far this character can go in her reality. And I enjoy working with her because of that. I think there are some rare directors who instinctively know actors. Lloyd Richards is one of those directors, and George Wolfe. I've learned so much with George. I call him my new hero. But it's the understanding that the actor has really come to the table with a lot, and you only get that really in theater, because film and television are directors' mediums. The theater is really for the actor. And however your brain works with the script, how you work through it, it is a great collaboration with the director in the theater. The actor has more of a say in decisions than in film or television.

It's your space. Just you and the audience. There's no camera.

And you don't have to hit your mark.

In Lackawanna Blues, *did you feel that you could shape the character in the same sort of way you shape it on the stage?*

Up until *Lackawanna*, I might do six scenes in a movie, but they'd be all very much in the same tone. But in this film, I had the opportunity to see how you can make those discoveries happen within a limited time, because we filmed *Lackawanna* in twenty-eight days and I was flying back and forth from L.A. to do *Law & Order*, so it was madness. It was fun, though. I loved it. I would leave *Law & Order*, go right to the airport, get to my hotel, drop my bags, get an hour's sleep, and go to the set. I did that for the entire month.

How did you manage that?

What *Law & Order* taught me was how to assess things quickly, because you don't have the luxury of the theater rehearsal. So usually you come in, you rehearse the scene a couple of times, and then you go away, they fix the lights, and you shoot it. And so your thoughts have to be quick because there're all these other things coming in. I can read the script and make gobs of decisions, but then there's the whole focus of the light, and what is coming before and what is coming after. And the director has a major concept, and then there are the other actors who've done the same thing that you've done, so are you gonna listen or be what I call a mirror actor—an actor who works everything out in the mirror and doesn't change it.

How do you deal in film with the actor you're talking to often not being in your line of vision?

At the beginning it was very disconcerting. But I think that after you've worked television, it allows your brain to bring up a face. It allows your brain to continue.

Was Lackawanna *shot in sequence?*

No.

So how do you do a scene today that takes place after the scene you do tomorrow?

The great thing for me in this one was that I was working with George Wolfe. And George had a total conception of what he wanted this film to look like, so there were some things that I completely relied on George for. I understood what was happening, but I didn't know where he wanted it to go. For instance, there was a scene—and I still

think I was right, and I'm sorry I didn't ask for another take a different way—but there was a scene where she comes home from this big
dance and she's waiting for her husband, who's a philanderer. And
he comes into the house drunk, and she's hurt. And the words
should have been said softer, because she says to him, "I'm not hurt.
You can't hurt me anymore." Which means to me, you don't yell that.
You say it. "You can't hurt me anymore." George had me yelling it,
well, not exactly yelling, but he had me use my big voice. And then I
understood why: he wanted the boy to hear me. It was important that
the boy hear this argument between the two adults. And the thing is
that, at the time, I was so busy trying to figure out how to make it
work against what I was feeling that I didn't even ask why he wanted
me to do it this way. But I let it ride. At that point I needed to figure
out how to do it, because it was so totally against what I was feeling.
And I said that to George, and he said, "Trust me. Trust me." And he
may have said to me, "The boy's there." But I just didn't feel it, and I
had to figure out how to do it to make it work for that moment. And
then when I saw it all together, it made perfect sense. But I still think
I'm right.

Doing it your way, how would the boy have heard it?

He wouldn't have heard it.

Maybe that was more important.

It was. To George, anyway, because the story is about the boy and
what he is experiencing as a young man.

*Have you ever seen these vintage paperbacks from the 1940s of Claude
McKay novels?*

Yes, yes.

That's what the images in Lackawanna *reminded me of.*

The interesting thing about that is that I grew up in that period, so it was so easy for me to feel what was happening. Because the real, the overall story was about the decay of the neighborhood, and this was the last vestige of what had been. I knew that neighborhood. My mother used to have people come to our house all the time. We had people in and out of our house. They weren't quite that group of misfits, but it was a time when you kind of felt all of that was in jeopardy, and that's what I felt about the film: she's in a time when her very life is in jeopardy, and all the people she's brought into this home, their lives are in jeopardy. So it was an interesting thing to do, especially to work with George. He has a vision. He doesn't come into a piece without a complete vision. And what was so interesting too was that it was a first for both of us: my first major film role and his first big film directorial piece.

The whole thing started when Ruben Santiago-Hudson came to my office at the Public and said, "I have these stories." And he did them for me, and I said, "This is fabulous." And I called John Dias, the literary manager, and said, "You gotta hear this." He just performed it for us, and John started working with him, and then we went to George, and George said, "Great, let's do it." And Ruben started writing. It was an extraordinary part of my tenure at the Public.

Ruben loves Ruben more than anybody had ever loved Ruben, and he's just the funniest person that I know, because he loves talking about himself. I saw it at the Studio Arena Theater in Buffalo. I took my friends backstage because they wanted to meet him, and we were mesmerized by all the people we had seen onstage all performed by this one man. And so we go back, and he goes, "Oh, oh, oh, oh yeah, baby, you know, stay in touch, girl, 'cause you know I just sold this to HBO, and I'm gonna be writing the screenplay and there might be something in it for you." And a few years later, after we filmed it, I told that story at the Image Awards, and I looked at him and said, "Is this what you had in mind?" But it was quite extraordinary to see him do it and then to actually be in it.

How did the filming go?

The first four days, there were moments where George was in the middle of a bunch of people talking to him. That always happens in film, too many cooks in the stew. The cameraman, the producers, the director of photography, all these people who had this amazing experience were surrounding him. They weren't nervous about him; they were really trying to help. And you could see him taking it all in. Then something happened on the third or fourth day, where it hit him: he got the language. Because the language is different, and there are these barriers that you cross when you go from film to television or when you go from theater to film. He wasn't completely versed in the language at first, so what he was doing was listening. It was fascinating to sort of watch that happen. He was so attentive. And then he let everyone go. Once he realized what the language was, he just said—I mean you could see his head, because George always thinks faster than he talks—and he went, "Ah, ah, ah, ah, oh, oh, oh, okay ladies and gentleman, we're gonna have to shoot these three scenes over." And boy oh boy, did they pop afterward.

Did you suspect that there was something not right about those scenes?

It wasn't that there wasn't anything right about the scenes. It was my watching what was happening with George, that he was in this new space and all these people who had had more experience than him were trying to explain what was happening.

But you didn't feel that the scenes weren't working. They would have worked—

What it did, it taught him how to express himself, and so he could and he did. It was fabulous, because there was a different energy in it all: "Ah, ah, ah, ah, oh, oh, oh, I've got it!" You know, that kind of thing, the way he is, so enthusiastic. It was quite interesting and lovely to watch.

Let's talk a little about the future now, could we?

Next season I'm doing a play, *Come Back, Little Sheba*, in the hiatus from *Law & Order*.

Oh, that's a great role for you. Is this going to be all black or a mixed cast?

Doc and Lola will be black, so I'm sure the rest of it will be mixed. At first I was sort of frightened by it, because it's like, "Wow." You know, Shirley Booth was so big, bigger than life, and that's so in my head because I've seen that film a hundred times. I really love the film, and it never occurred to me that I would ever do the part. But it is a major challenge that I'm really looking forward to. And I made a decision that as long as I do *Law & Order*, every other year I would do something in the theater, and this year's my vacation year. I think I earned it, though.

Is there any other role you'd like to play?

Someone asked me that the other day. I don't think so. Things have sort of happened with me, and I've been able to roll with the punches that way. There isn't necessarily a role that I want to play. But then someone suggests Lola and *Come Back, Little Sheba*, and I'm like, "Oh, oh, yeah I'd like to do that."

What would you have done if acting hadn't worked out for you?

It's hard to put yourself there when you don't need to, but it was always in my head that there are many things you can do; this is something you want to do. You can find other things to do. And again, I haven't been tested so I could speak it. Doors just kept opening. For me, to be in this entertainment business had been in my head since I can remember having a thought. But what it would be specifically was something totally different. So when I go into work, I go in with this attitude: I'm doing exactly what I said I was gonna do. How many people can say that? And not only am I doing it, but quite successfully. So what would I be bitching about? And certainly there are things to moan and groan about, and I do my share of them, don't get me wrong. I think you know me better than that. But by and large, when people work with me, they work with me again. Because when I do bitch and moan, its usually *about* something, 'cause I try not to waste energy. That's something I've learned. It's being tactful. It took me a while. And especially now, I think I know it better.

Dianne Wiest

We did two interview sessions at Rosemarie's apartment with Dianne Wiest, and each time she arrived exactly on time, explaining that since she lives across the street from where we're doing the interview, she knew exactly how long it would take to get here. Today she is wearing a starched white high-necked blouse, tight black pants, and loafers. She is limping slightly, the result of a knee sprained while running up and down the stairs during the Brooklyn shooting of an independent film she is making with Billy Crudup and Mandy Moore. It is a freezing, intensely bright day. Dianne cuts through the cold with the same warmth and combination of girlishness and womanliness that has made her a beloved presence on the screen and stage. During the interview, there is a quiet insistence on her own pace. She will not be rushed; she thinks about her responses and does not answer glibly. When she describes a particular incident, she relives the original emotions of that incident. Her feelings are always close to the surface. She holds nothing back, and that is a hallmark of what she values most in acting. She seems, as a person and as an artist, to let herself be known, to risk embarrassment and foolishness for the sake of originality and purity of feeling. We sit at a large black table, Dianne in front of the window. On the wall to her left are a series of original costume sketches by Santo Loquasto, Beth Clancy, and Marina Draghici. A bunch of green grapes is offered to Dianne, and she accepts. Once the interview starts, she doesn't eat any. She apologizes in advance for not being the right kind of person to do this interview. We assure her she is quite mistaken, and we begin.

Let's talk about when you knew you wanted to be an actor. Did your childhood support that in any way?

I remember very clearly the first time I was onstage, although it wasn't a stage; it was at West Point, New York, the military academy where I grew up. The closest I have to a hometown. I was a member of the Brownies, and they were doing a little skit. I was supposed to come on and sing "Daisy, Daisy, give me your answer do." And I remember thinking this: I'm no good; this is very very bad. I knew I was terrible, but I loved it. I remember that feeling, that moment, that room as though it were yesterday. And I was eight years old. It just became a crystal clear childhood memory. I went to the Catholic church in Highland Falls, and there was some kind of procession where we all put on our best dresses and carried candles and went behind this canopy that covered the Eucharist; then there were the priests and the altar boys and the incense. I was marching along to the music, and I thought, This is something I've never experienced before. It was a little otherworldly. And I thought, Well probably I'll become a nun; this is the thing for me, to be a nun. And then I became interested in ballet at about age nine and started doing little ballet performances, and some of them are very clear in my mind. I went to high school in Nuremberg, Germany, and there was an army base community theater type of thing. I did a dancing part in *Guys and Dolls*. I had a line, but I remember thinking, It's much easier to dance than to speak. There was no drama department, but my high school English teacher, Mr. Ferguson, decided he would put on plays. The first was *Our Hearts Were Young and Gay* and I was Cornelia Otis Skinner, and the next was *Pygmalion* and I was Eliza.

Did you know it was something that you could actually do in the world?

No. No. I had no idea that I could do it in the world, that I was talented, nothing. I just knew that this was what I wanted. And I was not to be deflated, much to my parents' dismay.

And how did you proceed?

We came back from Germany. My dad was stationed at Walter Reed Army Medical Center, and I went to the University of Maryland for a semester and a third. I thought philosophy was really interesting. And I loved English. But I never went to the classes. I never left the drama department, except to go across to the dance department. And so, luckily, this traveling Shakespeare troupe came through—called the American Shakespeare Theater. They had cast in New York, but they had lost the actress who was to play Adriana in *The Comedy of Errors*. So they did local auditions.

It's like you ran away with the circus.

I did. I ran away with the circus. Two U-Hauls, a station wagon. We set up our sets, I ironed the costumes, we did our own everything, and we went to a lot of gymnasiums, community centers, and little colleges. I did that for probably a year. It folded somewhere in the Midwest, and we were stranded. It was Thanksgiving. And my dear mother said, "Oh, bring everybody home!" And so I did.

You were in your teens.

I was nineteen.

Your parents thought this was—

They were alarmed. Their attitude was . . . go back to school, which I heard all the time. But I think inside, it was . . . let her get this out of her system. I came to New York right after that with a hundred dollars in my pocket—my parents didn't give me any money—and no place to live. And my friend Clay Haney put me up, and then I would just go from place to place . . . sleeping on the floor. I think my parents' feeling was that if they didn't support this, I would come to my senses, I would get sick of being poor, and I would go back to school.

But you never did. They didn't reckon with your determination?

No. Not at all. I think they were very frightened for me, and you know, having an eighteen-year-old daughter now, I am in great sympathy with them.

When did they feel, Oh, this is okay. She's okay?

Probably not till I started doing film work. And probably not until Woody Allen. At regional theaters, when I could support myself, I had a little apartment. And I was doing steady work. I think they weren't scared then, but I don't think they were happy until I was in movies.

Did you see plays growing up?

I think I was in them before I saw them. I remember once we traveled up to Scotland, where my mom's parents lived, and we had a stop-off in London and we saw *Lock Up Your Daughters*. And that's the first play I remember going to the theater and seeing.

Did you connect that with your need and desire to act?

No.

Did your parents recognize that you were good at this?

No. In fact, I wasn't good. They were right. And I think that when my parents came to see the traveling Shakespeare theater, they were very alarmed.

How did you get from one job to another? It's interesting, because you didn't study.

The children's company at the Long Wharf Theatre in New Haven was actually my first steady job. It was much like the traveling Shakespeare troupe. You just went around, you put up the set, you put on your costumes, and you were different characters in different plays. And you went to all these little schools. I was a princess in *The Lion and the Thorn*. I knew I wasn't good. And then they did this circus play, the name of which I can't remember. But my character's name was Winnie, and I was an overweight, tightrope, bareback rider type of character. I had a tutu, and they padded it out. And I got enormous laughs. It was the first time I thought, I'm funny. I had to hide in a trunk behind a piece of scenery onstage, and I remember thinking, Oh, dear god, please let me always act! I was just in love with it.

Having gotten this laugh, did you recognize that you knew how to do something that made people laugh?

I could repeat Winnie, whatever that was. I don't remember going out there and not getting laughs, although I certainly have had that experience, being funny one night and then not knowing what happened to the laugh the next night. But that didn't happen with Winnie. I think because it was physical comedy, and I had a funny voice, and it was for kids, you know? The next year, Arvin Brown asked me to be in the main company at the Long Wharf with John Cazale, Joyce Ebert, John Cromwell, and Ruth Nelson. Beautiful, beautiful people. I had to audition for Gorky's *Country People*, and I remember wanting that part so much. I wanted it desperately. I remember the audition very clearly, and thinking I'd done okay but not great, and then Arvin called and said, "We would like you to do it." And my joy was just so pure and crystal . . . wanting something so, so much, and actually getting it. I'll never forget that joy. That was a peak.

I keep hearing you saying, "I wasn't good."

I wasn't.

Then how—

This is what would happen. In *Country People*, I was very good for half the run, and then it fell apart. And Arvin would come, and he'd sit me down and say, "What's the matter?" I realized that I had lost what I had, because I had yet to acquire much technique—except by the repetition of doing bad things.

Did you ever find your way back in Country People?

I found it a little bit. And I would just twist myself into a rag for this emotion. That's what I would do.

How apparent do you think it actually was that it fell apart?

Very apparent.

So you would force an emotional thing to happen.

Which isn't very good acting, because you'd feel all the force.

What do you mean, feel the force?

The audience would know. Forcing something is overdoing, which was the only thing I knew how to do, really. So if inspiration didn't come . . . And you know how infrequently it does. I was not a good actor for a very very long time.

How did you get better?

I was trying to figure out a way, desperately trying to suck up any kind of learning. Not being clear enough in my own mind to say, Why don't you stop and go to school, Dianne? But somehow that just never entered my mind. Even to just come down to New York and go to an acting school, I said, How will I live? So I just kept doing bad work.

Was there a time when you had an "aha" moment?

It was gradual. I had no technique. And I think what would happen is, I would have an inspiring audition, or at least a good audition, and I would get a job. This happened at the Guthrie in Minneapolis. John Hirsch cast me right away. I'd never done Shakespeare, except for my traveling Shakespeare troupe. So here I am with this role in *Midsummer Night's Dream*, Hermia, with a cast of clearly superlative people who had done a *lot* of Shakespeare and had a *lot* of training. So

I show up, and these people are just amazing, and I open my mouth to read and it's humiliating. But luckily, there are voice classes and movement classes at the Guthrie, and I began to get a little training, but not enough fast enough. And I couldn't make the connection. I think it was the intimidation of being with these incredibly wonderful people, my lack of confidence—which wasn't my strong point to begin with—and my real lack of knowledge about anything to do with meter. I didn't even know what I was talking about—"like to a double cherry"—and how you figure it out. It was very bad, and I remember John Hirsch screaming at me, "How was I to know you were this bad? How was I to know?" And I thought, He's right. I tricked him. I tricked him at my audition. And how could he know I was this bad? Recently I ran into Linda Carlson, who played Helena, and she said, "Remember when you were John Hirsch's whipping boy?" And I hadn't been cognizant of the fact that I was the whipping boy, because I felt so bad. But having my feet held to the fire for that long, and just repeating that bad/good work night after night, I must have learned something, you know? And from those classes. So that by the end of the run, Roberta Maxwell said to me, "You have come a long way." And I thought, How lovely of her.

Linda Carlson told me that a year later John Hirsch told her he thought you were wonderful. So I think maybe by the end you really pulled it off.

I guess I did. Linda was wonderful. I mean she really knew what she was doing, and I remember being so envious of her, this young actress who really knew what she was doing. You know, it was amazing. Everybody else too, but she was the one I was so connected to in the play. One thing I was able to do consistently well, Rosemarie, was at your audition at TCG for *The Prime of Ms. Jean Brodie* in Louisville. I gave a consistent performance all through the run. It was effortless. I don't know why. It required nothing; I think because the character was a schoolgirl. Also I had a Scottish accent, and that's the first accent I used. I think that was a help. Somewhere in there, Zelda Fichandler came to see us in *Midsummer* at the Guthrie. Zelda was interested in me for Arena Stage. She said, "What do you think? How do you think you are in this play?" And I said, "Not very good." And she said, "You're right." And she said, "Do you think you would be able to do *The Hostage* and *Our Town*?" And of course I said, "Oh, yes. I can do it; I can do it." Not really knowing if I could. So I went to Arena Stage and stayed for four years. Again it was trial by fire because there was no training there. Great roles were handed to me. I'd rehearse all day; I'd perform at night. The first one I did, *The Hostage*, I played the little Irish waitress, Teresa. I remember at first not being able to do it, and I thought, Why can't I do this in an Irish accent? Why can't I do this? And then I went to see a play in Washington somewhere, and the acting was so bad, and I remember sitting in the audience thinking, Gee, why doesn't she drop everything and just say the lines? I remember thinking that very clearly, and then I was able to do *The Hostage*.

What would you do those days when you didn't know what you were doing? What would you do when you got the script?

I would try to feel what the character felt. I would imagine what they felt.

And you've since found that that's not the way?

Yes. I have.

When you said that, I was just thinking, Well, that must have been a tough way to do After the Fall, *to feel what Marilyn Monroe was feeling.*

And yet that was an effortless one.

What do you mean by effortless?

I guess I mean I never dried up, let it go. It never left me. It's like I dug a track, and I just had to roll down it every night. But I wasn't a Marilyn Monroe type of gal, you know? And so much of the play concentrates on this beauty and seductiveness she had. Joey Tillinger was the director. And Frank Langella was Quentin. And they didn't know what to do with me, how to costume me, and Joey one day looked at me and said, "You're not glamorous." So they let the whole thing of glamour go. I had short hair; I had a padded bra, but just sort of regular clothes. Everybody gave up trying to make me be sexy. Thank god they did, and then I was able to let all that go also.

But I saw pictures of you in the role, and you looked fabulous. You looked like what the character was supposed to look like.

Oh, oh.

I thought it was remarkable that they cast you, because you got inside the character like no one else could have. I mean, you didn't look like Marilyn Monroe, but you looked attractive and sexy, and you found her need.

I did, yeah.

When you find something like that, something that you say was effortless, do you mean that you find something true in the character, and then, knowing that, you can't go wrong? Is that what you mean? That once you're on this track, when you've got something that's really it, you know when it's true?

I guess so. Although by the same token, I think I've known things were true and not been able to act them. You know? I'm sorry to be so inarticulate.

No. You're very clear about what works, what doesn't, and how you work; that's what we want to know.

It's why I'm so frightened of teaching. Because I don't know how to articulate things, although I have a lot of the lingo now. But for myself, I still have trouble applying it. The whole process is still strange to me.

I know that each role is different, but is there any fear that you'll never find it, or fear that you'll lose it altogether? Or is that fear gone?

Not entirely. No. It's not entirely gone.

How was it to work on roles day and night at the Arena Stage? Did you feel—

Elated.

Elated.

Elated.

But at this point, you must have had confidence in what you were doing.

I did.

And that came through the doing.

It's that repetition . . . Oh, year after year—four years of major roles. But what happened after a couple of years is I found myself beginning to get sloppier, exhausted, drained, not sharp, not knowing how to get sharp. I saw it all begin to drift away.

How did you make your performance happen when the person over there or there or even the director was just not up to what you knew?

Yeah, there was a lot of that also.

How did you survive?

It's very difficult because I'm a very reactive actor. So that if something's going on and if I'm not getting something back, I think I usually sort of twist it. It's like: I need to love you and I can't, because I see you're not even there. So I'll twist it, and go how I hate, hate you so. I'll put all of that feeling of dislike and disregard and disrespect into the words of love. And I know the difference, but nobody else does. [She laughs and laughs.]

They just hear—

They see passion.

And they hear the words of love.

And I'm going, you know, motherfucker. Not really. But you—you flip it. I haven't had to do that for years and years and years. But I have had to do that.

Well, yes, I would think, as you were coming up, there would have been a mixed bag of actors.

Oh yes.

And have you had the same sort of experience with directors?

Yeah, directors—I just out and out fight with them.

How do you fight with them?

A part of me shuts down because they seem to me so emotionally il-
literate. They don't know what the hell is going on. I mean, never
mind what's going on in your character, they don't know what's going
on in the play. And a part of me just shuts them off. I don't let them
in. And the other part of me is . . . if I'm being forced to do something, I try very politely to explain why I think it might be better done
this way or that way, or that this is what I'm thinking or feeling, to try
to convince them, which you can't always do. And then, I think, in
the end, when I realize that I'm being forced to do something I really
don't truly believe I'm doing well, I have to go through this sort of—
it's almost like an onstage pout. You know, I'm out there, and I'm
thinking, This is awful. I'm not going to do it. And of course I have to
do it, and this is where I'm a bad actor with my fellow actors, because
I just can't do it this way. And then, you know, you have to get over
that pretty quickly and then just go and do it your way.

When Woody Allen cast you as the grande dame actress in Bullets Over
Broadway, *I believe that you said you couldn't do it.*

Yes, I did.

So how did you get to do it?

Well, this is what happened. Woody sent me the script and said I'd be
perfect for that part. This is so dear of him. So I read it, and I
thought, What the hell is he dreaming of? This isn't for me. I had no
idea what he was thinking. So I put on these beautiful costumes, and
the first day of shooting comes and goes, and Woody says, "Come
to the cutting room." He said, "Look at this," and I looked at the
dailies, and it was awful. I mean awful, just a stupid woman saying
these meaningless lines, trying to seduce beautiful John Cusack.

And I said, "I don't know what to do, Woody." And he said, "Well, think of something." I said, "I really don't know what to do." He said, "Well, you've got to think of something." I said, "I think you should replace me." That's as best as I could come up with.

What did you think you were doing?

Nothing. I didn't know what to do. I really didn't know what to do. Because the whole thing about film is you have to be as truthful and as much sort of *there* as you can be. You just have to be there. So this character of a wild actress, that's as best as I could do, this wild actress. Just sort of be this wild actress. Well, you know me. I'm not a wild actress. Well, I forgot about "acting." And so the next day, we were sitting on the set, both of us in despair, saying this is truly awful. And I said, "I think you have to replace me. You have to fire me and get somebody who can do this." And he said, very loyally, "No. I think it's something to do with your voice." And I remember coming toward panic that morning, determined that I would lower my voice, but really not knowing what the hell I was going to do. So we went back and reshot the same scene, and I was determined, and I lowered my voice, and suddenly, with this "fake" voice, I could do anything. Anything.

Like the accent in The Hostage.

Exactly. It freed me. It freed me.

So you went down to this lower register.

I went to this lower register. It had nothing to do with any truthfulness, anything at all in me. I became this wild actress. It freed me to be outrageous, like Winnie—and I seduced this guy.

I thought the same thing about you when I saw In the Summer House—
because of the voice.

I didn't feel good about my work in *Summer House*. I had stayed off
the stage for at least two or three years. But I had Joanne Akalaitis as
director, who, although she's not an actor's director, has a terrific
sense of staging. And she had Catherine Fitzmaurice, who is this
great voice teacher. So I was working with Catherine, but I felt that I
could get the character if I'd had another month of preparation before I even met them . . .

What do you feel you didn't get? What part of the character?

I wasn't in command the way I thought I could be. I couldn't make a
choice and stay with it. On that balcony, when I open the show, it
would be like in rehearsal: I would get an idea. Say I was thinking of
being able to have Hitler locked up in a prison. I had a million ideas,
a very different idea every day. Well, gee, that's all well and fine, but
eventually you have to perform night after night the same choice.
And because I kept drawing away, my choices would never abide by
anything throughout the whole play, and it was a long play. And Jane
Bowles is a great writer, but she's not a playwright at all. You had to
sort of drag the play around, and I never could get on top of it the
way I saw Franny Conroy get on top of it, the way I saw Liev Schreiber
get on top of it. Those were flawless, brilliant performances. Mine
was not.

*I agree with you, Dianne. You were wonderful, but you didn't have com-
mand, and I didn't feel safe with you, as I have felt.*

Exactly. I wasn't safe.

It was always alive, and you're always interesting to watch. But I just didn't feel safe.

Exactly right. Exactly right. I remember Joe Papp saying that to me after some audition that I didn't get, which seemed to be so true, but he ended up saying, "You're always interesting."

It's more than that.

No, but that's thinking that he couldn't give me the role, because I'm not in command. And this is where all that lack of training comes in. And I think college is a rite of passage that gives you confidence. I think all of that comes back and gets me. It got me there in *Summer House*. But then you start working again, and then you have your confidence, and god knows I have learned some things by now.

Does comedy still seem easier to you? More natural?

It's been a while since I've done anything really funny. It also depends on the type of comedy. It has to be a character. It's got to come from a physicality. I'm not a wit. You wouldn't want to put me in a Nöel Coward play.

But you could be in a Nöel Coward play, because you bring the bottom to the character. Everyone's sharp, but people who often do Coward don't have something supporting it.

Yeah, yeah. Maybe. I don't know why I even said that; I can't remember even seeing a Nöel Coward play. Anyway, it seems like a nice name to drop. But—like the character in *The Art of Dining*, where she was clumsy, shy. That was effortless. She was such a wonderful character. But I remember being in the middle of that woman—who is dropping things, embarrassing herself—and thinking, These people are laughing at me; this isn't funny. Because of course she didn't feel funny at all. She was in huge humiliation and pain.

They were laughing at you and loving you at the same time.

Yes. But you still do feel you're being laughed at, which is a little sad.

Do you think training would change that?

I don't think Noël Coward people mind that you laugh at them. Whereas the characters I do that are funny, even in *Bullets Over Broadway*, you're kind of ashamed you laughed at her. I don't know how to explain it more than that. But she is inside and she's just trying her best. I don't know why it comes out funny. I mean I do know. In *The Art of Dining*, you've dropped the lipstick in your soup. But the laugh . . . it doesn't feel funny.

But do you know as you're doing it that you're doing comedy?

I absolutely know I am doing comedy. I absolutely know, and I know that there's a huge 180-degree switch between approaching something like *Bullets* or *The Art of Dining* and, you know, approaching O'Neill.

Well, it's the context, because there could be a scene in a very serious play in which the character drops her lipstick and spills the soup, and the audience could be in tears.

Absolutely.

Since you're a very truthful actress, and call on yourself, are there some things you wouldn't want somebody to see? Or do you see acting as the vehicle to show everything you know?

No, I don't. A lot of what you know emotionally is tedious and boring. What I'm feeling emotionally is not what you want. What the audience wants is what is written that I bring myself to, and whatever that communion is. It's not me with my emotions overpowering the writing, saying, You know, this is so tragic or so funny. This is what you should look at. It's me feeling for whatever the scribbles on the page are and bringing what knowledge of human nature and myself I have to bear. But myself is a very limited topic. It's what I've read and seen and experienced of other people.

There's was a moment in The Goddess *with Kim Stanley when she picks up her crying baby, and it was really frightening, because she was so angry I thought she was going to hurt the baby. And I wondered, Who is this woman—meaning the actress Kim Stanley—that she knows this murderous hatred?*

You can imagine all kinds of things. This is what we do all the time. We imagine what it would be like to be in that situation and capable of doing anything that human nature is capable of.

What is asked of you in stage acting versus film acting? The process, how you use yourself, what's easy for you, what you enjoy more. TV acting too.

Back-to-back I had these two experiences. I was cast in Wendy Wasserstein's last play at Lincoln Center, *Third*, which was very very difficult for me to do. I kept on saying to Wendy and Dan Sullivan, the director, that I was miscast. Luckily, he never thought that, but what I felt during rehearsal was, I'm in a room with this incredibly gracious, wonderful, intellectual Dan Sullivan, and here I am, and I just said, "Hey Dan, guess what? I have no idea." Wendy's play required a Nöel Coward thing that I was not going to be capable of giving her, because I'm not sharp. And so I had a very hard time. It was my intention to read everything she mentioned, which is what I love to do—I love to research. But I'd gotten this small film, just seven days' work, right before rehearsals started, which cut out three weeks because I had to prepare for this very low-budget film. In the film, I play a mother from Queens over the decades. Poverty-stricken. The director is Justin Theroux, who's got a wonderful way with actors. In preparing for this, I had to figure out the accent, and I had to fit all this together because it was a last-minute job. And this is not in my repertoire; I haven't played this kind of woman before. It wasn't familiar; I hadn't done any research around it. It was a real story of poverty in this apartment, and how these people were happy there. And there were these wonderful young actors. And somehow . . . it required no acting, if you know what I mean. It was Justin's first film. But what an eye. He would constantly say, so kindly, "Just make it simple. Just make it simple." Which I did. And he told me afterward, after the film had been put together, that he always chose the most simple takes. And that was a lesson.

Then I go into Wendy's play, and I think, Okay, you've learned simple things, and then I realize I'm terribly miscast. I had to turn somersaults on my toes to do that character; it was so hard for me. And again, I always felt like I was a little bit behind: I didn't get ahead of it; I didn't get on top of it. And what I want to say about the young people I've been working with, say over the past, certainly the past ten years—they come in, and these are highly trained actors. They've not only been to college, they've been to conservatory programs. They come in and I watch them work, and I'm still envious. They come in and they have the skeleton of the character. And through rehearsals, you see them. Maybe they're trying a different hair color or a different costume, but because of their techniques, they have something constructed which no one can take away. And I come in, and I have maybe, you know, a left hand and a right ear and a couple of eyes, and I go about and I try to do it, but I never had that whole self-image. Hence, your comment and Joe Papp's comment—"You're always interesting." Because it's always a little off, lopsided, never, say, on top of it, except once in a while.

The character you played in Kathleen Tolan's play Memory House *was very articulate.*

Yes, she was.

And without the deep-seated humanity that you bring to it, the character could have been cold and nasty rather than a very loving mother. So I think that when the script says one thing, actors can bring this other thing to it, rather than telling what's already there.

What I wanted to say to certain critics is: You think I can't do anything else. In the meantime, I'm rehearsing Strindberg's *The Father* with Al Pacino. You know, I can do the wicked witch. I can, very easily. It's not that I can't. I can't explain more than that, but it's not that I can't act people who are cold, manipulative, and mean. I haven't gotten the chance to do that very much in film, god knows. And so in Wendy's play, the mother was a very cold and manipulative woman. And when Ben Brantley called me something like "melting and warm," I wanted to say, I'm not miscast; this is a choice.

Through all this, is there anyone you knew that you could talk to? Another actor?

My most consistent person is Kathleen Tolan, who I've known since the Public Theater, in Tina Howe's *Museum*, and who has been my eyes and ears and just this most beautifully honest friend. She is my dearest friend outside of it all. But also I think, because she has such an ear as a writer, she has become my dearest critic, my most trustworthy critic.

What are you thinking of when you read a script the first time?

I think, Okay, what set this all in motion? And the thing that sets a thing in motion happens before the screenplay or play in a good story begins. And without this thing, whatever it is that you discover, the story would never take place. So that's the first thing. And then, somewhere, something's going to turn. And that turning affects everybody, in the play or in the screenplay—everybody, without exception. If it doesn't affect everybody, then you haven't got it yet. So there's something that happens before it begins that affects why it rolls out; then you'll find something in turn that affects everybody; and then that rolls it to its conclusion. And the last thing that happens in this story, whatever it could be, is the reason the whole thing was told. Okay, so when I first look at something—I can't help looking more at my character's participation—but if you don't look at the whole landscape, what you're bringing to it becomes very small.

By seeing its place in the whole, it enriches your way of seeing your role and how to explore it.

Yes. By seeing how this affects whatever these episodes are that happen, how they affect your character and what she does.

Then what do you do?

And then I go in and say, Okay, who is this? Why does she do what she does? What are her reasons? For instance, in this film I've only got three days of work on, I play a mom who goes from hot to cold with no reason at all. And I thought, I can be this. I thought, You just jump. You don't prepare; you don't think like her. I feel myself getting short of breath even as I talk about it. Her center—I hate that word—but her way of going about the world is like a shortness of breath. She can't get enough—I actually feel dizzy—she can't get enough breath. And that makes her very compassionate, and then something scares her, and she says, "Fuck you." So that's how I do it. It's got to be absolutely real. A lot of it's just in your face, and then for that I need images. For instance, the director had me—I don't know whether it'll ever be in the film—but he had me make up a whole thing about when Mandy Moore, my daughter, was little, so that Billy Crudup would understand what she was like and what a good soul she was. Except I'm so self-involved I don't remember what she was like. Who knows what the fuck she was like when she was little? Who cares? But I feel like I'm going to bring him around if I can convince him. Do you understand? So then the director said, "Just make it up." And I said, "Oh, nobody's told me to do that since Woody." I thought, Oh, wow, that's wonderful. And then of course I froze, and I couldn't think of anything. I'd never even laid eyes on Mandy Moore before I shot. I didn't know her. What do I do? I go back to my children, and stories of Kathleen's children, and stories of my own childhood.

You got your big television experience with Law & Order. *How did you engage with it? What went right? What went wrong? Why did you leave?*

I've been thinking about that because I knew you'd want to talk about it, so let me see what I can tell you that might be useful to other people who are in some kind of a similar situation. What happened with this: I was just finishing making a film in Ireland, and I got the call from Sam Cohn, my agent, saying that Dick Wolf called and he wanted me to replace the great Steven Hill—who I worship—on *Law & Order*. And I thought, Oh, my gosh. I was extremely flattered and everything. Now, there are a couple of problems. One is the only television show I ever watch with any regularity is Jim Lehrer, so I didn't know *Law · & Order*. I know Sam Waterston, who's a good friend, love Sam. Great, just enormous admirer of Steven Hill. So

Dick and I talked, and I said, "Could you send cassettes so I can actually see the show?" I was embarrassed because I know what a huge show this is, but anyway. And he did send me some cassettes, and then I talked to him, so unfortunately, this whole thing began in a huge bubble of ignorance on my part, and then another bubble of ignorance on Dick's part, because he didn't know me at all.

Why was he hiring you if he didn't know you?

I think he was cashing in on me. I mean I'd won the Oscar recently, but I had never done any television, and he got me. And I don't think he was especially a fan of Woody Allen's or that he comes to the theater. It was a very peculiar choice, especially in retrospect.

What did you think of the show when you saw it?

I thought, Well, this is sort of interesting. But I didn't really know . . . I mean I knew what the cops were doing; I knew what the lawyers were doing, but I really didn't know—as brilliant as he is— exactly what Steve's character was doing, except in this one scene when he went to see his dying wife. But I didn't know how unusual that scene was, that it was the only time the character ever did anything out of the office or personal like that. So I talked to Dick and I said, "Dick, will you write this for me?" And he said, "Absolutely, I will. Absolutely." And I said, "Do you think we could have a little comedy in it? A little . . ." You know, I was trying to get myself scooched in there so I felt like this would be a woman with a point of view, a sense of humor, and not me trying to be Steven Hill. Well, of course, if I had been really familiar with the show or if I had really studied and talked to people, I would have known better. I just talked to Sam, and he said, "Come. Do it. We'll have a great time." I didn't do my homework.

What do you mean, your homework?

I didn't find out what would really be required of me. At the same time, both Ed Sherin, who'd been there for years and years and the chief writer, left the show, and in comes Arthur Penn, who I've done a play with, who I love, but there's no real chief writer anymore. There's a bunch of writers. Everybody was sort of up in limbo. There was new leadership. Huge changes. And the promise that I took so seriously, that they would talk to me about developing the character, went out the window. I was just, you know, sort of lost in the shuffle. And I kept on thinking, Well, surely somebody will do this before we start shooting. I remember being jet-lagged after I'd been in Ireland for months and not being able to get to *Law & Order* people to find out what it was I was needed to do. I remember the humiliation of not being able to find my way in this, not being able to figure out what I was to do in this vacuum, that the character—I didn't know who she was. Nobody cared, though, who she was; you're just supposed to come in and say, "Casey versus," you know, "the state of New York," and, "Go interview somebody." That's all that was required, but I didn't understand that really, and once I did understand it, I really couldn't believe that this person I was playing week after week didn't have anything to hope for, didn't have anything to fight against. She just had to walk this thin—and this is where I really did get into trouble— political line. I don't know what Dick's politics are, but it smacked of being a Republican show. It's always for the law. But then there came a show where I have to say, "I want the death penalty for a minor." And I just refused to do it. And that created a huge, huge thing. At that time Arthur had left; there was no one in charge. The writers are all in L.A. and they're concerned with: you said "and" instead of "but." There was no spontaneity allowed, which had been sort of my mainstay in any sort of film acting. I was just absolutely lost, and then they wanted me to say, "I am for the death penalty for a minor." And I said, "I can't do it." And Sam helped me through all of this, but he had to do

a lot of things in the show that he doesn't agree with politically. And I
saw that he stepped up to the plate and did it, and I said, "Okay, I have
to step up." And I really, physically, could not do it. And he said,
"What the hell is wrong with you? You're an actor." And I said, "Hello,
it's me doing this." In retrospect I see how much of the character I
never had, because it really felt like me. I had no reason, no perspective, no political clout, no reason to say this. And so, I thought, I'm
not saying this. And I didn't. And I was absolutely wrong. What they
did allow me to do in this speech where I said I'm endorsing the death
penalty for this kid—because otherwise it would destroy the whole
story—was say, "This is against every personal conviction I have ever
held." So they allowed me to say that. And then I said, "But as a repre-
sentative of the law, this is what I'm obliged to do." But from that
point on—and it was pretty early—I thought, I'm not going to ever be
comfortable here. And I never was. I had a three-year contract, and
Dick did say, "I'll let you out whenever you want to go." But of course
they couldn't wait, I'm sure. I could hear the cheers when I said good-
bye. It was a happy ending for all concerned, but you know, it was such
a bizarre series of events.

Do you think part of it is because there was no one in charge?

Everybody was frightened to tell me anything, lest it got back to Dick.
It was also an atmosphere of extreme fear. People were falling left
and right, there was huge chaos, and it was just the most peculiar situation. And the directors they were bringing in—some of them, most
of them, were from the technical end, like they would be camera-
men. And so the direction I would get would be something like,
"Don't feel so much." And I know what they meant. They just wanted
me to say, "Casey versus Miller." And I couldn't manage to do that. I
didn't have anything to wrap acting, performing, around, because I
had no objective from show to show. I had nothing to care about.
That's the best I'm able to explain it. I had nothing to act. I remem-

ber asking should I have an affair with Sam. But no, no, I couldn't even look at him kindly. And I think it was my ignorance going in: this huge hit show and that year of all the spin-offs, and me saying, "Couldn't you change it a little?" and of course, why should they change it? It would be kind of like reinventing Coca-Cola.

If you had read a screenplay about the same issue, would you have turned the part down because of this position on capital punishment for minors?

No. There would have been a character. But this was me. It felt like *I* was speaking. I couldn't say in front of millions and millions of people listening that anyone with any stitch of morality would endorse that position. It didn't come out of anything. It was just there, saying capital punishment for minors, yea!

Have you wanted to study acting in the last few years?

I took a Shakespeare workshop just last week at the Actors' Center because Kathleen said, "Go down to the Actors' Center." And I thought, Oh, I don't know this man who runs it, Michael Miller. But I went there, and I was very shy, sort of cut off and I said, I'm uncomfortable. But then I heard that Lloyd Richards was there, and I went into his class. And then I started sitting in on Earl Gister's classes. And then Earl said to me, "Take the teacher development course this summer. It's intensive, intensive. You know, nine in the morning to ten at night, with a Russian director," and I did that, and that got me thinking about teaching, and now I just go there as much as I can. I'd like to teach acting, but I'm very shy to do it, because I feel inarticulate.

What of your experiences as an actress can you particularly bring to a class?

Well, you know, it depends on where the student is, what the class is about. I think I will be able to show them how to get their minds off themselves, which is a huge thing—I think the first thing—crippling self-consciousness that we all fight against all our lives. I could also be a great encourager of risk taking. My risk taking has often come because I just didn't know what else to do, so I jumped off the diving board and hoped to land. And sometimes you do, and sometimes you don't; sometimes you swim, and sometimes you just go under. But I think that would be important for young people—not to stay safe, which I do see a lot of. Out of my own shortcomings I have become a risk-taker, but out of their strengths, perhaps they could become risk-takers.

How should young actors approach a scene? What should they be thinking about?

On what they want, whatever that is for this particular scene. On what their action is. And then there are tons of possibilities about how you go about getting after something.

A lot of young actors are afraid. They want to do it "right." How do you convince a young actor who's fighting that, that right is not interesting?

I think the first thing you would have to do is tell them they're okay being the person they are and bringing that unique soul onstage. That's what's going to be interesting about them, this one unique human soul, unlike anything else. Their thoughts are unlike anything else. How they'll pick up a glass is unlike anything; they are unique, and that's what's going to be interesting for people to see. That's what people want to see. That's what you've got going into it. And so, once you tell kids that just by virtue of existing, they have something fascinating, and once they can get their minds off themselves, they're going to be in an area where they're going to be free.

Ruben Santiago-Hudson

We're in a friend's apartment on the Upper West Side of
New York with an unobstructed view of Zabar's. It's
Ruben Santiago-Hudson's neighborhood—he lives in a
duplex just a few blocks away—and he is on time and raring to go. He
doesn't want anything to eat or drink. Let's go, let's go, he seems to
be signaling. He's built like a welterweight boxer, handsome and
compact. His body seems to be in motion even when he's sitting
still. He positions himself at the head of our table, practically vibrat-
ing with the anticipation of telling his story. From the moment we
turn on the tape recorder, his passion for acting as communication,
as catharsis, as storytelling, is vibrantly clear. With very little prompt-
ing from us, he launches into an always colorful and vivid monologue about his life in the theater. His conversation careens between
the poles of self-congratulation and an evangelical appreciation of
the role of the actor as a conveyor of truth. And Ruben has a lot of
stories to tell. He is a man with a mission. From the imagistic way he
talks, from the urgency of his need to communicate, it is no wonder

he has added writing and directing to his theatrical arsenal. No one form is quite enough for him. He is dedicated to the role of theater—particularly theater that tells stories of the African American experience.

How did it come together for you? How did you come to be an actor?

I was a very good reader, and I was always looking for people to teach me. In Lackawanna, they had a little thing called Loveland: a community center where they had a dance troupe, several R & B groups, theater workshops, conga groups, and we would go around to other community centers and we'd perform. So when I went to college, I just continued to do it because I enjoyed it so much. I didn't know I'd make a living doing that. I thought I probably could be an athlete, like all the black kids from the ghetto, but that didn't pan out. I never had enough talent. I could beat most people, but I always ran into somebody who jumped better, shot higher, was quicker. But onstage, I didn't run into anybody that awed me. My freshman year at Binghamton I was not having a good time. I was doing theater, but they were kicking my butt because everything I auditioned for they never gave me. They did *Guys and Dolls*. Everybody in the theater department said I should be Nathan Detroit!

You'd be perfect.

They gave me Harry the Horse. So I said I'm not gonna do Harry the Horse. I just got tired of not fitting in, so I was gonna transfer to a black school. And Lofton Mitchell pulled me to the side one day—at the time he was in *Bubbling Brown Sugar* on Broadway. He said, "Why you going to transfer? Where you gonna go? Howard University or some black school? Do you have Lofton Mitchell there, somebody that's gonna care for you and be around for you?" I said, "I barely saw you since I been here." He said, "Yeah, 'cause I'm doing this *Bubbling*

Brown Sugar, but hang with me, hang with me." So I tried to hang with him, but I got kicked out of school that next year.

Why?

Academically. I was just troubled. A man named John Yelldell—he was the guy who ran the equal opportunity program in Binghamton— let me know, under the table, that they would let me go to another school, but I couldn't tell anybody, so I wouldn't get kicked out of the whole SUNY system. "You got to sign these papers, and I'm gonna give you a chance, but you can never tell anyone I'm giving you this chance. You've got to promise me you're going to give it your all now, 'cause you've got too much talent. I see your whole background, I see your mother, I see you're raised in a rooming house, I see who you are. You're a 98, 99 student, brilliant student, and now you're getting kicked out of school, 70 averages, C's and D's. I'm gonna throw you a lifeline, but you got to promise me you're gonna make something of yourself." He said, "Where do you want to go?" Well, I had been kicked out of there for the semester. I wanted to go home. Nanny had cancer; they just removed her breast. I had had my second child, I was nineteen years old, and I was just having trouble. So I said, "I'm gonna go home." I had a buddy that was going to Buff State, so he said, "Sign here, go see so-and-so when you get there." So I went to Buff State to try to get my life together. And they were doing a play called *Our Lan'* by Theodore Ward, and that put me on the map in Buffalo. I stayed one semester, and they let me back into Binghamton, but I came back with a whole different passion.

And the school was on your side again?

I came back to Binghamton very serious about everything, went right into the theater department. There was a grad student they had hired in the directing program in Binghamton, a brother. And he wanted to direct *Sizwe Banzi Is Dead*. So he cast me, and he cast this African brother. At the same time, Alan Simpson gave me Ferrovius in *Androcles and the Lion*, so I'm doing *Sizwe* in the studio theater and *Androcles* in the Waters Theater.

That was a big turning point.

Sizwe Banzi turned it, because there was a sixteen-page monologue, and the theater department was just like, "Whoa, this guy's for real . . ."

It sounds to me like you did this yourself. In terms of knowing what to do with a script, how did you learn to make a moment?

The whole thing in growing up in the rooming house, I had the most colorful characters I've ever seen. All of them had these little idiosyncrasies, like Shaky Winfield was always shaking, and Shirley Brooks always talked real fast: "ShutupandtalkdontstopcauseicomefromTennesseethatshowtheytalk." So I picked up everybody's style, and I would mimic them.

When you actually started to do roles, were you doing imitations of people?

No. I never did imitations, because I always had this need to cry out about life, share this pain and joy that I had in my heart. I never had to imitate it. I have this pipeline that goes straight to my heart. I never faked.

You found your way very early. So acting saved you.

Yeah. I found a way, but it was all these guides that kept saying, "Get on this path, stay on this path."

When you saw a play, did you say, Oh I can, I can do that, that's a profession?

There's a director right now tells a story about me walking in to see a play he was directing in Buffalo and meeting him afterward. "I'm Ruben Santiago, I can do that." "Young man, I like your gumption, but this is real." And he laughed in my face. But he's called me to recommend him for many a job.

Did you ever have any specific training?

I have two master's degrees and a doctorate. My bachelor's is in theater, my master of fine arts is in acting.

What things did you actually learn in school about acting?

I learned a tremendous amount. You'd have to be crazy to go to school and not learn anything. I was a good student. Especially of something I love. I love theater.

You had such powerful instincts. You knew the hearts of these people, and you were able to get inside them. Was there anything else that helped you?

When I came back to Binghamton, I found teachers who believed in me. The majority said, "No, I don't believe you can make it as an actor." But Don Burrows and Percival Borde, the great Caribbean dancer, they believed in me. Don said, "What're you gonna do when you graduate?" I said, "I'm gonna go to New York and try to make it." He says, "Nah, New York is not the place. Get into the University/Resident Theatre Association [URTA] and get some scholarships. Get a master's." He said, "Listen, I been a judge at the URTA for the last eight years. The talent you're bringing is rare. You just go and do a couple of pieces: a tragic piece and a comedy piece and sing a song, and then let's see what happens. You gotta win in the school, then you gotta win in the region and the state, then you go to the nationals. But you'll win it."

And you did.

Yeah. Then I said, "Where should I go?" He said, "Now just hone the craft. Do some of the things you normally don't get a chance to do. Go do some Molière. Go do some Shakespeare. Go do some Feydeau, Beckett, and Brecht." He said, "Why don't you go to a company where you might actually do that stuff?" So he gave me a list of places where he had taught or lectured or knew people. He named about eight universities, and he said, "Let's write them a letter first, let them know to keep an eye on you, so when you get to the nationals, they'll come and they'll watch you 'cause they'll know you're interested." I was the only one from Binghamton to come down here to the Roosevelt Hotel, and I had sent letters to about eight schools, and Don said, "Listen, this is the way it goes: after the auditions at noon, they're gonna come and call your name, and that's who's interested in you. Then you have appointments, from hotel room to hotel room." He said, "Some people get none, some people get one, and some people get eight. You'll do good." So I said, "All right, I'll do it." So I get to the Roosevelt Hotel, they call my name out, I look at it, and I had thirteen universities wanting to see me. All the ones I had said I'm interested in, and they all offered me full scholarships. I talked to Don about it, and he said, "What do you want to do?" and I said, "Shakespeare, I want to do Shakespeare." He said, "Go to Wayne. They're a rep company. They'll do three Shakespeares at a time. It's a factory. There's so much Shakespeare you'll have done ten of them before you leave."

You chose Wayne over NYU or Yale?

I was going to go to Yale, but Lloyd Richards was taking some time off. And I wanted to be with Lloyd. So Wayne was my next shot because I wanted to do rep. And Don Burrows said, "If you do rep, nothing else gets harder." I went to Wayne, and that's where I met Terri Turner Phillips, who said, "When you get to New York, go see Rosemarie Tichler."

Did you do a lot of classical roles at Wayne?

Before I left Binghamton, a professor told me that I couldn't do classical theater, because my lips were too big. And I'd never be a good Shakespearean actor.

This was a white man who said this?

Of course! He said, "So you would have to cut the corners of your mouth to round the vowels and the O's." And I said to him, "I don't believe that." And he said, "Yeah, well, go to the theater in downtown Binghamton; there's a professional group there doing *Member of the Wedding*, and there's an actor there." So I went to speak to him, and I'm looking, and sure as hell the corners are cut in his mouth. I said, "You got the corners cut in your mouth?" and he said, "Yeah, that's the way black actors, when I came up, we had to cut the corners of our mouth." And I'm like, "I can do it without cutting the corners of my mouth. My lips can get out of the way, and I can say these words."

I'm aghast. I've never heard anything like this.

So I went to Wayne to prove that I could do Shakespeare. I remember being in the auditorium the first day. I was the only black student. Terri was there working on her doctorate, and Vaughn Washington was working on his doctorate, and I was working on my master's. So they said, "Introduce yourself and tell us what your goals are." And I stood up, and said, "My name is Ruben Santiago, from Lackawanna, New York. I want to be a professional actor, and while I'm here, one of my goals is to play some of the wonderful classical roles in the canon." And one guy in front of me, who was in the company, just busted out laughing. And he whispers to me, "You are going to be a spear-carrier and a fan boy, that's what you're gonna be." He told me the truth! He told me that he knew the way things were. And I said, "I will not do that. I will get my bus ticket and go the hell back." And he said, "We'll see." So the first play was *Caesar and Cleopatra*, and I was the fan boy. The second play was *Pygmalion*, and I was Bystander #2; the third play was *Wild Oats*, and I was Ruffian #1. The fourth play I was a rug bearer, and I was onstage with Terri, who was playing the maid-servant to the queen. And this other young white actor, he was plain stumbling over his words, and I'm sitting there carrying the rug. And I looked at Terri and said, "I can't take it no more. I'm going." She said, "Do not walk off this stage." And I got up and walked off the stage.

Why did they want you if that's what they were going to use you for?

They've gotta get a certain amount of color in a theater company in Detroit. So Vaughn grabbed me and said, "What the heck are you do-ing? You don't do that! You've got a chance to get sixty thousand dol-lars' worth of education. Don't you walk off!" I said, "I'm as good as anybody on that stage, and I can't take it!" I said, "That boy is stum-bling over those lines, and I know those lines. I can do that!" He was like, "Just relax . . . let me talk to the white people. I can talk to them better than you can." So Vaughn goes into the meeting, and he comes back to me and he says, "What do you want to do?" And I said, "Something that can show I can act." "Like what?" I said, "Like *Native Son*." And he goes back in the meeting, and he comes out and says, "Good news and bad news. Good news is you're gonna do *Native Son*. But we've gotta do it in this theater that's been closed for three years, called the Bonstelle Theater. It's empty, it's rats, it's dope fiends, it's shoot-outs. And we've gotta open a theater up." I said, "I'll open it up, I don't give a damn." We go to the theater, pull in the parking lot, weeds are all over, glass is all over, people standing out in the front. It's absolutely barren, it's empty, everything is run-down. So a guy opens up the door, and we go in, rats are running around. It smells like piss at the door. There are coals; fires have been started back there. The guy turns on the lights. And I look up at this theater. I'm looking at the rats running around on the stage, and I see that balcony, and I say, "This is where I should be . . . I'm gonna fill this place up." And we put on *Native Son*. It hadn't been done since 1943 with Canada Lee. And we packed it! Broke all the records. I played bigger towns, broke all the records in that theater. They wanted me back at Wayne. I said, "I don't wanna go back." I done tasted glory. Thousand people every night packing this house!

Were they ready to offer you roles now?

Yeah. The first thing they offered me to come back was Dr. Caius in *Merry Wives of Windsor*. It was a terrible role. First time in my career I got my ass kicked in reviews. I couldn't do the accent, I didn't un-derstand the role, I didn't like the play. And then they let me go back to Vaughn, to the black theater touring company for Wayne, and I did everything I wanted to do. I did *Home*, I did *Wine in the Wilderness*, I did *Purlie*. I did everything I wanted to do, and that was it.

Then you graduated, but they never gave you the parts you wanted.

They didn't, no.

They never let you play with the rest of the white actors.

No. And I said, "Why don't I get a chance to play these roles?" They said, "Because we *think* you can do these roles, but we *know* he can do it." I said, "Why, because he's blond and blue? Give me a chance, I'm in school. Let me try it." They said, "Maybe eventually, but we know this person can do it, and we don't know if you can, we think you can." The thing is, I didn't stop working. I worked on all those classical plays they worked on, and I did 'em for myself. I worked the language every day, I worked my scenes every day, I read the plays every day, and I prepared myself. And I was ready.

And after you graduated—

I stayed in Detroit and formed my own company with the other brother who was working on his doctorate, Dr. Vaughn Washington. We took the plays after the university put them up, and we'd buy the sets from them or let them throw them away and take them out of the garbage. We would rent trucks, and we put a great newsletter out to people: "This is what we do. We got something for your budget. If it's $500, Ruben and I will come in and read Malcolm and Martin. If it's $150, Ruben will come in and read poetry from Paul Laurence Dunbar. If you have $12,000, we'll give you a musical. If you got $2,000, we'll do *The Island*, with Ruben directing. We will do *Raisin*. We'll do *Tambourines to Glory*, whatever you want for your money." And so we would do it at the university, get all the rehearsing done, 'cause we couldn't afford rehearsal space. I was giving the actors more than they were making in Detroit.

How long did you do that?

Two years. I was doing *Home* on tour. Woody King had the national rights and was touring it, and he happened to come into the same town I was in, Jackson, Michigan, or one of those little black towns. And Ron Milner told him, "You've gotta go see this guy do *Home*. I mean, your show is okay, but whoever you got, this guy in this play will come and teach him how to do *Home*." And Woody says, "Bullshit. I've got a New York national touring company, ain't no boy up in the sticks . . ." And Ron says, "Go see him." Woody walks in to see me in my dressing room that evening, offered me to come to New York and take over the role from the guy who was doing it.

Is that how you got to New York?

Come to New York, go to Woody's office, Samm-Art Williams, who wrote it, decides he wants to do the play, so I don't have the role. I've got two hundred dollars in my pocket and nowhere to go. I walked into the Equity union—I had my Equity card—so I go to the Equity lounge. I'm sitting there trying to figure out what to do. And I see Leonard Jackson, who I recognize from *Five on the Black Hand Side*, and I knew there was a man in town who I had worked with when I was a kid, who ran the African cultural center. So I see Leonard, and I go and ask him about this guy. And Leonard says, "Oh, I know him. He's a doorman over at . . ." And Arthur French is with Jackson. I don't know Arthur French, I just see this tall black man with this raggedy beard. So I said, "Yeah, I'm just trying to find him. I'm one of his buddies from home." They said, "We don't know him. We don't know where he lives," and Leonard says, "Well, we know the vicinity he lives in." And I said, "Well, could you take me near where he lives?" I've got my suitcase with me, and we walk down and they drop me off on the corner of Forty-third and Ninth, Manhattan Plaza. I'm standing on the corner of Forty-third and Ninth with my suitcase, and Leonard says, "Young man, he lives in the area somewhere around here."

Who was the actor you were looking for?

His name was Ed Lawrence. So I stand on that corner looking at people for hours. And all of a sudden this guy comes by, and I said, "Ed Lawrence?" He says, "Who wants to know?" I said, "Ruben Santiago from Lackawanna." He said, "From where?" I said, "From Lackawanna." He said, "Do you know Lackawanna Smitty?" I said,

"Yeah." He said, "Do you know Howard Elliott?" I said, "I went to school with his daughter. Miss Magdalene is his wife." He said, "Who is your people?" And I said, "Nanny." He said, "What you want, boy?" I said, "I'm looking for a place to live. I just need a place to crash for a couple . . ." He said, "Listen, you're from Lackawanna, you know Howard Elliott, you know Lackawanna Smitty, Nanny's your people, come on with me." He takes me in his house, he gives me a sheet and a mattress. He says, "You only can stay two weeks." And I said, "Thank you."

In the actor's home! [Laughs.]

That next week I got the Theater for Young Audiences production of *Play to Win*, where I played Jackie Robinson, at $150 a week. I literally hadn't eaten; that starving actor thing was happening. And right after that, I booked something else at Crossroads, and my salary was $220. At the same time, I kept going to Negro Ensemble, saying, "I should be in *Soldier's Play*." They said, "Well, there ain't no Puerto Ricans in *Soldier's Play*." My name was Ruben Santiago, no Hudson. I go to Puerto Rican Traveling Theatre. I said, "Hi, you know, I should be with you guys, I'm Puerto Rican." They said, "Do you speak Spanish?" I said no, so they said no. I said, "You can't use me in Puerto Rican Traveling, you can't use me in Negro Ensemble. Where can I go?" So I hung around and hung around waiting for Doug Ward to come off the road with the national tour of *Soldier's Play* so I could audition for him. Sure as hell, they have auditions in December for replacements. They don't give me an audition. My godmother says, "You gotta add a name so they know you black and Puerto Rican." I said, "What name? My name is Ruben Santiago, my father's name is Ruben Santiago, my son's name is Ruben Santiago. I'm Ruben Santiago." My mom said, "Don't be a fool. You've got other names too. What's your mother's last name? Hudson. Put that on there too. Put any name you want, put Jones, put Schmo . . . just let them know your heritage." So I put

Hudson on there. I go in, put my name on the list. So I come in, I read one role. Doug says "Look at this." I look at another role, I read that, I read Cobb, I read Peterson, I read Davenport . . .

This is all in Soldier's Play?

My manager calls, says, "I've got good news, Rube, good and bad. Which one, good or bad?" And I said, "Give me the good, then I can deal with the bad." He said, "Good news, they cast you in *Soldier's Play*." I said, "Yeeeees! What's the bad news?" He said, "You're the understudy of everybody." The guy said, "You were so good, you knew everybody's role . . . understudy everybody." I said, "I'm not onstage?" He said no. "Not even the littlest role?" He said no. "But you're in the show, that's what you wanted, you're in." I said, "I can't do that." He said, "What do you mean you can't do it? You wanted to be in, you're in!" I said, "I can't do it." He said, "How much money you got in your pocket?" I said, "I've got like five dollars and seventy-five cents." He says, "Do you want this job or not?" I said, "Well, how much money?" He said, "When you understudy, it's $350 a week and $300 per diem." I said, "If they let me onstage in the littlest role, I'll understudy everybody. Just let me onstage, I just gotta be onstage." "Okay, I'll tell 'em." He tells them; they give me a role. But I understudy everybody. That's how I got into *Soldier's Play*, I got a role playing Bernard Cobb, friend of C. J. Memphis, and I ended up as Peterson; then I ended up as Davenport. I played all the roles I wanted to play. And off the road they plucked me to play Theo in the twenty-fifth anniversary of *Ceremonies in Dark Old Men*. They took me off the road, put me in that play, off-Broadway, but I finally landed in New York. When I did *Ceremonies*, there was a lady, I'll never forget her, named Edith Oliver, a critic for *The New Yorker*, who said in her review, "This is the next big thing. This Ruben Santiago-Hudson is the next Billy Dee Williams."

Do you read reviews?

Yeah I read 'em. I laugh at 'em, I get mad at 'em. Yeah I read 'em.

Do you read them while you're performing?

Yeah. It does not change a thing I do.

It doesn't change a thing you do, really?

It changes things I do offstage, because I get mad or I get happy. But on-stage it changes nothing. I'm very very disciplined. But she said that about me, and that kind of put me on the map. But the thing is, I did learn a technique, I did learn a style. I did study Lessac and Linklater for voice. I did study Stanislavsky. And took little bits of it all and devoured it, and found out what stuck, and came up with what worked for me.

Let's start with when you get a play like Seven Guitars. *Had you ever worked with August before?*

No. Chasing him.

Did you tour that play before it came to New York? I know he works on the scripts as the play moves around. How much participation did you as an actor have? Did he reshape the play or role?

August reshaped it tremendously with me, once he heard, once his ear got attuned to me, 'cause the role was not written for me; it was written for Rocky Carroll. But Rocky went to do movies, so it opened up. And I had been writing them letters—August and Lloyd—haunting the theaters, haunting their auditions, trying to get in. You know, I'm that kind of guy. I want to be in. I felt that I should be in and get a shot. I auditioned for *Two Trains Running,* in which Fishburne did the role I auditioned for—of Sterling—but they remembered me. So when Rocky pulled out, my agent was pursuing an audition for me, and they said, "Oh, we're looking for him." So I came in and I won the role. Once I started doing it, August probably thought Rocky would come back, and that was the plan. But once we got into the Goodman Theatre, August said, "I can't hear anybody else's voice but yours. You're Canewell." And that's how I locked into the role, because I really took it and made it my own.

Did it mean that you would discuss the role with him, or was it that what you did, showed him what the role was?

He knew what the role was when he wrote it; then he entrusted it with his director, Lloyd, who knew what the role was equally to August. And then, after three months of me breathing, living, waking up, doing everything I possibly could, living inside this character, wearing his shoes, wearing his hat, and feeling his heart beat, I told him who he was by just the way I did things. And then we would have debates about certain things, about my character.

Did you feel that you knew the character so well that you could argue with the writer?

Not argue, but bring up points. Insight.

Like what?

Well, I remember one time he wanted me to pull my knife out on Floyd when Floyd pulls his pistol out and says give me my money. And I said, "That's not who I am." He said, "Well, somebody pulls a pistol out on you and that's who you become." I said, "I don't think so," and he said, "Why not?" I said, "Because I have a line that you wrote, that says, 'All I want is three rooms, a garden, and a woman who knows how to sit with me and the dog, what else could a man want? I mean, if I was Rockefeller, I could want more money, but what else could a poor man want?' I never said anything about being rich, and I would never kill Floyd about that money. I would give him half the money just if he asks, because I found it, far as I know. I don't know it's his. But I would not threaten his life over this money. I don't care about it. My feelings are hurt, and I will fight him down to the dirt, but I won't kill him."

Did he hear you?

You don't see a knife get pulled in that play.

What if he hadn't? Could you have done it?

I did it. I showed him. I did it with all the compassion I could possibly do. I got into the scene with all my heart, tried to convince myself that I should pull the knife out and threaten Floyd, and I popped it out. We looked at each other and we had a standoff, and then, you know, the scene went by, and Lloyd said, "Go back to doing what you were doing." That's one instance. Other things would happen, a lot of times things happened.

What happens now when you direct this play?

I tell 'em, "Show me," if they have a different idea.

If August heard you as the voice of that character, what do you hear when you hear another actor playing it?

I tell them, "Show me. Show me something. If you think you've got something to show me, show me. And if it tells the story as purely and clearly and as strongly and truthfully as my version of it, you got it, but you've got to prove that to me." Because I know how this thing works. I said, "It's language driven, it's not plot driven. It's character driven, it's poetic, it's musical. And you've gotta play the music. Anything you bring to me other than playing the music, if it's getting in the way, if it's commenting on the work, then I'm not going to accept it. But if you can bring something to me to rediscover, a new, fresh, but honest, truthful, poignant, profound, and clear look, then you got it. You've gotta bring it." And if he shows it to me, it's his. So yeah, I hear 'em. But I know August Wilson's language.

Back to that . . . You get a script.

I'm a research-driven person. I try to fill myself with as much information as I can and let it burst out through my character. And I know who I am. I know the time, I know the place, I know the people.

What do you do if you are working with actors who aren't at the level of heart and commitment that you are?

I lead by example. If you don't step up to the plate when you are onstage with me, you will get blown off the stage. You will be embarrassed, because I'm going to look you right in the eye, and I'm going to give you all I've got. And I expect that from whoever's on that stage, and if not, you're going to stand out pretty bad. I mean, commitment, responsibility, these things that go along with theater. Theater is sacred to me. There's a responsibility to that. I tell my cast that all the time. I'm not going to let you squander the opportunity, and I'm not going to squander the opportunity. So come in prepared every day, challenged every day to go another step. Wherever you fall, we're going to remedy. Give it all, give it all. The more you invest, the more you get out. If you fake it, you're not going to get anything out.

That's as a director. How about as an actor?

Right now, when I walked out of my house, I had ten August Wilson plays sitting on my desk, and I had the whole Shakespeare Folio on the left side, his sonnets on top of that. That's what was sitting on my desk when I walked out to meet you. And before I left, I peeked into *Two Trains Running* and put it down and then came.

You really like to live in those worlds with those words, right?

My son Trey, he's ten years old, he says, "Daddy, you're always working." I said, "Because somebody's coming behind me every day." No one works harder than me. I'm constantly looking for another opportunity to learn more. If I don't work the language, if I don't read Shakespeare, if I don't read the sonnets, then how am I expected to walk up onstage? Things about the characters' lives are common to me, because they're common people and royal people, and the common people are the ones who I am. The language is not common to me, so I have to find out what they're saying, so I can say it clearly, and I love the way it rolls off my tongue.

Let's talk about one of the Shakespeare things you did.

I did *Measure*. Begged them to do, almost cried to let me do Brutus. Rosemarie, you were there then. I was literally kicking down doors. Please give me an audition. You don't owe me the role, but should I bring my Tony in and stand it as a doorstop just to let you know? I didn't get an audition.

The director knew you. It would be very hard to turn you down. He told me, "I'm not going to cast him." I said, "He can't change your mind?" And he said, "I know it's not what I want."

The last thing I asked him for—"Can I walk in and say hello? I don't need to read one word. I just want to shake your hand and say good luck, and if anything happens that you might need me in any role other than Brutus, if you might need Ruben, please call me, I want to be a part of this." He said no. Not to say hello to me! It hurt me—not only hurt me, but disrespected me. So when I met him—I'd never met him in my life—I'm standing with Kevin Kline at the play. Kevin says, "When are we going to do something again?" I said, "You name it. You got all the power. You don't need to call. Just tell me when you need me." And I said, "You know, I wanted to be in this play so bad, and the guy wouldn't even say hello to me, the son of a bitch. If I ever meet him, I'm going to tell him that was disrespectful." And then he comes down the stairs. Kevin introduces us. "Son of a bitch, you rotten mother . . . aw man." And he said, "Why are you talking to me that way?" And I said, "I asked to say hello to you and you deny me? To say hello?" I said, "You don't owe me shit, but respect . . . and you didn't give me that, so right now what I'm giving you is no respect." And I say, "Good luck," and I sit down, and Kevin says, "Did you tell him how you *really* felt?" [Laughing.] No, because he hurt me. I've had people come to me, 'cause I'm a director now, and they send messages: I know this guy, we're friends, he's gotta see me, give me one minute. And I say, "Let. Him. In!"

That's because you're an actor.

I've had people say, "I've gotta get in this role, I have to get in," and I said, "Let them in." Or I take an actor and he'll be fucking up an audition, and I'll give him a note. And he'll do it and he'll leave. One time one of the producers said, "Why do you take time? You know the person can't play the role." And I said, "Because that person came down here, and I want to let him leave bigger than when he walked in here."

Let's go back to Shakespeare. Mary Zimmerman directed you in Henry VIII. *How did you work? Did you read, or did she offer it to you?*

I read.

Did she have a concept? As an actor, did you just fit into her concept?

I think she got a little prodding too. I think George prodded her, and you all got me in there, and she saw what I was bringing, and whoever didn't take the role left it with me.

But if the director has a concept and you have to fit it, how much of yourself can you actually—

I'm an actor. I'll fit into any concept you want to do. I'm not going to buck the system. There are things that I believe. If I believe in something, I'll fight for it. If it's important to me. I don't fight about any little thing. I don't need to fight. There's something to be learned about every director, there's something to be learned from every actor. I want to learn it, but if something is not true, I'm not going down that path, you know? I'll try it, and if I say it don't feel right, I say it don't feel right.

Did you work with a voice coach? Was that Deb Hecht? Was she helpful?

Yeah, she was helpful. I mean, I needed all the help I could get. She gave me good help. The best help came from John Dias. Just answering questions I had about the time, the period, what does this word mean.

In terms of scene work—

Well, I did a lot of research, reading everything I could about Henry VIII, every little anecdote, every little note, every letter I could find.

I have piles of information about it. Some I brought into my character, and some I didn't, but I had the information. So I knew about his behavior, things he had done, things he couldn't do, what he was good at, what he wasn't good at. Where he fell short and where he rose very high. I did my research. So I knew the character inside and out.

You've done a lot of television and a lot of film too. How is that a different process for you, and what is your feeling about those media?

Television is so afraid of the African American heart. The soul of the black people. I've never been whole on TV. I'm one thing, whatever they see me as. I'm the tough sergeant cop, or I'm the bum that's drinking wine, or I'm trying to find a serial killer or something, but I'm never whole. I never go home and hug my wife and say, "I love you" or "I'd die for my kids" or "This is precious to me" or "This is where tears come from" or "This is how loud I can laugh." Never. So it's really working a job. I like the challenge to make that kind of stuff work and try to give flavors and inklings that I am a whole human being, and sometimes it gets in the way. This last film I did, I was sitting there with one of the stars. I'm hired to be her partner, to protect her from the serial killer she arrested who's out on the lam. I've been on the force ten years longer than her, and not once in the movie do I add anything to the equation, do I say, "We should keep an eye on this guy" or "That could be evidence" or "Listen, I'll go around the back, you go around the front. You need me, just give me a holler." Nothing that was intelligent. All I said was, "Where we going?" "You think that's the guy?" "Why are we following this person?" "What's that?" "This is evidence." "Why do you think this is evidence?" "Because it's a footprint." Finally, after about three weeks, I'm sitting there and I say, "Why'd you all hire me?" "You're such a wonderful actor . . ." "Yeah, but what have I added to this movie? You really could have done this without me. She didn't need me. I'm supposed to be her protector, but she's already kicked me in the ass, beat me up, knocked me down. She's already told me I act like a little baby. I keep asking questions. I have not once given one inkling that I might be a good cop. But I've been on the force ten years longer than her, and I'm hired by my superior to protect her. And I can't even protect her from me. Why am I in this movie?"

Did they make any changes?

They said, "When you see an opportunity for you to add something, go ahead and add it." I said, "It ain't going to work that way. You've gotta tell me . . ." I said, "I'll tell you what. I'll find a way to make it work. I'll find a way."

You raised it, and they didn't respond, so you found a way?

And they said, "You're right. Where does that happen, show us where it happens." I said, "I'm a writer. You don't want me to show you where it happens, because I'm going to rewrite this shit." So the first time it came up was when she goes to beat me up, all her whole hundred pounds jumping on my two hundred. And I'm like, "Well, I don't think that could happen. I think she could knock me down. I'll take that if it's a leg sweep. If she hits me in the back of the head with a gun—which was going to be very personal—if she does that, I will not finish this movie unless I get her ass back. People don't get hit in the head with guns and slapped in the face and spit on without retaliating. 'Cause it's an insult to every black cop that's been a cop for the last twenty-five years, with a little partner that's fifteen years younger than him. So let me have some pride for all the little young black cops in the precinct and all the brothers who've been there twenty years. Let me have a little bit of pride." "Well that's the way the movie's done. It's in the movie that you get your ass kicked." And

I said, "I didn't take the job because I said I didn't like that scene, and you said you'd change it." Movies and TV are very hard.

I've never heard that you had a reputation of being difficult, but do you think you lose any roles because of this?

I lose every day, but I'm always gonna stand up for it. I'm representing a lot of people.

Do you have a desire to create roles for yourself, as you did with Lackawanna Blues? *Or to cast yourself in Shakespeare or other great roles?*

I can pretty much do what I want to do in the theater outside of New York. But I can't afford to go outside of New York. It's like I love theater. I just love it. If I can get that out of me I'd have been a rich man. I'm directing now, and writing, and acting. But I'll never get anywhere waiting for other people to give me an opportunity. I don't care how good I am. There are theaters in this city that practice exclusion. So I can't wait for them to give me a job.

Would it interest you to take a steady role in Law & Order?

Love it. I'd take a steady role in anything in New York. I will back up into a corner and sit in that corner and play that role to take care of my kids, and do my theater at night. I've literally called the powers that be that run New York shows, Dick Wolf, and said, "I'm the last actor in New York. I've been here for twenty-four years, and you have all these shows, why don't I get a shot at a regular?" They needed a police captain, so I said, "Give me a shot." "Oh, we're going to give it to Eric Bogosian." I said, "What has Eric done that I haven't?" He hasn't played as many police captains as I've played! The one I just finished was a police lieutenant. You know, domestic disturbance, Billy Cooper on *Another World*. I'm a cop, cop, cop, I told Dick. I will walk in there and cop that cop. Michael Hayes, the series on CBS: cop. Three pilots I've played cops in, several movies. What has Eric Bogosian done as an actor that I have not? And I love Eric Bogosian. Just give me a shot.

You have to create your own work.

That's why I'm writing and directing. So I don't only create my own work, I create work for other people in the same position I'm in— that need to be seen, that the country needs to see, 'cause they're such gifts to the arts, to the theater, and to film or TV or whatever. They deserve it, and who's going to make that happen? So I'm gonna see if I can make some of that happen.

Did the success of the HBO version of Lackawanna Blues *open up doors for you in television as a writer?*

No. No, my phone has not rung.

HBO hasn't offered you or asked you to write something else?

No, but I went and pitched them something. I went with another producer who had a deal, who couldn't find a writer to write this novel. And he took me in on my treatment and we sold it. But no one called us and said, "What do you want to do next, son?" Nobody called us and said, "Can we get a first-look deal with you?" *Lackawanna Blues* had more viewers than anything they had on HBO last year. More than *Empire Falls* at sixty million. More than *Warm Springs* and *Sometimes in April*. Anything they had. I mean, when do you get your Happy Meal?

But you sold something?

The producer sold it. I'm the hired writer. You know, I'm shopping, trying to make stuff happen. I'm trying to change distorted images of my people that have been created through cinema and TV for so long. And there are a few soldiers out there trying to fight that fight, and they're more powerful than I am, they're richer than I am. There's an article about Spike Lee in *New York* magazine today, about what he's doing, and he got filthy rich doing it. I have to suffer. I mean, every day someone's telling me, "Rube, don't say nothing, don't let people know how you feel." I said, "Why not? Everybody else does. I want to make a difference." As an actor, I can't. As an actor, I can bring you a tremendous amount of joy. As an actor, I can bring you whole human beings of color. As an actor, I can take you on a journey that takes you out of whatever your responsibilities were that day. But I can't change the conditions of my people. And as a director I can. As a director and a writer I can. It's tough. I love acting, and I want to act, but it's not a position where you can really change a lot. I'm waiting to be chosen. I'm going to the dance, I'm all dressed up, and I know the steps, but who's going to take my hand? It's confusing sometimes—you give your heart and life to something, and you wonder, when is the payoff? If I were as good as I am in any other field? I explain that to actors. Your competence does not equate with your success. So all you can do is look for what you know is going to be there, an opportunity to play a great role. Everything else is gratis; you don't know what else is coming behind you.

You continue to act, obviously. What do the writing and the directing feed in you?

I've gathered all this information over the last thirty years of acting with all these wonderful people, and I'm bursting with it, and now

I'm giving it to the people that're close to me. So I'm teaching through my directing. I'm quite meticulous about what I see and what I do, quite prepared to give it to people, because the journey doesn't stop because Lloyd died, because August died. We take the Lloydisms and the Augustisms, and we take our isms and add it on to somebody else. We take and build from that foundation they gave us, and hand that off and say, "What you owe is that you hand that off again." You fill somebody else's heart up with what you have, and their mind and their brain and their intellect with what you have. And so that's why I love directing. I'm passing it on. I'm a product of those people.

It's a great tradition.

I don't approach any role without going to my notebook from *Jelly's Last Jam*, or the notes Lloyd gave me from *Seven Guitars*. I look at the notes that were given to me by a lot of directors and I sift through a lot of stuff and I see something that stands out. And sometimes it not only informs you about how to be an actor, it informs you about how to be a human being, especially when you're working with somebody like Lloyd. Every day in rehearsal I'd give a Lloyd quote. My actors in *Seven Guitars* thought they had a bad show the other day. They stumbled on some words, they knocked over a bowl on the punch line and didn't get a laugh, somebody tripped going up the stairs. Words got messed up and somebody was late on an entrance. But the show was good because they were that committed to it. So I come in the next day, and they said, "Do you have notes tonight?" and I said, "No notes tonight. Tomorrow, let's meet at a certain time for an hour." So we meet, but instead of meeting in the auditorium, I tell my stage manager, "Set all the chairs on the stage, on the set." So we set all the chairs on the stage and we sat around in a circle and I looked at 'em. I said, "So, uh, how did you feel about the show last night?" Everybody gets quiet, and they all told me how they felt about the show.

They kicked their own asses. And so when I said, "I love you all. I love every person in this play. I love you. I love you for your commitment. I love you for your honesty. I love you for your truth." I said, "And I love that you all are reaching for the highest rung of the ladder every night. And anytime you don't hit it, you feel that you failed. And that's why I love you. But the thing about that is that failure is not an incurable disease. It ain't cancer, so we're here to fix it. Whatever you all need to reach for that rung again, I'm going to give that to you, but you've got to dig into your heart fully." And I said, "On your worst day, you got a good show. On your worst day you're one of the best shows in town. On your best day, you're the best show in town." And I said, "Right now, tonight, look at last night's play as target practice. Tonight we hit the bull's-eye. There are 160 seats in this theater, there are 180 sold, and there is a 40-person waiting list. And our job is to make sure that each ass that sits in those seats gets a theatrical experience unlike any they've had, and that we honor August Wilson in the highest, best, strongest, most profound, truthful way we can. And we're gonna get that shot tonight, so let's start working." And that night was just off the chain. I get chills thinking about it now. One actor pulled me in the corner, and he said, "That day when we came in. I was prepared to get my ass run out, and you made me feel so good." I said, "I've been where you are. I've walked offstage and felt less than I'm capable of doing. So I would never criticize you. I would just let you know what's possible. You're in this role because I know what you can do. And you've shown me, many a night, what the peak of this role is. And one night you fall short, I'm still betting on you."

Have enough directors said that to you?

They don't have to. Nanny said it to me. People who lived in my house said it to me when the world told me no. And so when I go out, it intimidates people, and maybe everybody don't like the fact that

I feel confident I can do what I put my mind to. It don't make everybody rest comfortable. But that's not who I'm trying to make rest comfortable; I'm trying to make me rest comfortable. I'm trying to go out on that stage and take whatever angst, whatever anger the world is kicking me in the face with, and turn it into something positive. Either that, or I can take a gun and kill thirteen people. Now if Charlie Parker had killed thirteen people, he never would have played a note. And if I had killed thirteen people, I never would have been the actor I am. I find another way to take what life dishes to me and turn it into something beautiful, and that's my art. That's where the blues came from. That's where Romare Bearden came from, William H. Johnson, Paul Laurence Dunbar, Langston Hughes. That's where George C. Wolfe came from. That's where Lorraine Hansberry came from and August Wilson. Out of what life had given them, they turned it into something beautiful. You take an August Wilson play. Trust it. Do not question it. Do not think you're gonna cry, do not want to cry, do not want to be emotional. Want to say these words. Close your eyes and see what happens. Never start a speech and know where you're gonna end up. Just start the first step. And that's the way I did it when I played Canewell, I took the first step. Then I end up in this place. I'm like, damn, how did I get here? Then when I walk off the stage, I'm like, Oh, that felt so good. I don't ask nobody nothing, I don't have to. I'm not doing it for you, I'm doing it because it's an actor on that stage looking across. That's who I'm trying to appeal to, that's who I'm reaching. You get it if you're an audience. Hopefully, it pours out in the end 'cause I'm leaving blood on the stage. If it's three hundred shows, three hundred little pieces of me are gonna be left on that stage, and I've gotta rebuild it the next day. I gotta go to the gym, I gotta sit with my kids, I gotta go throw the baseball. I gotta go to a movie. I gotta rebuild me. I gotta read some poetry, I gotta read some Shakespeare. I gotta let it go. Rebuild that piece I just gave. But that's my sacrifice. That I can give you a piece of me. I'm not gonna fake it. I'm gonna give you something that you keep forever. When I die, there'll be thousands and thousands of people that I've given a piece of myself to that will never, ever forget me. If you come to see me in one performance, you know that I didn't hold back anything. I gave you a piece of me. And hopefully in some little way, that made you a better person, because it made me a better person being able to do it.

Meryl Streep

★

I t's a very bright day in early spring, and we're scheduled to meet
Meryl Streep at the Cupping Room, a local SoHo coffee bar, at
three o'clock. At about a minute after, we spot her crossing the
street, talking on her cell phone, and waving to us. She's wearing
sunglasses, jeans, and a white sweater, with her hair up. She looks—
at the same time—exactly like what one thinks Meryl Streep looks
like and nothing at all like the culture's version of a movie star; a
quick glance around tells us that no one but the two of us even no-
tices her. Her schedule is full, she says: a film coming up, a personal
appearance at a charity function that evening, and she's just moved
into a new apartment. We confide our concern that the restaurant is
too noisy. "Let's see," she says, and strides up the stairs to scout it
out. We trail behind her. "I think it's okay," she concludes, and we
look around for the best table. The restaurant has emptied out
somewhat since we first looked, and the management is nice enough
to turn off the music so we can use our tape recorder. If anyone rec-
ognizes Meryl, they behave exactly as New Yorkers usually do around

celebrities: they ignore her. We decide on a tiny corner table and order iced tea all around. Meryl is very blond and fair-skinned, with delicate features that are sharper on film than seen across the table. She is thoughtful when answering our questions, frank about what she doesn't know about her craft, down-to-earth about her celebrated status, quick to laugh at herself and to make us laugh. Her sentences are remarkably well formed, free of hesitations and circuitous construction, and she has the timing of an expert comedian. With her small hands folded on the table in front of her, she speaks softly, confident that everything she says will be heard.

Did you want to act before you went to Yale?

In high school I did musicals. I had a good singing voice, so I thought I would be a music major at Vassar. When I got there, I saw very quickly how many people in the music department were also good at math, because music *is* math. Composition and all. So I was quickly dissuaded from being a music major. And I just followed a course of liberal arts study. I'm interested in everything. I think that's one thing a lot of actors share. They're curious people. I was very interested in everything. Except math. I'm not proud of that, but . . . it sure would have come in handy later on in my career. I was in a play in my sophomore year at Vassar, and my friends told me I was very very good and I should do that.

What was the play?

It was *Miss Julie*. I didn't know anything. I really didn't. But I do what my friends tell me. When they asked, "How do you know how to do that?" I don't really know. So that's where the mystery starts: I know how to pretend to the level of belief. That is the thing children know, and then we forget as we grow up. Some people don't forget it as well or as much.

Did you sense that you were good?

I think that I had a power of some sort onstage to move events, which I didn't really have in my life. And that was very attractive. But I really don't know what I was doing. I did have a couple of things in my bag. I was a good, fast study—really really fast in terms of learning lines, and there were a lot of lines. It was just something that was really really easy.

Did you go to the theater?

My mother took me to the musical theater. I don't think I ever had seen a straight play until I was in college. Because she loved musicals, and so did I. I still do.

When you went to these musicals, did you think you wanted to do that?

Oh yes. I was obsessed. I was the lead in all three of my high school musicals. Daisy Mae in *Li'l Abner*. And I was Marian the Librarian in *The Music Man* and I was Laurie in *Oklahoma*. I clearly liked musicals. I didn't think about the acting part. I thought about the singing part, the showing-off part, and the dancing part, and all that stuff. And then I got serious about everything, including acting. I really loved design. In fact, my degree and my thesis at Vassar were in costume design. It was 1971, and I was sort of a hippie, I guess, and I had a boyfriend at Dartmouth and I was acting in a little summer theater up there. That's when I got impatient for it to be better, to be more serious, or to take something by the horns or be where people were doing it in a more rigorous way. I was waiting on tables, so I applied to graduate school because I thought if you wanted to do something, you go to graduate school. I sent away for the applications, and the application to Juilliard was very expensive, forty dollars. And Yale was fifteen dollars, so I applied to Yale. And I wrote them a snotty

letter at Juilliard as well. "Obviously, you're culling your class . . ." I
was very snotty. Because I was paying for it! I mean, I got loans and
scholarships from Yale and that's where I went.

*I remember talking to Jerry Dempsey, who was at the Yale Rep, and he said
to me, "I don't think we taught Meryl anything."*

Oh, I disagree with that. It was a grab bag. The things that I honestly
really think about now and rely on are physical things. Carmen de
Lavallade and Geoffrey Holder, Wesley Fata, my movement teachers,
who taught me relaxation and strength and rest, and Moni Yakim,
mime. The mask class. With Marge Philips we read sonnets and she
taught us that a thought is a breath and a breath is a thought, the
same thing. You have to make the breath last through the entire
thought. These things I truly still use. Even when I'm not reading a
verse, it's a very good rule. In the singing class, where people were
not singers, Betsy Parrish said it doesn't matter, singing is expression, it's undiluted, unobstructed by your brain and all your neu-
roses. It's pure. It's music. It comes out from the middle of you. I
learned all those things. But acting, however, I don't know. I don't
know how people teach acting. I've read lots of books about it and I
just can't make any sense of it. I don't parse things the way they do.
Everybody does it a different way.

Did you reject the notions that they taught in acting classes?

There was not a method that anybody taught in the acting classes.
While I was there—for three years—they would hire the acting
teacher each year and then hire another one the next year, with a
whole new regime, who would teach us a whole other way of doing.
There were fads. There was story theater. Then there was Bobby
Lewis, who read all the parts for us before we began. He was
adorable. You could learn from everybody, but as far as coming away

with a method . . . I went to Russia last year under fishy circumstances to accept a Stanislavsky award. And I had never studied the
Method! I appreciated it, I told them I appreciated it, but I haven't
employed it. I am absolutely terrified each time I start a new thing,
because I don't have a way in. In my life I felt I've done so many different kinds of things that ask for different approaches. I don't know
how you can approach each role the same way.

How do you start? You get a script—

One thing that I did learn at Yale—or not so much learned as agreed
with—is Brustein's idea that things are written at all different periods and times, but things want to be heard at certain moments. The
time in which you live calls for certain kinds of voices to be heard. So
I think that part of what I do when I read a script is, I think, This is
relevant to now, for whatever reason, or this needs to be heard now.
It's a fluid thing. A play is always seen in the context of its time.
What's going on right then. That's how we receive it as an audience.
In the moment of our communal anxiety or pessimism or despair, or
whatever is going on. I don't necessarily think about that, but I rely
on it—my inner hum, my awareness of where I am in the world right
now, right here—and something resonates in the script. So that's
what happens. Sometimes I hear a character speaking in a part, and
I feel like I have to embody that or be it or say that. I don't know what
it is. How do you fall in love?

*It's a great talent, actually. You've picked good parts. What if someone
had all this talent and lacked the judgment that you're talking about?*

It's a sense or sensibility. It's very complicated. It also helps to have
the confidence of an early success. Things worked out for me very
quickly, very early, very fast, so when that builds on itself, you have a
certain amount of confidence—not that you'll ever work again, be-

cause I always had the feeling with each job, well, that's it. But every actor has that. I at least had the confidence that I was saving my money. I was always very frugal. I was always very careful about that. And I thought, Well, maybe I can make my living at this. I didn't know that right away, and I wanted to make a living.

You pick the play or screenplay . . . then is there something particular you do next, or is it dictated—

Sometimes I read it once—like *Sophie's Choice*—and I did not pick it up again until our first reading, because it was too hard for me to read.

Did you read the novel?

I read the novel after I read the screenplay.

Did you do research? Did you read about Poland?

I learned Polish. I didn't do research on Poland. Alan Pakula did that and Styron did that, and that was the context into which I stepped. I just wanted to feel that I could live inside the language and the music of it, and that I could put on any kind of clothes. I did Berlitz. I had a lady come and do a blitz, every day.

How much rehearsal did you have?

I don't remember those things. We sat around and talked about it. Alan was like a rabbi. He talked about the exegesis of the text. It was pretty thick, the script. The movie that he showed us was five hours long, and I loved it! I read poetry, lots of poetry. I felt she was a romantic character who lived emotionally, and poetry speaks that way to me. I listened to the music that Styron had them listen to.

Then you take The Bridges of Madison County. *It doesn't even seem like the same person played those two roles, because of the physicality. Sophie was thin and luminous; you could see through her skin. And then there's this middle-aged, lusty, buxom Italian woman. Was the way you went into that very different?*

I don't think I had very much time to prepare that, but I had a person in my mind who was so vivid in my childhood, a lady who was a child bride from the war. Her husband, tall and blond, brought her back, and she spoke with a very thick accent. My mother loved her. Her name was Nucci, and she said, (accent) "Take out the gerbbege." Her children were named American names: Chreesee. Jaakee. Brrrrucie. She was just in my body. I was fascinated with her.

Then once she's "in" you . . . I don't mean it's easy, but—

She's just already there. A lot of them are already there.

They're already there. Tell me another one—

Everybody. Like the girl in *The Deer Hunter* or Madame Arkadina— they were already there.

With Postcards from the Edge, *because the character was your age and looked like what I think you actually look like, people talked as if that were really "Meryl."*

Yeah [laughing].

Estelle Parsons said, "You never see me in anything I do. I'm always acting, always a complete character."

But I would say you always see me. You always see me.

Was someone in your mind for that character too?

Yeah! Carrie Fisher. All the time. I mean we don't look anything alike, but I was thinking of her, also knowing that I wasn't "doing" her. I wasn't interested in that. And Shirley didn't want to "do" Debbie. We very consciously made the physicality very different. I don't know. How do you approach a script? Every script is very different. I find that I have terror every time because each one asks a different thing. I do trust the thing that I immediately recognize—a scent, an inner *yes*. I don't really abstract why or take out the reasons. Usually what I do is, after I think, I want to do this, I give it to my husband, and if he agrees, I do it, because we are very different people, but if we agree . . .

If he agrees, you do it?

No. If he can see why, I do it.

Has he dissuaded you?

Yes.

Can you tell what?

No!

But by dissuading, do you mean he's shown you the error of your ways, that it's not what you thought?

He'll say, "Why would you want to do that?" [Laughing.] Then my inner *yes* crumbles. But usually we concur, and when we haven't, in the end I'm relieved when he disagrees, because there's something obviously missing in me that he fills up.

Have you done things that you're sorry that you did? Or that you felt you hadn't got a grip on? In terms of this voice from inside? .

Yes, because I've done things for other reasons than "I need to do this." To work with people I admire. Or that I should do it. And that has not worked out. Even with people I greatly admire.

How do you deal with it once you're doing it? How do you save yourself?

Thank god it hasn't happened very much. But I take it out on everyone. And I am miserable.

Would I see it on the screen? Could I tell?

I don't know.

You've never been bad.

Yes. I've been boring.

Is there a role you felt you didn't achieve?

I think I was bad in *Still of the Night*, which was a noir film directed by Robert Benton. I love him, and we had made *Kramer vs. Kramer* together, and I really wanted to work with him again. Jessica Tandy was in it.

Why did you think you were bad?

I didn't have anything to do. I couldn't figure out what to do. There was no character. The noir femme fatale is essentially a type, and I was bored by her. There was so much attention to lighting and how my hair looked and being sleek and gorgeous, but what do I do? What do I convey? What's the person about? What's the inner life? It's not about the inner life, dear. It's all about being misconstrued. You think the woman's this, but she's not. But what is she? No one cares. She looks great.

Any other roles you felt you didn't achieve?

Probably, but I can't call them to mind. Unpleasant circumstances . . . forget about it.

Denial.

I'm sure. Denial is very very valuable.

Why did you do The River Wild?

I did that for lots of reasons. I never saw any kind of adventurous physical roles, and I had little girls, and there weren't lots of roles like that. And Curtis Hanson is a fantastic filmmaker, and I thought it was going to be really interesting.

There's one line that jumps out that you make so hilarious—when you say to Kevin Bacon, "You and your pathetic life!"

I remember it.

There was such a spin on that line, it seemed that this kind of acting is something the movie didn't really even need, and yet there it was.

It was a little bit of class hatred in there. I'm sort of not physically terribly brave, so I thought, Let's put it up there.

Was there a temptation all these years to go back to the stage?

Always. I told my children that they're the reason that I "sacrificed," but they couldn't care less. And when I went back and did *The Seagull* after twenty years, I was really terrified. That was one where I read so many great plays—I thought I wanted to do something in the park and it would be for free, but that was the one that spoke to me in that time. Interestingly, it was the summer of 2001.

Was it your idea to do that somersault?

Oh yes. The cartwheel, I'm sure. I remember Irene Worth in *The Cherry Orchard* always wanted to have more stamina and be more vivacious than any of the ingenues, and that completely reminded me of her. She was so dear, and she sent me a little pince-nez that some famous Russian actress, an old, old lady who had played Madame Arkadina, had given to her.

Were you trying to establish a tradition of doing a physical stunt in every Chekhov play you did?

I fell down in *The Cherry Orchard* on every entrance or exit. That was a little thing I set for myself: the idea of the clumsy maid.

When you act on the stage, do you keep it alive in that you never know exactly what you're going to do?

Not really, no. The other actors don't like that. Not on the stage. There are more surprises allowed in film. You can change staging. Onstage you can't change blocking, but you can change how you embody a line. You can't really decide you're going to move upstage this time.

Do you have more control when you act on the stage?

On the stage, yes.

So how do you exercise control when you act in a film? Can you?

No. And that's the great secret of acting anyway: you give up. You give it up all the time, and that's when you do your best. You relinquish control, you know?

John Lithgow told us a very different story. His method was that you do your best work in the master shot so they always have to cut to that. They can use it as a guide for how to cut.

Oh my gosh. Well, he's so smart and is involved in a level of understanding . . . I just don't think that way. I think, Take one shot, maybe take two, it will be better, at least I'll get another chance. When are they going to start? I wish I had a coffee. That's what I think. And then I get another chance. You beg for a third take. The theater is more thoroughgoing an exercise. It's a different art.

Did you feel you had to rev yourself up or get back in shape when you did Seagull?

I didn't think about revving myself up. Some nights, when it was ninety and I was in the corset and we were getting ready to go out, I thought, Well, I have a choice now. I can either play the moment, which is soggy, hot, and disgusting, or I can fight with it. And each approach is valid. Because at least you're located where you are. You're either fighting the reality or you're grounded in it. But you're there. You're there. The thing about the stage is, it's really happening in front of them, so they're living it with you. I guess that's true in film too, but you don't feel the presence, the breath of the audience on your neck.

Is there any sense you get from the people on the set? The crew? Are they paying attention?

Sometimes, and that's encouraging when they do [laughing]. The best is when you do something and they go like this [mimes wild laughter].

You said before, it's a different art. Can you talk about stage and film acting?

They're not fundamentally different, because fundamentally it's the same thing. And when it's first born . . . the first reading of a movie, it's like a play. You just connect, that's all you do. You just connect with the other people. That's all you have. You don't have the sets and costumes. But in the doing of it, it becomes very different. Acting on stage, it's amplified life. You don't think about it that way; you just have different muscles working.

It seems natural for you to know how far to pitch your performance.

You live it so much in rehearsal. You make it there. And then you re-animate it every night. But on film you can make it right then. And you don't think about sending it out there. And in fact, when somebody comes and says, "Can you give us a little more volume," I get so resentful. I say, "No, I can't give you more volume." I'm not thinking that way. But onstage, of course, it's not a problem.

How do you cope with the delays, the technical life?

I think I was frustrated with that when I started, but I felt so lucky to be there that I didn't start complaining until I got much older. And then it's always the same thing: hurry up and wait.

What do you do? How do you keep alive?

It's a real mystery.

Do you sit by yourself? Talk to other actors?

I do different things at different times. Sometimes I want to be by myself. Sometimes I want to eat. I don't know. Sometimes I think, Well, I have a big emotional scene today. I should get ready [laughs]. I don't have any idea how to get ready.

You're just confident that it'll be there when it's time to be there?

Yes, and then when it's not there, then I have *shpilkis* [Yiddish: rampant anxiety]—that's the only word. I go nuts inside. I sweat and worry and say, "I need a moment." I go into my trailer, and there's nothing there that will help me. Nothing. It's a horrible way to make a living. And then I think sometimes it's like . . . because I'm not religious . . . it's my church. And then I get very humble, and I realize I have to lie down and offer my neck in front of it, and that's why I say it's giving up.

I haven't heard any of the other actors we've spoken to say anything like that. They seem to be reaching for a way to hold on to it, not let it go.

We all try to push and pull, and ask it to come, and force it, and hold our breath and sweat, but I think in my experience it's me, and whatever it is that I do, it's when I give up that it appears. I can't push. I'm here. Where am I? Who is this that's with me in the scene?

How much do the other actors help you?

Everything. They're everything.

And if they're not?

Even if they're not, they're everything. I put my entire life on their shoulders whether they like it or not. That's all there is.

What about directors?

The director can set up all the circumstances. They've done it already. But they're not in there. No matter how much they want to be, they're not in that encounter. They can change the sort of question that you're asking of the other person in the scene. Mike Nichols is the most brilliant at that. He reads what it is that the encounter is. He reads what you're asking—not literally, but what you're asking. And he'll say . . . I can't remember any of the things he said. I feel bad about it; I know that he's vital, but I get rid of the instruction almost the minute I hear it. Like actors say, "I know I know I know." I don't want the consciousness of the instruction in my mind. The minute it comes out of his mouth, you go, "Yeah yeah yeah. That's right." And I've already incorporated it. I don't want to think about it in the scene, so I promptly forget it, so I can't tell you anything he's said. I can't give the specifics of it, because I do throw it away.

That's very clear.

Actors want to know it, and then they don't want to know it. If you were to stop and think about it, you would be a theater historian.

Have you started to work on Mother Courage?

I should have [laughing]. Plowing my way through the book Oskar [Eustis] gave me about the Thirty Years' War, or whatever the war is. I know it's important on a certain level, but I'm really interested to know what George Wolfe's take is and what Tony Kushner's take is on this play, how and why they're going to make it a present event that has to take place in 2006 in the summer in New York. That's what I'm most interested in, because I can fit myself into that, and that'll happen when we start.

Whatever research you do before that will just fall in.

I don't know where I get this reputation for doing so much research. I don't. I have done nothing, zero at this point. I'm just pretending that I've opened the book that Oskar gave me. It looks at me every night from my bedside table.

Have you ever been interested in directing?

I always think I would like it a lot because I love actors. I love what they do. And I've watched so many wonderful directors and appreciate the things they do. I don't know that I would have any gift for it. A director's job is a longer job than an actor's. An actor starts, exercises his chops and huffs and puffs, and it's done. A director's job is more cogitation and delegation skills.

What do you tell your own children about being an actor?

I've told them lots of things. Nothing goes in. Well, maybe some things go in. I mostly tell them don't get discouraged, because it's very discouraging. And don't mix up the criticism or the rejection of the work with the criticism or rejection of you as a human being, as who you are, because it's very easy to get mixed up. We *are* the violin, we are the piano, the architect's paper, the sculpture. It's our own bodies, and it's very hard not to. Kids now have to look a certain way. It's just ridiculous.

What makes people stay with it, people who are insecure? I've come up with three things: sheer will, talent, and luck. Sheer will is really it. You can't get up in the morning and not think about it.

I don't have that. They almost kicked me out of Yale because they said I didn't have that. And it was something that was true. They have these evaluations, and they said, "You don't have the requisite ambition. You don't want it hard enough." It was something I recognized. It was a fair criticism. But I didn't think I needed it necessarily, to be an actor and a happy person.

Was that the year you did a lot of work?

I did a lot of work every year. That's because of the way the school is set up. The directors and playwrights get to pick the cast they want for their senior projects. So the same people sometimes work over and over again. It's not ideal. It's not fair. It's a trial by fire.

I had auditioned you for Trelawny of the "Wells," *and you came for a callback. The train from New London was very late.*

Yes, I was at the O'Neill Playwrights Conference.

Joe Papp and A. J. Antoon and I were waiting.

You were the one who gave me a chance. Joe hadn't seen me. That was you who called me back.

And you were late, and Joe was going to leave, and I went out for a last look down the street, and there you were, walking, not running—

Well, I didn't want to get sweaty.

And you walked in, and I was incredibly impressed with how you apologized simply but didn't whine, and then you went and just did the work. And you didn't let the tension and the fear hurt you. And I thought to myself, There's no stopping her. I thought you were extraordinarily talented and that you could do that. I never forgot how self-possessed you were. Do you have a memory of that?

Well, I gave up. It was so late. I thought, They're not going to hire me. I'm going to go, but it's doomed. Doomed. I'm a very big pessimist. That also helps.

You just let it happen.

Yeah.

Sounds like your method.

We spend all this time trying to make everything perfect, but I remember the first performance of *Trelawny* and I'm thinking, My student loans are going to be paid off! And I'm so nervous in the wings, getting ready to go on, my upper lip was trembling, and I was trying to stop it, but I couldn't. I went out onstage and I was playing this extremely confident creature and swanning around. Michael Tucker was already onstage, and we had a scene together and he was also very nervous. His face was bright red, and that just made me more nervous. And I knew John Simon was in the audience. Those were the days when they came opening night; everybody came one night. It was before Joe laid down the law. And then Michael caught something on his sleeve, and it fell over on the table, and I caught it before it broke and I put it back. And from that moment everything was just fine because something real had happened, and it pulled us right onto the table, into the world. And then all the work we had done in rehearsal and the life we had lived and who we were, we just located ourselves in the tactile world and there we were.

In Angels in America, *if someone didn't know that you were in the film, or didn't know the conceit of playing several roles, they wouldn't have known it was you as the rabbi.*

Well, you know how that worked . . . Probably if I'd had a year to worry about it, I would have worried about it. I got that part so late. We'd already started rehearsal and everything was already cast, and Mike [Nichols] said, "Do you want to play the rabbi too?" Sure. I didn't even think about it. I didn't have enough time to worry about it. Got a couple of tapes of people from different parts of Latvia and listened to them speaking about their lives. A couple of people gave me their grandfathers' recordings. I feel like I discovered my inner old man. That's who I am. I wish I were that wise and funny and could just point things in one direction the way I want to. He's a wonderful character. It was no work to do that. It was just me.

You've got an easy job.

Yes I do, except the beginning is very scary. The beginning is hard. Before I did the rabbi, I thought it was fun and I'd learn the lines and think about the opening scene where he's officiating at the funeral. It's very powerful and very linked. I always think about my grandparents, all the time. I catch myself staring at old people. I'm interested in old people. I remember being afraid as I came out of the trailer. I had my whole getup on. I had very tight rubber bands around my wrists to make my veins stand out, so I could look down at my hands and convince myself that I was old. I *felt* like this person. I felt like it was difficult to cross Seventy-ninth Street. It *was* difficult. And people stopped their cars a different way than they stopped for me. I did have a moment of fraudulence when I got up and started to speak, and then I realized that none of the people knew who I was. They really didn't know that I'd walked down the aisle, and none of the extras had any idea who I was. I knew it. Then it wasn't a problem.

Is there anything you want to play? Do you think that way?

No.

Well, with Arkadina—

With Arkadina, I was on a search. I read all these parts, and that was the one that spoke to me at that time. Maybe if I read it this year, I wouldn't feel that way.

Your youngest is fourteen. Are you going to do more theater?

The summer is when I'm going to do that. It's too hard to be away every night. And all weekend.

When she's in college—

Then I'll play Juliet.

You could do it! You and Kevin.

That would be very interesting. I'd love that. What would we know? What would we bring as old people? That would be so interesting, wouldn't it?

What about Lady Macbeth?

I'm not mad enough yet for Lady Macbeth.

Kevin Spacey

★

The first sound we hear when we knock on the door is excited barking. The door opens, and a small black dog rushes out to greet us. When we're done being licked, we're greeted by Kevin Spacey. He's in New York from his home in London—where he is artistic director of the Old Vic—to do publicity for his latest film, *Superman Returns*, directed by *The Usual Suspects* director, Bryan Singer. Kevin introduces Mini the pooch, who quickly loses interest in us and curls up in a chair in the living room. Kevin is dressed in a gray T-shirt, gray slacks, and a gray cabbie's cap, and he's barefoot. His suite is on the forty-first floor, and on this clear day we can see all the way to the lake in Central Park.

When did you think, Oh, acting is wonderful. I want to do this?

I started to perform in junior high school. The first thing I had to do was a pantomime to music. So there was no dialogue. And I created a pantomime to the recording of the theme of *Deliverance*. I created a bank robbery on horseback. I used a chair as a horse, and I remember I fell off it and everybody laughed. When I got to the end of it, I did something that also made them laugh, and then they burst into applause. Literally, I was like a dog that hears a whistle that no one else can hear, and I perked up: What is that? I would say that acting in the first few years of high school was very much just fun. My parents would come and see me, and all my classmates would make fun of me, and it was just fun, it was just a complete class clown having a ball. It wasn't until the second year of high school that I got cast in a production of Arthur Miller's *All My Sons*. I played George, the brother who comes back and confronts his sister about what has gone down, and disrupts the whole thing. I think it's just one scene. The Drama Teachers Association of Southern California—that's seventy-two high schools—chose three productions every year that represented the best of high school theater and transferred them to a weekend seminar at a college. This production of *All My Sons* had been chosen as one of the three best. And it was at this performance that something happened: I walked off the stage, and I felt I had affected an audience. I had had an impact in playing this character. I hadn't had that experience before. Something on that day, with me and that audience, just clicked. And I remember going backstage and sitting on a chair in the wings. There was an audible kind of boo as I left, and then they applauded the performance. And that was the first time that I thought, Oh, well, maybe I can do this.

Did you feel something between you and the audience as it was happening?

I think I absolutely felt something was up, but it wasn't until I left the stage that I began to register what I had just experienced. And what an important moment it was to realize: I no longer wanted to be an actor. For the first time, I realized I *was* an actor. That has always stuck with me as a significant moment.

Were your parents supportive of this?

Yes. My father was not in the arts when he was young. He was a photographer for a while and he became a writer for most of his life, but he never was published as a writer. He was working on the great American novel, as he called it, but he worked as a technical procedure writer for aircraft corporations. My mother was always in the arts. She was a dancer in school, and she participated in school plays, and she was a big lover of theater, so from a very early age she started taking us to the theater. They were both incredibly supportive and came to every show and drove me to auditions and all of that. As the years continued, I started to do it more actively in high school.

Did you see a performance at some point when you were young and recognize, That's great. I want to be up there?

Yes, many many times. But it's funny, because that weekend actually turned out to be a significant weekend in my life in terms of the next step I took. The previous night, I had watched onstage Mare Winningham and Val Kilmer from Chatsworth High School. And I remember sitting in the audience watching and thinking—because they were from a different school—God, I would love to work with them, they were so good in this production. And when our play finished the next day, I was backstage, and the show was over, and a gentleman came up to me and introduced himself as the drama teacher at Chatsworth High School. And he said, "You know, I shouldn't be saying this, but I'd like you to transfer to my school." So I did. And my final year of high school was doing plays with Val and Mare and directing things.

Did you and Val apply to Juilliard together?

No. He went straight to Juilliard from high school. I stuck around Los

Angeles trying to audition for really bad television shows and doing stand-up comedy. It took nearly a year and a half of Val's letters to me saying, "You've got to come and study if this is something you're really serious about doing. You gotta audition for Juilliard." So I did.

So you didn't go to college?

I went a little bit to college. I went to Juilliard at nineteen.

Was Val right? What did they teach you?

Oh, he was absolutely right. It was the right decision. I arrived in New York in the summer of 1979 and got right into school in September. We had a pretty remarkable class. When I was there, it would have been hard for me to acknowledge what I was learning, because what I have learned since is that great training doesn't happen while you're there. It happens when you're out and you're experiencing what it's like to work with directors and what it's like to work with other actors and what it's like to try to serve a playwright. And it would only be years later, after I left Juilliard, that I would be in rehearsal for a play, and a director might say something to me or a moment might happen with another actor, and I would go, Oh my god, that's what they were talking about. That's what they meant. Because, you know, until you have a context to put it in that is your own and your own experience, a lot of things you learn just lodge in, and they're in some bubble in your brain until you actually need to learn what the lesson was.

I always felt that the really great Juilliard actors were at their best ten years later.

I know exactly what you mean. The technique, I think. I don't know this for a fact, but from observing it and having been through it and having accepted a lot of it and fought a lot of it. And this is ultimately why I left: I think what they tended to do was in a sense decide, in whatever way they did, what kind of actor you were going to be, and then they wanted to strip you, in some degree, of your personality. To turn you into a kind of neutral figure and then build on that. Now, when you're seventeen, eighteen, nineteen, twenty, twenty-one, twenty-two, that's an incredibly brave thing to be able to do to yourself, to sort of let go of things that are you. And in many cases, I would agree with you in that I think it took some people a very long time to be able to break through that, in a sense, deconstruction, and find themselves again.

Did you stay for the whole training?

I left after two years. I went back afterward and saw my friends in their fourth year, and there were a number whose personalities were still strong, whose sense of themselves was so clear that they managed to not be stripped. We had twenty-eight in our class, and we all may have been undeveloped, unfocused, unclear, but there was a group that was talented and a group that was unique, and some of them survived that process and some of them didn't. I think it has a lot to do with where you are as a person. I got through it, and for whatever reason, when I decided to leave, I felt I had learned what I came there to learn, even though I couldn't pinpoint what that was. I just felt I was anxious to work.

What made you leave after two years?

Well, actually there was a conversation. Because I made up my own rules. What I mean by that is, for example, I would not go to all the classes—like history of theater—because I'd be rehearsing a play or I'd be rehearsing a scene. So I was called into Michael Langham's office. He was the head of the department, a wonderful British director who ran the Stratford Festival in Ontario for many years. And he said to me that every single aspect of the school had to be a priority and I could not make these delineations. And I remember thinking, I have been coming to this room twice a week for Mr. Langham's Shakespeare class, and you have been spending your time and energy to tell us how we have to carve out what's important in the text. How we have to emphasize certain words and throw away the rest. Are you telling me that I'm not able to do the same in my life? That I can't make a priority that this is more important to me than that? Because you keep arguing that if you make it all important, it makes no sense, it has no value, you don't carve out what's important then. So there was a kind of stalemate.

And that was it? You left the program?

I literally went downstairs and packed my bags and went to Marian Seldes's class and told everyone I was moving on. I suspect that if I'd stayed, he probably would've kicked me out in a couple of months. But as to the question of what did I learn: I think what I learned more than anything else—and which I am enormously, enormously grateful for—is technique. What I learned was how do you get up every night for eight weeks, or twelve weeks or fourteen weeks or six months, into a run of a play and always be alive and always be there and always have your breath and always be energetic and always be ready to respond even on those nights when it doesn't hit you, and somehow the performance, the audience—you just feel it's not happening. It is technique that gets you through it. It is what you can do technically even if it's not connected emotionally on that particular night. I've been fortunate because there have been very rare nights where I felt that I had failed the play or the play failed me. I do have a caveat to that: I have a pretend tattoo on my chest—it's upside down so that I can read it—and it says "Blame the text last." Sometimes you feel like you failed the play, like you didn't serve the text. Sometimes

I hit a moment in a play where I feel I'm just sort of waking up. And there are a lot of things you can do to make sure you don't hit the stage cold: just getting together with the cast doing a line-through, also letting the day go and letting go of whatever other things are distractions, be they good or bad. Remember that you have to hit that stage with your foot on the pedal and ready to go.

Did you feel adrift or that you were free when you left Juilliard?

I had no agent, I had no job, I had no prospects. I didn't have much money. What I did was call you at the Public Theater. There was a lot of "Ms. Tichler is not in at the moment. Who are you?" "I'm an actor, I just left Juilliard." But I had met the director Des McAnuff, who had done a play at Juilliard for a fourth-year class. I was always hanging out with him, and I'd actually been in a fourth-year production because they didn't have another guy for a part. So I played Val's father. When Des was doing Shakespeare in the Park one summer, I thought, Well, maybe he'll remember me and I can audition. I really had to badger, and I don't know whether it was you or someone else who finally got so fed up with me, I can't remember. But I got a call: "Come in next Tuesday and be ready to sing and to do monologues." And I marched myself down to the Public, and I got my first part in the theater in New York. So that was my very first gig.

Was it a start? Did it lead to anything? Did you feel you had a place in the New York theater?

No. I was playing a messenger, with five lines. But I had a manager, and I got through playing in August, and I remember thinking, What the fuck am I going to do? I really really don't want to wait on tables, I really don't. So I went back to the Public and asked if Mr. Papp was there. He always used to take great interest in emerging talent, and he would come down to rehearsals and see a new actor and ask, "Where you from? What's your school?" So I'd had a few conversations with him over the summer, and I went into his office and gave my sad story, and he hired me on the spot. So I started working almost immediately in the stockroom, and then over the next eight months I worked in various departments. I got up to the contracts office. I was put in the publicity office with Richard Kornberg and eventually in Mr. Papp's office.

It was just office work at the Public? No acting?

While this was happening, I got an off-off-Broadway play at Dance Space. And I got my first New York review: *The Village Voice* came to review the play and wrote a very favorable review in which the reviewer compared me to both Marlon Brando and Karl Malden, which made my friends call me Marlon Malden. And Morgan Jeness showed Joe that review, and the next night he came to Dance Space and saw this play that I was in. And the next day, he called me into his office and fired me. And I remember saying, "What have I done?" And he said, "No, you didn't do anything. You've been working here now eight months or so, and you've gotten very comfortable with the hundred and twenty bucks we're paying you, and last night I went to the theater and I saw an actor onstage, and that's what you should be doing." So he pushed me out, gave me a month's salary, made me go out into the world. And the nice end of that story is that four months later, he and Gail were in the opening night audience of my first Broadway play. So I look at Joe as a huge—not just influence—but a huge mentor. The play was *Ghosts*, with Liv Ullmann, the disastrous *Ghosts*. It was an interesting experience for me. I got to see some of that backstage stuff you see, or read about, because conspiracies are flying around. John Madden was the original director of that play, and he got fired when we were at the Kennedy Center because he and Ms. Ullmann didn't connect, and John Neville, who was playing Pastor Manders did, and before you knew it, John Madden was fired and—

Neville took over—

I wanted to quit because I felt it had been unfair; I felt Madden had been fantastic. For god's sake, he was the guy who got me my Equity card, just through an audition. Anyhow, the whole link to all of that was that one of the things that Joe did, one of the jobs I had at the festival in the late term of my employment there, was when Dolores, who answered the phones, took her lunch. I knew how to run switchboards, because my mother had been a private secretary, so they had me sit at the switchboard desk. And Des was now at the festival directing—and he used to walk by me every day back and forth on his way to lunch. So he recommended me to go to Soho Rep and meet this director, and I ended up getting that play, *Barbarians*. That play, the casting director of *Ghosts* came and saw me, and that's how it started.

At what point did you feel that you could say no to scripts, that you really felt, I want to do that, and not that—

Much to the distress of my agents at the time—'cause I eventually did get an agent, and I eventually did get a manager, who is still my manager to this day—I actually started turning down things very early on. I turned down things that my agent didn't understand. Movie opportunities. I was just like, "I just don't wanna do that." It's not that I knew what I wanted to do—because very often you can't know what you want to do until it's presented to you—but I knew what I didn't want to do.

What was that?

I didn't want to do stuff that I thought was just commercial crap, where I would make money and get a credit. You know, there were a number of different philosophies about how you make a career. One was you do everything anyone asks you to do, and you just accumulate things and hope to god something works. And that kind of felt for me like a shot-in-the-dark philosophy: you just keep shooting and hoping to god that you hit something that connects. I didn't cotton to that, but I did cotton to the idea that if you were as specific in your choices of what you did as you were as an actor in a role, then you might find things that were right for you, that would challenge you and be interesting to do. So I turned down a lot of things and, as a result, got a reputation. Who does he think he is? How dare he turn down this part? So you do odd jobs when you can. After *Ghosts*, I left New York, because the honest truth is, at the end of that production I just wasn't good enough. I wasn't good enough to play in the leads I wanted to be in. And there I was, in this big Broadway opportunity, and the play wasn't a success. It ran for a while, but it wasn't a success. I survived the reviews, but in my own assessment of myself I wasn't good enough, and I decided that I needed to go learn. I needed to go work in a place where I wouldn't gain a reputation. I needed to be able to go someplace where I could fail. Because I felt I'd just failed on Broadway and that that opportunity wasn't gonna come around again that quickly. The truth is, people make assessments really quickly, casting directors do, and producers do and directors do. You walk into an audition and you do a bad audition and it goes on the card, it goes in the computer, that it wasn't good. Next time you wanna go in for an audition, they look at the card and, "Oh, no, he's not good." But I was very ambitious, and when I heard that someone I knew was up for a part, even if I didn't know the script, my attitude was, Goddamnit, why wasn't I included? And my manager sat me down one night and said, "Do you think you're a good actor?" And I said, "Well, yeah, of course." And he said, "No, but do you think at this point, at twenty-one years old, do you think you're as good as you're going to be?" And I said, "Well, no, of course not." And he said, "Well then, why do you want to go out and show everybody who you are now? Why don't we target the things that are right for you, rather than you not having read the script at all and assuming you're right for every part that's out there? Why don't we actually target specific things and start to try to build a career a little more quietly and realize that it may take ten years?" And when I started to go back and look and examine the actors I really admired, it was pretty noticeable that every single one of them didn't really make their big breaks till they were in their thirties.

Like who?

Henry Fonda was thirty-one when he did his first movie. Hoffman was thirty-one when he did *The Graduate*. Nicholson was thirty-four when he did *Easy Rider*.

What were they doing until then?

They were building their craft, they were working, they were doing plays; they were building strong enough foundations that they were gonna run with it.

What did you do?

I left New York and I did regional theater. I went to the Kennedy Center, I went to Williamstown, to Seattle Rep. I went to a lot of places to just try and learn, to act and do a small part or a big part.

Were you holding your ambition in check, or did you feel you were direct-ing your ambition to do these things?

I was trying to direct my ambition, and I was trying to get out of my way of thinking—of comparing myself to other people, which is deadly. It took me a while to do that. I came back to New York a couple of years later, in '84, and met Mike Nichols, who auditioned me for the national tour of *The Real Thing*. He came sauntering down the aisle of the theater after I did my reading, and he said, "It was very good. Where are you from?" And we had a little chat, and he said, "I'd like you to come in and read for *Hurlyburly*." And he asked me to under-study the Harvey Keitel part. And I was like, "He's supposed to look like he can beat the shit out of everybody. He's a fucking tough guy." And Mike was like, "It's all about attitude." And I took that assign-ment, and I worked and worked and worked, and in a couple of days I got on. And Mike came and saw it, and he came backstage and said, "That was really terrific. How soon could you learn Mickey?" And I said, "Well, I kind of already know it." So I learned Mickey and went on as Mickey more than anything else, because Ron Silver, who was playing at that point, got a movie called *Garbo Talks*, and he left the cast for six weeks. So Mike came and loved it and said, "How soon could you learn Eddie?" So I did literally every male part in that play.

When you say you worked at it, how did you do that?

When you're understudying, it tends to happen this way: you re-hearse in a rehearsal room. You don't necessarily get onstage, be-cause if they rehearse onstage, they have to call the stage crew, so that's an expense. Nine times out of ten, you get thrown on the stage. You come in on a Saturday, and they say, "You're on!" and you have no rehearsal on the set. So I used to sneak into the theater. I would go in and pass the doorman and then go to my dressing room and go down the other way, and there was always this sort of one light on the stage and I would rehearse very quietly all of the moves on the stage in the early part of the afternoon. I got caught once. I was onstage, and the stage lights went on, and Bill Hurt came out of the wings and looked at me and said [imitating Bill Hurt], "My my my, what do we have here? A dedicated actor. What *are* you doing?" "I'm understudying, I'm learning." And he said, "Well, do you know it? Do you know the lines in the script?" I said yes. And he said, "Well then, let's do it, what *is* the *point* of doing it alone?" So I ended up rehearsing with Bill Hurt, and we became friends after that. And I have to say, that experience of understudying was incredible. To work with Nichols, to work with that stage management, and to work with those kinds of actors: Frank Langella came in at one point and started playing Eddie. It was a remarkable education, you know, to get up every night on a Broadway stage and do a performance, and nobody knew who I was. I wasn't famous, I was just an actor. And it was one of the best experiences ever just in terms of learning and training and that consistency.

Do you have one way that you approach a role? Or do you—

It is decidedly different every time. When I did *Long Day's Journey*—I'll give you an example. I spent an unbelievable amount of time reading every fucking thing I could get my hands on about O'Neill. I just had a fucking library. I still have it. I read everything, I studied everything. Now, looking back, some of that stuff was useful and valuable and helpful, but I think a lot of it was probably useless and confusing because there were so many opposing views of O'Neill.

It was critical stuff you read?

Critical stuff, and biographical stuff. And then when I did *Iceman Cometh* years later, I decided, Somewhere in there, it's all there. I'm just gonna trust it. And I didn't read a thing. I just trusted the play and the director and whatever my instincts were bringing to the equation. That's an example of two completely different ways to approach O'Neill plays.

When you did Iceman Cometh, *how did you start? You got the script, you read it—*

About nine months before we were gonna begin rehearsals, I had been asked if I wanted to do this play. I thought, I saw *Iceman*, I saw Jason Robards do it at the Kennedy Center. I'm not gonna read it. I'm not gonna prepare for it in that way. So I didn't read it. I only read it on the plane two weeks before rehearsal—the next year on my way to London. And I read the play again: Omigod, I'm out of my mind to be doing this play, I thought. This play is a monster. I had completely forgotten just how fucking monstrous it was. And so I spent two weeks being quite nervous about it, you know, as we were marching toward the first day. And then I walked into the rehearsal room and met this company of actors that Howard Davies had put together. And twenty minutes into this read-through, I went, Oh, he is so brilliant. He has created a whole world. I knew I was in the safest hands I could be in. The process of working with Howard—the way in which he prods and guides.

Talk about that more. What do you need from a director?

What I need is a director who has a very clear idea of what the play is about, has an opinion about the play. Who understands the ideas the writer is attempting to get out, and who is able to describe that vision, to see how something is starting to shape. To understand—no, that's going too far in this particular direction. There was a quality that Howard and I both agreed could possibly be very useful, which was an evangelical attack. That Hickey was absolutely and passionately so determined about trying to save his friends from his own fate. There was a preacher in it, and it was written that way. I really allowed that sort of fervor to drive the play. I had the experience in *Long Day's Journey* with a director, Jonathan Miller, who wanted the play to move at a very very fast clip. We actually overlapped each other in dialogue when I did this production with Jack Lemmon, which they didn't care for in America, because they felt, How dare you not let us hear every single word that O'Neill wrote? In London, they loved it, it was exciting. We had a more successful run in Britain than we did in the United States. I need a director who is not only able to know what note to give to you but at a very specific moment, at a time when you are ready to take that note. Sometimes directors who are not skilled, who don't fully appreciate the process of what is happening to an actor's brain in the course of rehearsal when things are beginning to percolate—ideas are beginning to get laid down, you're beginning to explore things—give a note too early, before you've assessed and found and tried and failed a whole number of things. If they give a note that's so specific that you can't possibly know what to do with it, then it's a waste of a note. It's the directors— and I've been fortunate with Howard Davies or Sam Mendes or Trevor Nunn, whom I recently worked with on *Richard II*—who know the precise moment to give you a note. And sometimes it's not till the second week of previews, when you're now living it and trying to connect the dots, and you're trying to carve the arc of the character's experience more and more each night so it becomes richer and deeper and more meaningful to you and therefore to an audience. Then the director just comes up and whispers this thing, and some- times when I hear it, I know I've been doing what that note is about for six weeks. I've been doing it for six weeks, and he hasn't said a thing to me about it until that moment, and I go, "But I've been do- ing that for all these . . ." And he'll say, "Yeah, but I think you just needed to get through what I saw you do last night, and now it's time for you to try this way." And Trevor's in my head, because it's so re- cent, with so many moments like that. I had a huge argument about

Richard II, particularly because it's known for its poetic rhythms, and Richard loves the sound of his own voice, and it's all very flowery, and I just said, "Bullshit, you know, bullshit." I don't believe that it's about a guy who is in love with his own voice. I mean, yeah, it's about a guy who's kind of heard his own voice most of his life and nobody's ever said, Oh you're really wrong there, oh king, sir. So he's certainly got a sense of position and that he has this divine right to be the king, and nothing will ever ever take it away. But when that starts to be pulled away from him, when the very thing he's been his whole entire life is taken away from him, then I don't think it's about flowery poetry and enjoying the sound of his own voice. He's fucking fighting for his life because without his kingship he doesn't know who he is! And that's of course what the journey is, because the journey of Richard II is an external journey for most of the play, until the abdication scene, and then on a specific line where he says "There lies the substance." He has to go inside of him. He makes a realization that his journey now is an internal one, and that's where the play shifts, and it becomes about a king becoming a man who would be a better king if he were still king. And even though it's called a history play, that's to me what makes it a great tragedy.

Did you and Trevor develop this together?

We'd spent about four years talking about what play we'd like to do, and there were a lot of choices on the table. He had a modern take on the play. He wanted to use it in a sense of showing the corridors of power, showing how politicians use the media for spin. In the production, he was using cameras onstage, and John of Gaunt's speech was not done in a room with six people. It was done on television repeatedly, again and again and again, in order to get half the country for something and half against. And I thought this conception of the play was so relevant and potentially something that a younger audience would be able to follow. Trevor did a lot of textual cuts, cutting an enormous amount out of the first scene, cutting two characters out and bringing in sections of *Henry IV, Part One* for Bolingbroke's story. So it was really a beautifully crafted stand-alone play. And when I discovered that it was a play Trevor had never directed, that's when I decided that's what we should do: we should have an opportunity to have a first experience together rather than my being his third Richard III. You know: let's do it because we've never done it.

Has it ever happened during your career that a director wasn't helping you?

When I came back to New York from regional theater, I got cast in a play at a very well known theater with a very well known director, and we went through three weeks of rehearsal and it just wasn't working. And I thought, This is not going to be a play that I will be good in. This is not a good experience. No one is communicating. I don't see the vision of this play. I thought I did when I read it, but now in rehearsal it was a new work. And I quit. I would say my biggest complaint about directors—and this is going to sound odd because most of the time I've been very fortunate—is when they want you to do something, they have an idea about how you should attack a line or attack a scene and then cannot give you an argument for why. They just say something like, "I like it that way." I don't care if you like it that way. I need to know as an actor who's serving a writer why you like it that way, and what is the intention, because I don't get it. When directors cannot make an argument to an actor about why they want you to do something, then it's very hard to trust them, because there's nothing being expressed, there's no relationship. And sometimes you say, "Well, why don't you just show me?" And then usually they stop.

How did you apply all that you learned about being an actor—and all that you know about what you like and don't like in directors—in directing yourself in Beyond the Sea?

Well, I wasn't alone. The truth is, on that kind of film, which is an independently made movie, you bring on people who become your codirectors, whom you trust: whose eye and talent and taste and vision of what you're trying to put together can help you succeed. I had a script supervisor, an art director, a production designer, a camera operator. I have a producer, an associate producer. People I turn to every day. I have a vision about the film, but when it comes to individual scenes, you really do have to rely on a lot of other people.

Did you watch dailies? Did you have to reshoot because you felt, Oh, no, this isn't what I meant? The job seems so difficult.

It was actually the best job in the world to direct, especially film. What I try to do is make sure I give myself choices in editing. If you're doing a scene and you have an attack, there's a particular mood you're trying to evoke, that's fine, do it the way you think it is. But then, start fucking with it, do a line softer, do that line differently, come at that line in another way, because ultimately you're gonna be editing. What a director and editor do is craft a performance based on the material they have, which is dailies. I know that in several cases I shot a better movie than was cut. Because the choices they used were the most sentimental, the most weepy, the most dripping with sincerity. There were harder, tougher choices made; there was an enormous amount of material they could have used and cut in such a way to make a better movie. There is no doubt in my mind. So when you're not producing, you have no control whatsoever. And no matter how many times you tell them, "You're going to get killed if you release it," they say, "We tested it, and the numbers look great," but what does that mean? These numbers don't mean anything. You went to a shopping mall and those people told you they liked it, but they had a free movie and some popcorn, so what do you expect? So it is always about getting into the editing room and having choices so that you can decide where a character is. We have very very well known actors, who you can go watch in movies—and it's why when they do theater and they're not able to cut it, here's the reason—they showed up on that day and they did that scene with energy, and they showed up the next day and did a scene with energy, and then you cut it all together and it's like a flat line. These actors don't understand or appreciate story arc, arc of the character, ups and downs, highs and lows, what a character knows there that they didn't know here, how a character starts to change through the course of the piece. That, to me, is the funnest thing about making movies—being able to get into the editing room and have choices.

And when you're acting, and you have no control, you're aware of giving the editor and director choices?

Yeah, and sometimes that works to your advantage, and sometimes that works to your disadvantage.

Is there any way to control your performance on film?

I think the performance starts to be crafted after you move around, you bring the camera in, you start to do two-shots. You start to develop the performance in the course of the day. In a master you can be very broad, but when the camera starts to come in, you have to start to decide, How do I want this to appear, how big is this, how small is this, how quiet is this, how tender is this? It begins to shape itself as the camera moves around—making decisions about how do I want to play this, this is take four of that lens, we also have that camera doing a two-shot at the same time. Okay, we have enough of it that way, let me try something else. I used to watch Pacino, when we did *Glengarry Glen Ross*, and Al could do twenty-four, thirty-four takes. And Al would say [imitating Pacino], "How many are you going to print?" and the director would say, "Uh, we're printing three and eight and ten." And Al would go, "I would print twelve. I think there is something happening in twelve." And they'd print twelve and something was happening in twelve. I used to go to dailies. I was watching myself and learning about myself on film. When I did *Usual Suspects*, it was the first time a director, Bryan Singer, said to me, "I don't want you to come to dailies." He said, "Because you have to play so many layers of what is true and not true, I can't have you second-guessing what the audience knows and doesn't know. You have to trust me, that I'm telling this story."

I wondered at the end of The Usual Suspects *whether you were just playing the character of Verbal or whether you were playing the character of Keyser Söze playing the character of Verbal. I don't know if there are any moments when I saw Keyser. Are there?*

There are. Bryan looked at it this way. You are an actor playing a character who is playing a character. There were so many little moments when Bryan wanted clues. You could go back and see moments when I am looking at the bulletin board, but you don't know it's there. It was just one of those extraordinary experiences. He was so clear about what he wanted. It was complicated for all of us because Bryan had convinced people of certain things. Gabriel Byrne thought he was Keyser Söze and was very confused when he saw the movie. That entire thing was about how the truth can be right in front of your face, but if you're not looking at it from the right angle, you can completely miss it.

Beyond the Sea *seems like such a personal story.*

There's no doubt in my experience of that movie that it was a cautionary tale. It was about a guy who was incredibly ambitious and paid the price for it in his relationships. And yet he was this remarkably talented and now largely forgotten figure in American history. I thought his story was ripe for drama, and I wanted to make a movie that was about a guy who didn't play by the rules and who made up his own path despite the fact that a lot of people wanted him to be one thing. And I think that's something I recognized I had experienced, in that people tend to like you the way they discovered you, and then you start to move and shift yourself into other areas and do other things and find other challenges, which is all Bobby Darin was about in his brief fourteen-year career. He was a very different person than I am, but at the end of the day, that movie was as much a statement of mine—that you have to go your own way, you can't live your life for your career, for other people. You have to do the things that you think are right, and challenge yourself in the ways that you must be challenged in order to get better and to keep evolving, keep changing, and keep working on your talent.

How does this apply to you?

At the end of 1999, I got to this point. I had made a very clear decision ten years earlier to start focusing on film and see if I could carve out a career. I had done it. *American Beauty* was out, and I thought, It just doesn't get better than this, to find another part as remarkable as this in a movie as universally received as this movie. So now what am I supposed to do? Spend ten years making more movies, making more money, doing what, trying to top myself? I got to the point where I just was no longer interested in engaging in the game of my own personal career. It became meaningless to me. When the opportunity to go to the Old Vic to start a theater company and dedicate myself again to the theater and in a sense kind of flip it—well. I spent ten years doing movies and squeezing plays in. Now I'm spending ten years doing plays and squeezing movies in.

Is your work at the Old Vic strictly putting on plays?

No. We have a whole range of work that we do under the umbrella we call Old Vic New Voices. We have a large educational program, vast community work, workshops where we offer kids an opportunity to experience the artists and tools of theater as a way for them to start to build their confidence and sense of collaboration with their peers. There is a company in New York that I greatly admire, the 24 Hour Company, and I asked them to partner up with us to present the insane project they do where, in twenty-four hours, six ten-minute plays that didn't exist the night before are performed in front of a sold-out audience. Playwrights work all night, actors rehearse all day, and then we premiere these plays. It was such a great success that I said, "I want to do this for kids." We have a whole program called the Old Vic Club for emerging young writers, producers, directors, and actors between the ages of eighteen and twenty-five. You don't have to prove you're a professional, you don't have to have any credits. Just tell us why you want to be in theater. We audition hundreds of kids and pick a company of fifty: thirty-one actors, six writers, six directors, six producers. And they stay with us for three years. We support them and give them a foundation and a home. And to a person, each of them have said that, while performing at the Old Vic was an incredible experience, the best part has been what follows. The connections are starting to percolate, and that's great, because these people will grow up in the business together. We're really trying to develop the next generation of talent and not just help develop work for the Old Vic but for the industry. It is unbelievably satisfying and what I believe we can do. We're gonna continue creating these young companies every year, and it makes me feel that I am giving back to an industry that has given me so much.

After the Academy Awards were handed out, Annie Proulx, who wrote the original story for Brokeback Mountain, *wrote an essay, in which she seemed to be referring to Edward R. Murrow and Truman Capote, and she said, Isn't it easier to do a role based on reality than it is to create one? like the characters in her story. I was going to ask you, Did you think it was easier to re-create Bobby Darin, because he already existed, than to start from scratch?*

Well, I could tell you this. There are probably twenty examples of really great fictional characters who are remarkable, but we could also give twenty examples of great portrayals of people who lived. I will say this: it was easier maybe to work on Bobby Darin in terms of the scripts, because scripts existed. I'm not sure I could've started from scratch, but once I found the conception, the movie within the movie idea, which for me took it out of the realm of the more usual biopic approach, I was much more interested in making a movie that was a fantasy, one that used elements of other movies I have admired that literally are almost the same subject—*All That Jazz* and *8½*. Both of those films go into places: Is this real, is this not real? Is this a dream or not a dream, a fantasy or not? I wanted to use the basis of Bobby Darin's life and the idea of the way he expressed himself on-stage to extend into musical numbers, so that suddenly the movie became like an old MGM musical.

If Bobby Darin hadn't existed, if you wanted to make up a singer of that period, how would you have sung it? Because your phrasing was very accurate. You sounded just like him.

I think that whenever you're faced with playing somebody who really lived, there is a slightly different responsibility. And you also have to take some creative license. First of all, you have to make a lot of choices about what do I keep in and what do I keep out. How do I tell a story about a person who was, has some flaws, some arrogance, you know, did some things that weren't great? How do I maintain this person even if I want to show some of those warts? How do I do it in such a way that I don't lose the audience in terms of their sympathy or their affection for that person as a character? So there are things you leave out. And just as hard were the choices of songs, 'cause he recorded over three hundred songs. What do you put in? There was a lot of great material, but you can't use it all. So you try to pick things that you think help move the story forward rather than just doing another song—actually trying to advance the story. And I would say that there's also a respect that you want to have for the family, if there's family still alive. In a sense, it's not really gonna be this person's life story, it's the combination of a lot of events and things. For example, from a storytelling point of a view, I felt that to have Bobby Darin go to the Copacabana, which is the thing he always dreamed of doing, and not have Sandra Dee there, was structurally not good for me, even though he had played the Copa and had that experience well before he married her. I decided it would be more poignant in a sense that she should be there, and he should be singing to her on this incredibly important night. But that's not the way it happened. When you're making a drama, you have to kind of make those choices where you say, "No, I really want her to be there. I want this to be about them and not just another scene in a nightclub where he's having a great success." When it's about the relationship, it changes the nature of the whole enterprise, the whole scene, that whole section.

Do you read reviews?

I don't read reviews when I'm doing a play. I have them compiled. I haven't even read the reviews for *Richard II*, but at some point I'll read them. Later. I don't think they help at all.

There's no theater writer in London whom you respect at all?

It's not about respect. It's about you're in the middle of something that is a stream of consciousness for you. You're going moment to moment to moment, and you're not thinking of someone commenting on a choice you make. Even if somebody gives you a really fabulous compliment about the way you played something, suddenly something that you've just been playing is pointed out to you as a special thing. It can ruin the spontaneity, and it can make you start playing it because you know you're going to get the response the writer so lavishly praised you for. So I think it's dangerous to read reviews. Because the truth is that at the end of the day, the great reviews, are they gonna make you feel better? But that depends on who wrote it. What I always try to remember is this—you can take all of the critics and put them in the theater and they wouldn't fill one row, and to me, the most important critics are the public.

One more question. What do you think it was . . . Was there any compilation of things that made you act, made you need to act?

I think I learned very early on that making people laugh was a wonderful thing, so I was definitely the kid in the back of the class making the other kids laugh. Perhaps it was the experiences I had going to the theater as such a young child, and I became a movie buff very early on, so I fell in love with actors of another generation—Spencer Tracy, Jimmy Stewart, Fonda, Cagney. I was watching these late movies on television, just thinking they were the most incredible things I'd ever seen. And so I think I fell in love with the idea of being an actor, of being a performer, because I was a performer. And I could always make my parents laugh, and that was a great feeling, and it just sort of evolved for me into having fun with it to realizing I might actually have the talent to develop. And then I have to say it was only later, only after I'd been in New York for a number of years, that I actually started to think of the theater as a community and that there was a responsibility to that community. And that the choices you made contributed to this community.

You started out wanting very strongly to perform. How strong is that urge now?

It's still there. It's there in large measure because I'm now doing what I wanted to do from the time I was a kid. I had a dream of running a theater when I was really young.

Did you want to do it in the United States?

Well, I don't think I could do what I'm doing now in the United States. We're not subsidized. Let's say I had a thousand-seat theater on Broadway and I was trying to run a theater program. I would run into enormous expenses and costs. I also was in a place in my life where I wanted to live in another country and experience another culture, have a different experience. When it happened, it happened. It didn't cross my mind to come back to the United States and find out that somebody else had a better office. This is where I'm meant to be. Joe Papp had a huge influence and still to this day does, because I often think of Joe—what would Joe do?—but what I feel I'm trying to do now is to take all of the incredible good fortune and success that has come to me and to use it for something that's bigger than myself. And I want to create something that's gonna last long after I'm gone. So I feel like everything I've been working at and doing in my life has been leading to this. I'm in the right place at the right moment doing the right thing.

Philip Seymour Hoffman

Philip Seymour Hoffman meets us in the lobby of the Public Theater, where the LAByrinth Theater Company, of which he is a member, is in residence. He's dressed for a day out in New York in which lots of errands have to be run: backpack, bottle of water, cup of coffee, baseball cap, running shoes, layers of clothes. He's wearing a full beard, which is as blond as his hair. He is good-looking in an all-American way, solid and athletic, sturdy, the beard making him appear burly and avuncular. His manner is straightforward and friendly, with a kind of openness whose source and meaning become clearer as our conversation goes on; he is as an actor as he is as a man. We take the elevator to the second floor, where Philip greets the office personnel familiarly, trading a few quick personal bits with them, then joins us in an unoccupied, book-lined office. During the interview he displays a mixture of confidence and modesty; he is aware of and admittedly enjoying the heightened position he is in after his award-winning performance in *Capote*, but he also seems to have all the hoopla in perspective, his feet on the ground. While we're deciding how to arrange ourselves at the table, Philip is the one who moves it into place.

When did you think you wanted to do this acting thing? What was it that started you on this course?

I wasn't into acting as a kid. I played baseball and stuff. Then in fifth grade I was cast in *Tom Sawyer*, a musical in my grammar school. On the day we had to perform, my stomach was incredibly upset and I was saying, "Oh, I've got these horrible cramps." And my teacher said, "Do you want to go to the bathroom or something?" This was my first experience like it, and it was mortifying. Plus, I had to enter into the play with a stick in my hand, and I didn't have the stick, so I left the school to go outside and take a branch off a tree, and I didn't tell anybody, which is very much me now as an adult: I'll go do it myself. And I got locked out of the school! It was a weekend, so no one knew I was locked out, and I was running from door to door. The play hadn't started yet, 'cause I started the play. I was playing Becky Thatcher's brother. He starts out the play pretending he's a pirate, and I'm supposed to come down the aisle of the theater with a stick. So I'm banging on these doors, crying, just bawling, trying to get inside. And I get inside, and I remember going on, I remember starting the play . . . and everything going away. That's my first experience, and there was such trauma, even as a young child not having any interest in it. The trauma around having to start the event was so awful and the relief and the release were so extraordinary once it started, and I always remembered that. The nerves, the fear, the why-are-you-asking-this-of-me kind of feeling. It's a very complicated thing that goes through you, and it's hard to explain. People think you're an actor because, "you need the theater," but you're an actor for very complicated reasons.

You're saying that it still happens to you?

It's not as traumatic as it was then, but it isn't pleasant. The moments before having to act are still reminiscent of that time.

What's at the base of that feeling?

Well, nothing causes it. It's just that even at that time, I knew that I cared. That's what it comes from. I care. And I knew innately maybe what it might take to do it well, even though I'm sure I did it fifth-grade well. And that's what causes the trauma, because what it takes to do it well, I think, is great vulnerability. In front of strangers, you have to bring in vulnerability and privacy that normal people run screaming from. I think that for most people, it's one of their worst fears. If you're an actor, and it's something you want to do well, you are confronting that fear honestly. I don't think actors are different from other people. I think they still have that fear, but they know they have a need to create something and do something with it. But to get past that moment, you are dealing with something—to me it's quite primal—because you could get up there and not be vulnerable and not be private and be pretty bad. I think that happens a lot. And therefore there's not a lot of trauma, there's not a lot of anxiety, because you get up there and protect the shit out of yourself. Even at that age I think I felt this. I knew I had to start this play, and I knew I had to start it with a certain energy. And I knew that would take something of me that I wasn't kosher with. You know what I mean? I didn't like it, that that was going to be asked of me and that I was going to have to do it, the possible humiliation of it.

But you continued to act in school?

I did acting when I was a sophomore or junior in high school. And I had the same thing, but I was a teenager with a bunch of other teenagers, kind of a gang of people doing this theater in my high school. I still had the trauma around it, but now it was more focused on what I could do as an actor, because I had learned some things and realized that there are tools at your disposal that can help you focus yourself. There was a teacher at my high school, Midge Marshall, who was very serious about the theater. She wasn't doing just the high school musicals and stuff. I played Willy Loman in *Death of a Salesman* when I was a senior in high school.

How did she help you do Willy Loman?

Basically, she threw you and your young mind into a very complicated, adult, advanced play. It's very smart. Obviously you're not going to understand all those things and you're not going to do it all that well, but she got you intensely interested in what theater could be, because you were dealing with great theater. I mean that's a great play, and the ideas are there.

Did she talk to you about it?

What happened was that Dustin Hoffman was playing it at the time on Broadway, but the run was sold out, and I was in the city auditioning for NYU and this was the last day of the play's run. My mom called anyway, being the very persuasive woman that she could be, and found out that there was one ticket in a box. There are four loose seats in a box, and three of them were taken by a group, so this fourth one had been dangling there for months and no one had taken it. That was really a pivotal moment for me, seeing him do that. I left that performance and started kind of running, 'cause the energy was so extraordinary inside of me.

Had you already done your Willy Loman?

No, no, I hadn't. So I saw him do Willy and then I came back to my high school and I just ripped him off like you cannot believe.

What did you rip off?

Well, it was more his map, 'cause I didn't have an understanding of the man and the pressures of what that was. I did have an understanding of having a father, and these things. I was keying into Biff much more than I was keying into Willy. I was very moved by the play even when I read it at that age. "You're never going to be enough"— that kind of thing. And what you will do to make it look like you are what you aren't, how you can't be honest about yourself. All those things that come up with those son characters. Just watching Hoffman's logic through it, watching his map through it, I remember understanding and going, Oh, okay. So that's really what I ripped off, his logical map.

He wasn't really old enough or physically the vision of Willy that anybody ever had.

He wasn't, but I was seventeen, so to me he was ancient. You know what I mean? He was probably in his mid-forties or something at the time. He shuffled. I didn't do any of those things, but I just copied his logic. I remember being like, I'm gonna follow that guy. It was another lesson, it was something I didn't understand at that time, it was that logical map. That logic has a lot to do with succeeding in acting. You have to have a logical moment-to-moment life, so that one moment can't happen without the next, that the next moment can't happen without the previous moment happening, that there's a moment-to-moment logic.

And you have to understand that in an intellectual way before you start rehearsal?

No. I think you find that while you're creating a role. And so watching him was very helpful because I was able to key into something that I didn't have any grasp on at all.

You do an arc for your character and then go moment to moment?

I know the arc is important. How I get there is always a battle of will. Because I think every time I enter into a role, I want to find an easy way out like I did when I was ten. I don't want to go through that experience again, so how can I find an easy way out? How I go about finding the arc, the logical arc, is always different. It's always me playing games with myself to try to eventually get the will to ask the hard questions that are going to lead toward understanding psychologically why a person does what they do and how they actually do it, and then how do I make that all my own? There's no real written way to do that. You sit there and read the script, and then you go back and start from the top and you start to ask questions: What am I doing? What am I doing to the other people? How am I doing it? You ask simple questions of actions and things, just basic kinds of things like that, that will send you off on your journey. It'll get you thinking about all those things that'll get you to remember things about yourself. And then you slowly start to piece it together, logically, how this character moves through this story. But it really is just about looking at this person: What am I doing here? What am I doing there? What, ultimately, do I want?

Did you, in your training—whatever it was—did you have a lot of body and movement work?

I had some in college. I was a bit of an athlete when I was younger. I wasn't a great athlete, but I was a very physical kid.

My impression is that the second we see you, we know who the character is. You haven't said anything; you haven't done anything. You just look a certain way.

That's logic too, meaning everything has to have a sense of logic. If there's a gap of disbelief that you have, it's pretty hard to keep moving. If there's a gap, you really fall through it. You can't keep moving forward, because you just can't get to the next moment. And that drives directors crazy, that drives people crazy, because you'll literally be like, No, I don't buy it. What is that, it's a gap. The whole movie's gonna fall right through, the whole play's gonna fall right through. So sometimes it's a physical thing. And then you realize later in life, god, that's what my teacher meant when she was referring to Stella Adler: "If you're playing a king, sound kingly." And those are things you have to learn on your own. There are certain characters that you understand, that you just know, like say my character in *The Talented Mr. Ripley*, Freddy Miles. He's not rigid. Rigid doesn't fit the logic. He's not trying to control himself in order to control others. You know, whatever, I'm just making that up, but it's like, I know that's right. If it's not logically right, that's a gap and I'll fall through that gap. So in order to play through the psychological map that is here—and have it be personal to me—there's something I'm going to have to do to myself physically in order for me to buy it all.

Can you say what it was in that character?

It's like he's napping. He's living in a pre-orgasm world.

I always had the impression that he was just about to toss a scarf over his shoulder.

Yeah, he's living in a just-about-to-take-the-beautiful-woman's-clothes-off world. I mean he's cushioned, and he'd like to pull everyone into that thing. And that works well because Ripley comes in and would like to upset that thing he's quite specifically set up, that world he's specifically set up for himself, and that's a huge threat.

Well, those scenes with him and Ripley are very tense because the character is so tense himself, so controlled—

He wants to take away that world.

There was a wonderful moment when you come back, and he's at the piano. And he's playing something, and you're underscoring or mimicking him. Do you remember that moment? And I thought it just told the whole story about what you felt about him and what he was doing. Was that a happy accident, or—

It wasn't an accident, but it wasn't scripted that I would do that. I was actually supposed to play something. You were supposed to see that he had skills at the piano, which I did not. I was actually learning to look like I know how to play the piano for another film, *Flawless*. But I didn't have the time to learn that. So I had to come up with something else that would ultimately do the same thing, and I realized that, well, then he doesn't know how, and he's actually going to shove it in this guy's face, his bourgeois bullshit. Like, you love all these . . . you know, the trappings, this light. You know nothing about that. You're a fraud. And that's the other thing: it's not as psychologized, but the other thing with him being the way he is, you know, I can let everyone think of me as this laissez-faire, roving, expat party boy, but ultimately who I am is somebody that'll walk into a room and the minute he saw somebody, he *knew*. That's who this guy was. That was his talent. That's why he was so popular, that's why everybody knew him. And then the minute he meets Ripley, he knows: you're a fraud. He knew he was shit. He knew he was a fucking hack. He was a hack in life, and he knew that he had come to do something, and so you see him when they meet in that piazza. And then the very next scene, they're in the record store, and you see Freddy Miles look at Ripley, and the look on his face is like, I'm gonna kill you. Don't fuck with this, I'll kill you. And they haven't even talked. So I know from the script that that must be a part of who this guy is. And the most interesting part is by not showing it. That he would present himself to the world as one way, but actually, if you cross him, he's going to show you the other way. He's a very powerful man. He's the guy that's going to turn into . . . if he didn't die, he was gonna be an incredibly wealthy, powerful man of the world. I knew that that's who I was dealing with.

Going into the film, did you know everything you just said?

No. Those are things that you uncover as you're working on the role.

What if you shoot a scene, and a couple of days later, you're about to shoot another scene, and you think, Oh, now I see. Here's what I should have done.

You suck it up. Or you try to find a way with what you have left. Film is a lot about piecing things together, but you feel like, I missed that there. That was something I needed to express there. That was a moment I needed to fill, and I filled it I think inaccurately. Hopefully, not too off, but inaccurately enough. It didn't color enough. It wasn't specific enough. It didn't flesh out a certain thing that would have been appropriate for the psychological path again of this character's emotional journey. But you can look at the rest of the script. I've actually taken scenes and gone, I've shot these scenes, I haven't shot these scenes. I've taken out what I've actually done. I've shot these scenes that I think might be okay. And I've shot these scenes that are awful. I've actually had piles and looked at it. And why I did that is, first off, the thing you need to do: you need to face reality. You need to face truth in order to be vulnerable and private. You need to actually have that kind of truth with yourself. But you also need to look at it and say, Okay, what do I need to do with what I have left? So I can give this editor and this director the best option possible to piece together the performance necessary for them.

You do that during filming?

I've done it a couple times. And I've really gone and been like, I've got to look at this. I've got to look at the whole thing, 'cause I know there's a piece of me that I don't think I did it right. I don't think I did well. And some scenes I do think I did well. And I look at what I have left and see if what I missed here I can maybe pick up here, and that's something you can do in a film. Theater's not like that, of course. In theater, you have tomorrow.

Have you ever had the experience doing a play where you're not there, you're just sort of thinking about the laundry. And then you realize, oh—

Sure. Yeah. Somebody said it, not me: "Even the greatest athletes have off nights." Actors and athletes are very similar, and that's why I like that analogy. It's very similar, and I'm a big sports fan. They have to be private and vulnerable. They do, because . . . if you're not private and vulnerable in front of lots of people, you're nervous and you're self-conscious and you perform badly. So you have to have a sense of how to be yourself, and athletes are the same way. They walk out, and they exude who they are, and they just become incredibly expressive through their art form. It's very similar. And even the best ones, the most capable of creating an environment where they can perform at their peak potential, have nights where that's all of a sudden elusive to them. And why? It's elusive, and they don't perform well. It can be for many reasons.

How much structure—and how much freedom—do you need when you work?

Children seem like they don't want to be told what to do, but actually they do. Meaning, if you give me structure, it'll free me up. There's something in that, about life, you know, about life in general. There's something about, No, no structure, I wanna look at everything. There's something about that that's irresponsible and immature and actually is someone who doesn't want to create anything. The person who's trying to look for the structure, they're trying to look for their own structure, the one that'll work. Sometimes with certain roles, what will happen is that if you are able to give yourself a very specific structure to work into, it can free you up. Very much so. And sometimes when that's more elusive, when you don't have that, you feel very exposed. But if there's a structure, if there's something that you're working inside of, you can actually be incredibly expressive *and* incredibly exposed.

Can you give an example of that?

You ultimately need some kind of structure to work in, no matter what part you're playing. I remember reading the response to the Oscars by the woman who wrote the *Brokeback Mountain* short story, Annie Proulx. It's pretty fabulous. She was pretty pissed off. But she gets to this point about the actors—and I'm reading it, I was with her, I was very interested in what she was writing. I was thinking she was gonna talk about *Crash* and what her themes were, so she gets to the middle section, praising the actors, saying, I wonder what's more difficult: creating a character that already existed, or creating one out of the dark. And obviously she's commenting on me and on David Strathairn playing Edward R. Murrow. I stop and go like, I wish I had her number. Because I wanna call her and be like, "Well, I've done both. They're both fuckin' hard." They're both the same thing, meaning that you have resources with one, and with the other one, you have to find them. But either way, you're still gonna have to do the same thing inside those constructs, inside those structures that you're creating for yourself. And that, ultimately, is always gonna be the same, you're gonna run into the same difficulties. But it is an interesting question she posed.

Well, I think people don't understand acting exactly. That's what we're trying to do for people who are interested, trying to get people like you, who really know how to do it, to explain what it is and how you get to it. Because it's mysterious, yet it is a craft.

There are things you actually do, but like athletics, I think it's dangerous to talk too much about this, because it's an art form. It's why actors throw tantrums. It's why actors lose their minds. It's why actors are considered divas. It's why . . . whatever. Because they're the one instrument in the environment that is being controlled by a mysterious fucking force which happens to be the mind, heart, and spirit of a human being. They're not controlled by a battery, they're not controlled by a cord. It's hard to explain that, but it's true. If you were thinking, That joint isn't oiled, it's rusty! and you get pissed at it, it's just an object. That's what we are actually, if that makes any sense. You have tools at your disposal. You have a mind that you've soaked up with as much information as possible, and all those things help you get inside it. But the ultimate execution of it is something that is almost ninety-five percent will. All the work before that is you laying the groundwork, asking the questions, understanding what you need to do, understanding what you need to look at, creating the physical construct to help you with the logic, with whatever needs to happen, all the character work, all the emotional through line. Once you get there, it's will. It's like, Am I gonna allow myself to do this thing I was just doing alone, in front of you? And for me, there's a little part of me that's like, And screw you for asking me to do it [laughter]. Even though you haven't asked me, there's a part in you that has. As an actor, you have to do something to get past that, because there's a part of you that knows people are sitting there, or if it's on the set, they're watching, and there's always a part of me that's like, Ain't life grand, great, y'all are gonna sit there. You want me to do this thing. You know what I mean? That's the odd, crazy moment before, and then you do, and then afterward you're thankful. It's a very crazy thing. Afterward, you're thankful and you wanna hug all those people.

What you're describing makes me think that the audition process must be really really hard. You have to do this, and you don't even have the job.

Auditioning's a whole different beast, actually. Auditions, you just kind of tune 'em out a little bit, you know? Because they're there to give you the job or not, and you kind of would like the job, so you're just there to actually do the work the best you can. And it's usually only a few people. You're acting in front of the least amount of people that you ever have to, so it's actually a moment of just throwing down and trying to see what you can bring there, 'cause you haven't evolved that character. Auditions are very tricky, because people really want to see it. Sometimes they don't get the best people. They audition all these people, and they get the person that gave the best audition. And sometimes the best people for the role are the people who haven't found it yet, because that's how they work. They're just not there yet. When they get there, they're gonna be the one you want. That's why auditions are very tricky.

Let's go back a little. You get to NYU as an undergraduate. Did you learn some things there?

It actually was a very fruitful time.

What group did you go in?

It was the Circle in the Square. I graduated in 1989. Terry Hayden and Jackie Brooks and Alan Langdon and Tony Greco were really great teachers. I learned a tremendous amount. I learned everything I carry with me still today that helps me get into thinking and inside this construct that you have to build—who this character is.

How do you function when the other actors are not up to you, or aren't as serious about it as you, aren't as good, aren't as disciplined? How do you act with somebody who isn't doing it? How do you save yourself if the other actors are staring at you and nobody's home?

You have to save each other.

How do you do that?

Well, again, it's not something you really like talking about it. You just save them. You have to love the other actor on the stage; you have to, ultimately. How you love the other actor is actually by succeeding in your goal and affecting them the way the play is asking you. So I say: hurt them. Deeply. They will love you for it later. Because the more I hurt you deeply, truly, honestly, the better you're gonna act. That's the only way I know how to say it. If you have a decent enough actor up there—or you have someone like Meryl Streep, who's basically in on you, she's giving you—it's pretty hard to fuck it up. 'Cause if somebody's trying to save you, they're loving you with their complete conviction to affect you appropriately for that play, moment to moment. And one moment will not come unless the first moment has been succeeded. You just become one, that's what you do. When two actors understand that, you get something that is very exciting.

About her experience of acting with you in Long Day's Journey into
Night, *Vanessa Redgrave spoke about looking into your haunted eyes,
with all that history. Do you want to talk about your experience of playing
that role?*

It was just awful, an awful thing. I remember I got to work with Jason
Robards in *Magnolia* a few years before that. He had passed away by
the time we did *Long Day's Journey*, and I remembered that he did the
play for two years. I was in the middle of this run, and I was like, How
the hell did he do that? I guess he was still drinking at the time. Doing that play is everything I've been talking about times ten, where
you're literally entering an environment where the play cannot be
done—no play can be done—without a complete and utter giving
over. But this play cannot be done without you telling the deepest,
darkest secrets you have, and it is extraordinary. You can do it half-
ass and not have to do that; you see a bad production of a great play,
and everyone's like, "Why is this guy good?" And then you see a great
production, and you're like, Holy shit! Can you believe the person
even wrote it, that the person even existed? Like O'Neill, That man
existed? That man created this? And that's all it was. It was just one
night after another, knowing that everyone was gonna have to do that
kind of work.

And the preparation for it, was that worth it?

The other actors are everything. And the feelings you go through
with other actors during the run of a play like that, you really become
closer to them than you do to people you've known all your life, and
then the play ends and you don't see them again. And it's a very odd
experience. It's like you have your life in my hands and I have my life
in your hands—in front of an audience. Robert Sean Leonard is one
of the great listeners of actors. I'd go into the last scene, and the
minute he hit me, I knew what was coming. And if I had looked at

him and he wasn't there, it would've been awful trying to get through that. But every night, that's what it was, the emotional logic, what's leading him: if only his mother would love him like she loved him when he was seven, when he walked in, gave the kid the chicken pox, and the kid died—if only she would love him the way she loved him before that day . . . that was bliss. It was heaven. But from that day on, it's been torture. It was literally him wanting that, and Edmund coming along, and because of him and the morphine, he literally has been carrying that weight. But it all came down to that kernel, that's how it plays out. It's primal. He's writing about the first time your head hit the bosom of your mother, and what that feeling was, and how that feeling . . . the idea that love like that became butchered, became tattered and torn. And that's the stuff you start thinking about . . . but then it's you and the text, and you can sit in class and talk about that play endlessly. "Well, this is Jamie . . ." But ultimately you just gotta go up and do it. That's a different thing. I remember an acting teacher saying, "Eventually, you gotta decide to do the play every night." It's one of the best pieces of teaching I ever got. If you don't decide to do it—and sixty percent of actors don't decide to do it—they go do it anyway. The minute you decide to do it, it's you doing the work to create the will to walk onstage.

What does the kind of acting that you just described cost you?

Your nerves get frayed. It was the same thing in *True West*. That play really takes it out of you—not the same, but similar. Something about Sam Shepard gets under your skin. You're digging into that well so often that your nerves become frayed, you become jittery, and I think anxiety and panic attacks become more frequent. If I were a doctor, I would say these are the signs that a run should probably end soon. That doesn't happen to everybody, but I do think with plays of that nature, that is the kind of trade-off that will happen. Where you're in the middle of a performance and you have a full-blown panic attack. And you're pale and sweating. No one knows it but you. It's just the things that are there. Your body doesn't know, so your body will start to behave in weird ways sometimes.

We wanted to talk a little bit about your directing, but mainly in terms of your acting. What was it that led you to direct?

Mostly I direct the playwright Steven Adly Guirgis. We're both with LAByrinth Theater Company. In 1997 or '98 he wrote five scenes of a play and said, "Read these." And I really liked them. And he was like, "Do you want to direct it?" He hadn't finished it yet, but I was like, "Sure! Yeah," you know, so I directed that. And I've directed since. And it's a very freeing thing. As an actor, it's a necessary thing for me to do once in a while. It's not something I want to only do, because actors need other actors to act well, but actors also need to be concerned with themselves, taking care of themselves, dealing with themselves, so there's a certain self-centered nature to it even before you enter into the arena of actually performing. Directing is the exact opposite. Directing is fantastic because your job is to make sure everyone does their best. So you have a vision and you're seeing it through, making sure the play is performed and expressed in a way that is the most potent and as clear as possible and all that. But ultimately for that to happen, you need everyone to do the best they can do. So you find yourself in the position of assisting others to do the best work they've ever done, and there's something incredibly satisfying about it. I've always enjoyed when I've directed, and because I'm able to watch the other actors, I learn about acting. It's satisfying while you're rehearsing and you see performances take off. You're like a dad or something. Wow, you're so fucking proud, and that feeling you can't compare. But directing is ultimately unsatisfying. Once opening night comes, you're like a distant cousin. So it's not nearly as satisfying in that way. You don't actually get that same see-it-through payoff that a play gives you as an actor.

How much did you have to do with making Capote *happen?*

I didn't write it. I knew Bennett Miller and Danny Futterman before the script got to me. Two years prior to that, Danny had gone to Bennett with the idea, and Bennett was like, "Good luck." And two years later he came to Bennett with a script, and Bennett liked it, and then they thought, Who'll play it? And they found me and I read it and I said I'd do it. So I was on the ground floor from the producing aspect of it. I didn't come in saying, "I wanna play Truman Capote." Trust me, when they came to me with that script, I was like, "Are you fucking kidding me?" I literally almost just said no on the spot, 'cause I was like, "That's ridiculous." I had to be convinced.

Tell me what other roles you want to play on the stage or on film. Do you think of it that way, or do you see what comes your way?

The next role I want to play is the next role I want to play, I guess is the answer. I don't know what that is until I actually see it. It has to be in the moment. Life has to flow. If you don't let life flow, it's hard to create. You can't control creation. The minute I try to control what I'm going to act, what parts I'm going to play, they become something that I don't want to act. It becomes a heady thing. It becomes, If I just play that part, then I'll play that part, and then I'd better be over there. It becomes something that's just structure and math, not creative.

Are there certain people you'd like to work with, certain directors you look forward to?

There are certain directors I've worked with before that I'd love to work with again. But you never know what the experience might be like. You think, I'd love to work with that person. But then you're with that person, and you're like, God, why did I want to work with that person? or, Why would I want to work with that person? Or you work with that person, and you're like, Wow, that person's fantastic. I mean, that's just been my experience the whole way. You really don't know what's going to happen most times. You might have an idea it's going to be a certain way, and it's not. So I always say the director I want to work with is the next director I'm working with.

So you don't think, When I'm fifty-five or sixty, or whatever, what would I like to be doing in this world, in acting? You don't think, Will I be ready for my Lear? Vanessa Redgrave said she'd like to see you play Lear when you're fifty—

God love her. *She* can play Lear. She's fantastic. She could totally play the female Lear. I don't think, Oh, I'm going to play that part. But I do think of a time when, maybe in a couple of years, I can do a play and a film every two years, directing other plays. A lot of my life is more about getting to watch. All I think about all the time is, God I want to see that! or, I'd like to go to that museum. That's when I'm in heaven. It'd be great to just create and give a couple of times every two years, give to people, and then have the rest of the time be where I can just take it in. But I don't have a thing about what part I'll play.

Let's talk about another film role.

Well, *Magnolia* was an incredibly personal tale. I think Paul is one of the great American filmmakers, and it's Paul's best movie, and a lot of people don't agree with me. But I think that movie is him doing something pretty extraordinary, which is creating opera without the music. I really do think that when you're watching the film, you're watching an opera, and I think people missed that. I don't think they understood that that's what they were watching, so they saw like, God, what's all this emotion? What's all this? When you know a director and you have history, things become more personal. There's always a lot of work that you have to do as an actor, as well as with the directors and scripts. That work can color your understanding of the environment you're working in, the character you're playing, and the perfection of the character you're playing. When you work with a director you have history with, though, and they're writing things for you, that work's been done.

So with Magnolia, *you came with a lot of history and a lot of connection to that.*

I knew what my role was in the environment. I knew a lot before I even read it. So it was actually one of the easier films that I've ever had to do, because what it did was, it created a feeling of how I feel when I direct, where I'm there to make sure the others do the best they can. I would show up, and I was there for Paul. It was something that really allowed me to get inside of a structure that was created with this character, Phil Parma, the nurse. It allowed me to get inside there and say, Okay. And that's what you have to do when you play parts. You have to make it something other than you to get past it all. And with him it was easy 'cause he was right there. Sometimes it's not that easy. You do have to find a way to say, This is for the audience. They're gonna get what they're going to get, and hopefully they're going to be pleased. I do think characters you play exist in the world. You have to have a humility and understand that even though they're fictional, these characters exist, these people exist, and you have to honor them. And I feel that strongly, and so in *Magnolia*, I was honoring him, and he was right there.

Is it more interesting for you to play characters whom the audience might find morally hard to take?

Unless you are playing a serial killer or pedophile. There are certain characters where the moral line is pretty distinct, but other than that, it's just judgment. Some people aren't going to be really upset about the prank caller guy I played in *Happiness*. Some people are going to be like, "Get over the problem." Some people are going to be like, "Omigod!" They're going to label him as if he should be in jail or something. So you don't know. I don't think about it like that, is what I'm saying. 'Cause to me it's not morality you're dealing with, it's judgment.

I just meant is it more interesting to you to play a character who is questionable.

What I'm saying is everybody's questionable. I firmly believe that.

But aren't there heroes?

And were they heroes since the day they were born?

They're heroes when we see them.

But what about when we don't see them? People make mistakes, people hurt other people. I'm not talking about characters, I'm talking about people. I'm dealing more with the fact that if you see a film and all you see is the hero side of the character, then you're not watching real people, anything that's based on any kind of reality. And so you're just basically going with it as a fantasy, and that's cool too. I like those films too. But that's what those characters are. I'm more referring to the fact that in a three-dimensional well-written part, the actor's job is not to worry about the morality of the characters. It's our job to argue for and to advocate.

What was the moment when you thought, I could do this for my life?

Well, my mom took me to the Geva Theatre in Rochester after that *Tom Sawyer* grammar school thing. It was a small theater at the time, but they brought in actors from New York. The first show I saw was *All My Sons*, and it was the first time I had ever sat in the theater and watched a serious play. And I was just over the moon, floored by what this was. I don't know if the production was any good. I was in the seventh grade, but I thought I had found something that no one knew about. I literally was like, "You're kidding me." That these people were getting up in front of me and making me believe something that wasn't actually happening. I really had one of those corny realizations: I have to come here as much as I can. And that's the thing, as an actor—we were talking about earlier—this kind of almost resentment you have toward the people in front of you when you know you're the one who's gonna ultimately have to be vulnerable and private and sharp. The thing that gets you, innately, is when you understand, What I'm giving is this experience I had in seventh grade. And so, you move past it, 'cause you know ultimately what you're giving is something great, if done well. Because that experience I had when I was a kid—I can't tell you how, getting back into the theater after that moment of being locked out was something I thought about almost all the time. When I saw *All My Sons*, and the father runs out at the end and kills himself, I thought, My god, my god. He just killed himself. I was crying, and I was twelve years old! I was, like, it's so sad. How did they do that in a dark fucking room?! That didn't make me want to be an actor. That made me a theater lover for life. And I think that's what I am. I'm a theater lover for life, a theater lover for life. I still prefer to watch.

Prefer? What do you mean?

If you're actually acting in something and you're a part of creating, you experience the release, the joy that you helped give to these people. It's extraordinary. But I would rather be sitting, watching, and just caving in to the fucking beauty. I would still rather watch Michael Stuhlbarg. I would rather watch you than act. I prefer to be that person—I prefer it! I prefer actually sitting there and watching great actors and great material take me away. It's the best fuckin' thing in the world, and my love and awestruck-ness with actors at that moment, it just has no bounds. Ultimately, it all keys back to why I'd rather watch, because why I wanted to do it is—I wanted to create it anyway I could. I wanted to be a part of it any way I could, and so I knew I could do this. I think I could do it well. In order to do it well, it's gonna be very difficult. But if I do this and I can do it well, then I will be a part of this thing that I know is probably one of the greatest things that exists, which is a moment in the theater. To be on either side, on the stage or in the audience, for that moment in the theater when something happens that we all know, which we're addicted to or in search of all the time. Which is that moment when a quorum of people on the planet are in one room and they actually, as a unit, are experiencing life together. It's something that is a transcendent thing that theater can offer. And when it actually happens, when it happens to you, you are in search of it the rest of your life. If I can do it well, I want to be a part of what that is, because there's nothing better than that.

ABOUT THE INTERVIEWEES

Frances Conroy

AWARDS

Golden Globe Award, Best Performance by an Actress in a Television Series (Drama), for *Six Feet Under*; Drama Desk Award, Outstanding Featured Actress in a Play, for *The Secret Rapture*; OBIE Award, Performance, for *The Last Yankee*; Outer Critics Circle Award, Outstanding Featured Actress in a Play, for *The Ride Down Mt. Morgan*; Screen Actors Guild Award, Outstanding Performance by a Female Actor in a Drama Series, for *Six Feet Under*; Screen Actors Guild Award, Outstanding Performance by an Ensemble in a Drama Series, for *Six Feet Under*; Nominee, Tony Award, Best Performance by a Featured Actress in a Play, for *The Ride Down Mt. Morgan*

MILESTONES

STAGE
The Skin of Our Teeth; *The Little Foxes*; *Broken Glass*; *The Last Yankee*; *Two Shakespearean Actors*; *The Secret Rapture*; *Our Town*; *The Lady from Dubuque*; *Othello*

FILM
Broken Flowers; *Catwoman*; *The Crucible*; *Sleepless in Seattle*; *Crimes and Misdemeanors*; *Manhattan*

TELEVISION
Six Feet Under

Billy Crudup

AWARDS

Clarence Derwent Award, for *Arcadia*; National Board of Review Award, Breakthrough Performance (Male), for *The Hi-Lo Country*; Online Film Critics Society Award, Best Ensemble Cast Performance, for *Almost Famous*; Outer Critics Circle Award, Outstanding Debut of an Actor, for *Arcadia*; Theatre World Award, for *Arcadia*; Nominee, Tony Award, Best Performance by a Leading Actor in a Play, for *The Pillowman* and *The Elephant Man*

MILESTONES

STAGE
The Pillowman; *The Elephant Man*; *Measure for Measure*; *Oedipus Rex*; *Three Sisters*; *Bus Stop*; *Arcadia*

FILM
Mission: Impossible III; *Stage Beauty*; *Big Fish*; *Charlotte Gray*; *Almost Famous*; *Jesus' Son*; *The Hi-Lo Country*; *Without Limits*; *Inventing the Abbotts*

Philip Seymour Hoffman

AWARDS

Oscar, Best Performance by an Actor in a Leading Role, for *Capote*; Golden Globe Award, Best Performance by an Actor in a Motion Picture (Drama), for *Capote*; Boston Film Critics Association Award, Best Actor, for *Capote*; British Academy of Film and Television Arts Film Award, Best Performance by an Actor in a Leading Role, for *Capote*; Broadcast Film Critics Association Critics' Choice Award, Best Actor, for *Capote*; Florida Film Critics Circle Award, Best Ensemble Cast, for *State and Main*; Golden Satellite Award, Best Performance by an Actor in a Motion Picture (Comedy or Musical), for *Flawless*; Independent Spirit Award, Best Male Lead, for *Capote*; Los Angeles Film Critics Association Award, Best Actor, for *Capote*; National Board of Review Award, Best Actor, for *Capote*; National Board of Review Award, Best Supporting Actor, for *Magnolia* and *The Talented Mr. Ripley*; National Board of Review Award, Best Acting by an Ensemble, for *Happiness*; National Society of Film Critics Award, Best Actor, for *Capote*; Online Film Critics Society Award, Best Supporting Actor, for *Almost Famous*; Online Film Critics Society Award, Best Ensemble Cast Performance, for *Almost Famous* and *State and Main*; Outer Critics Circle Special Achievement Award, for *True West*; Screen Actors Guild Award, Outstanding Performance by a Male Actor in a Leading Role, for *Capote*; Theatre World Award, for *True West*; Toronto Film Critics Association Award, Best Actor, for *Capote*

MILESTONES

STAGE
The Seagull; *True West*; *Shopping and Fucking*; *The Merchant of Venice*

FILM
Mission: Impossible III; *Capote*; *Cold Mountain*; *25th Hour*; *Red Dragon*; *Punch-Drunk Love*; *Almost Famous*; *State and Main*; *The Talented Mr. Ripley*; *Magnolia*; *Flawless*; *Happiness*; *Boogie Nights*

Kevin Kline

AWARDS

Oscar, Best Performance by an Actor in a Supporting Role, for *A Fish Called Wanda*; Tony Award, Best Performance by a Leading Actor in a Musical, for *The Pirates of Penzance*; Tony Award, Best Performance by a Featured Actor in a Musical, for *On the Twentieth Century*; Drama Desk Award, Outstanding Actor in a Musical, for *The Pirates of Penzance*; Drama Desk Award, Outstanding Featured Actor in a Musical, for *On the Twentieth Century*; IFP Gotham Actor Award; OBIE Award, Sustained Excellence of Performance (1985–86); OBIE Award, Performance, for *The Pirates of Penzance*; St. Louis International Film Festival Lifetime Achievement Award

MILESTONES

STAGE
Henry IV; *The Seagull*; *Ivanov*; *Hamlet*; *On the Twentieth Century*

FILM
De-Lovely; *Wild Wild West*; *A Midsummer Night's Dream*; *In & Out*; *The Ice Storm*; *Dave*; *A Fish Called Wanda*; *The Big Chill*; *Sophie's Choice*

John Lithgow

AWARDS

Golden Globe Award, Best Performance by an Actor in a Television Series (Comedy/Musical), for *3rd Rock from the Sun*; Emmy Award, Outstanding Lead Actor in a Comedy Series, for *3rd Rock from the Sun*; Emmy Award, Outstanding Guest Performer in a Drama Series, for *Amazing Stories*; Tony Award, Best Performance by a Featured

Actor in a Play, for *The Changing Room*; Tony Award, Best Performance by an Actor in a Musical, for *Sweet Smell of Success*; The Actor, Outstanding Performance by a Male Actor in a Comedy Series, for *3rd Rock from the Sun*; American Comedy Award, Funniest Male Performer in a Television Series (Leading Role), for *3rd Rock from the Sun*; Drama Desk Award, Outstanding Actor in a Play, for *Requiem for a Heavyweight*; Drama Desk Award, Outstanding Performance, for *The Changing Room*; Golden Satellite Award, Best Performance by an Actor in a Television Series (Comedy or Musical), for *3rd Rock from the Sun*; Los Angeles Film Critics Association Award, Best Supporting Actor, for *The World According to Garp*; New York Film Critics Circle Award, Best Supporting Actor, for *The World According to Garp*

MILESTONES

STAGE
Dirty Rotten Scoundrels; *The Retreat from Moscow*; *Sweet Smell of Success*; *M. Butterfly*; *The Front Page*; *Requiem for a Heavyweight*; *Beyond Therapy*; *Anna Christie*; *My Fat Friend*; *The Changing Room*

FILM
Cliffhanger; *Raising Cain*; *Footloose*; *Terms of Endearment*; *The World According to Garp*; *Blow Out*; *Obsession*

TELEVISION
3rd Rock from the Sun

Patti LuPone

AWARDS

Tony Award, Best Performance by an Actress in a Musical, for *Evita*; Drama Desk Award, Outstanding Actress in a Musical, for *Anything*

Goes and *Evita*; Florida Film Critics Circle Award, Best Ensemble Cast, for *State and Main*; Olivier Award, Best Actress in a Musical, for *Les Misérables* and *The Cradle Will Rock*; Online Film Critics Society Award, Best Ensemble Cast Performance, for *State and Main*; Outer Critics Circle Award, Outstanding Solo Performance, for *Patti LuPone on Broadway*; Nominee, Tony Award, Best Performance by a Leading Actress in a Musical, for *Sweeney Todd*

MILESTONES

STAGE

Sweeney Todd; *Noises Off*; *The Old Neighborhood*; *Patti LuPone on Broadway*; *Pal Joey*; *Sunset Boulevard*; *Les Misérables*; *Oliver!*; *The Cradle Will Rock*; *Evita*; *The Baker's Wife*; *The Three Sisters*; *The Beggar's Opera*; *Next Time I'll Sing to You Master Class*

FILM

State and Main; *Summer of Sam*; *Driving Miss Daisy*; *King of the Gypsies*

S. Epatha Merkerson

AWARDS

Golden Globe Award, Best Performance by an Actress in a Miniseries or Motion Picture Made for Television, for *Lackawanna Blues*; Emmy Award, Outstanding Lead Actress in a Miniseries or a Movie, for *Lackawanna Blues*; Helen Hayes Award, Outstanding Lead Actress (Resident Play), for *The Old Settler*; NAACP Theatre Award, Best Actress in a Play, for *The Piano Lesson*; OBIE Award, Performance, for *I'm Not Stupid*; Screen Actors Guild Award, Outstanding Performance by a Female Actor in a Television Movie or Miniseries, for *Lackawanna Blues*; Nominee, Independent Spirit Award, Best Female Lead, for *Lackawanna Blues*

MILESTONES

STAGE

The Piano Lesson; *The Dream Team*; *For Colored Girls Who Have Considered Suicide/When the Rainbow Is Enuf . . .* ; *I'm Not Stupid*; *Moms*; *Lady Day at Emerson's Bar and Grill*

FILM

Lackawanna Blues; *It's Nothing Personal*; *Loose Cannons*

TELEVISION

Law & Order

Estelle Parsons

AWARDS

Oscar, Best Performance by an Actress in a Supporting Role, for *Bonnie and Clyde*; Drama Desk Award, Unique Theatrical Experience, for *Miss Margarida's Way*; OBIE Award, Distinguished Performance, for *Next Time I'll Sing to You* and *In the Summer House*; Theatre World Award, Most Promising Newcomer; Theatre World Award, Best Debut Performance, for *Mrs. Dally Has a Lover*; Nominee, Oscar, Best Supporting Actress, for *Rachel, Rachel*; Nominee, Tony Award, for *The Seven Descents of Myrtle*, *And Miss Reardon Drinks a Little*, *Miss Margarida's Way*, and *Morning's at Seven*; Nominee, British Academy of Film and Television Arts Film Award, Best Supporting Actress, for *Watermelon Man*

MILESTONES

STAGE

Morning's at Seven; *Happy Days*; *The Pirates of Penzance*; *Miss Margarida's Way*; *And Miss Reardon Drinks a Little*; *The Seven Descents of Myrtle*

FILM
Looking for Richard; *Boys on the Side*; *Dick Tracy*; *Watermelon Man*; *Don't Drink the Water*; *Rachel, Rachel*; *Bonnie and Clyde*

TELEVISION
Roseanne (ABC)

Mandy Patinkin

AWARDS

Emmy Award, Outstanding Lead Actor in a Drama Series, for *Chicago Hope*; Tony Award, Best Performance by a Featured Actor in a Musical, for *Evita*; CableACE Award, Actor in a Theatrical or Dramatic Special, for *Sunday in the Park with George*; Nominee, Tony Award, Best Performance by a Leading Actor in a Musical, for *Sunday in the Park with George* and *The Wild Party*

MILESTONES

STAGE
Mandy Patinkin in Concert: Mamaloshen; *Falsettos*; *The Secret Garden*; *Mandy Patinkin in Concert: Dress Casual*; *Follies in Concert*

FILM
Piñero; *Impromptu*; *Dick Tracy*; *Alien Nation*; *The Princess Bride*; *Yentl*; *Ragtime*

Ruben Santiago-Hudson

AWARDS

Tony Award, Best Performance by a Featured Actor in a Play, for *Seven Guitars*; Black Movie Award, Outstanding Television Movie, for *Lackawanna Blues*; Black Reel Award, Best Screenplay, Original or Adapted (Television), for *Lackawanna Blues*; Christopher Award (Television & Cable), for *Lackawanna Blues*; Humanitas Prize (90 Minute Category), for *Lackawanna Blues*; Nominee, Emmy Award, Outstanding Made for Television Movie, for *Lackawanna Blues*; Nominee, Black Reel Award, Best Supporting Actor (Television), for *Their Eyes Were Watching God*; Nominee, Image Award, Outstanding Actor in a Television Movie, Mini-Series or Dramatic Special, for *Their Eyes Were Watching God*; Nominee, Independent Spirit Award, Best First Feature, for *Lackawanna Blues*; Nominee, PGA Golden Laurel Award, Producer of the Year Award in Long-Form Television, for *Lackawanna Blues*; Nominee, Satellite Award, Outstanding Actor in a Supporting Role in a Series, Miniseries, or Motion Picture Made for Television, for *Their Eyes Were Watching God*; Nominee, Writers Guild of America Award, Long Form (Adapted), for *Lackawanna Blues*

MILESTONES

STAGE
Seven Guitars (2006, as director); *Gem of the Ocean*; *Henry VIII*; *Seven Guitars*; *Measure for Measure*; *Conversations in Exile*; *Boogie Woogie & Booker T.*; *Ceremonies in Dark Old Men*; *A Soldier's Play*

FILM
Honeydripper; *Brother's Shadow*; *Their Eyes Were Watching God*; *Lackawanna Blues* (actor and writer); *American Tragedy*; *Shaft*; *The Devil's Advocate*; *Coming to America*

Marian Seldes

AWARDS

Tony Award, Best Performance by a Supporting or Featured Actress in a Play, for *A Delicate Balance*; Drama Desk Award, Outstanding

Performance, for *Father's Day*; L.A. Stage Alliance Ovation Award, Best Lead Actress in a Play, for *Three Tall Women*; Madge Evans & Sidney Kingsley Award for Excellence in Theater; OBIE Award, Sustained Achievement; OBIE Award, Distinguished Performance, for *The Ginger Man*; OBIE Award, Performance, for *Isadora Duncan Sleeps with the Russian Navy*; Nominee, Tony Award, Best Performance by a Leading Actress in a Play, for *Ring Round the Moon* and *Father's Day*

MILESTONES

STAGE
The Torch-Bearers; *The Play About the Baby*; *Ring Round the Moon*; *Ivanov*; *Three Tall Women*; *Painting Churches*; *Deathtrap* (over one thousand consecutive performances, landing her in *The Guinness Book of World Records*); *Isadora Duncan Sleeps with the Russian Navy*; *Equus*; *A Delicate Balance*; *Tiny Alice*; *The Milk Train Doesn't Stop Here Anymore*

FILM
The Haunting; *Digging to China*; *Home Alone 3*; *Gertrude Stein and a Companion!*; *Fingers*

Kevin Spacey

AWARDS

Oscar, Best Performance by an Actor in a Leading Role, for *American Beauty*; Oscar, Best Actor in a Supporting Role, for *The Usual Suspects*; Tony Award, Best Performance by a Featured Actor in a Play, for *Lost in Yonkers*; British Academy of Film and Television Arts Film Award, Best Performance by an Actor in a Leading Role, for *American Beauty*; Drama Desk Award, Outstanding Featured Actor in a Play, for *Lost in Yonkers*; Lawrence Olivier Award, Best Actor, for *The Iceman Cometh*; London Film Critics' Circle Award, Best Actor, for *American Beauty*; London Critics' Circle Award, Best Actor, for *The*

Iceman Cometh; National Board of Review Award, Best Supporting Actor, for *The Usual Suspects* and *Seven*; New York Critics Circle Award, Best Supporting Actor, for *Seven*, *The Usual Suspects*, *Swimming with Sharks*, and *Outbreak*; Outer Critics Circle Award, Outstanding Actor in a Play, for *The Iceman Cometh*

MILESTONES

STAGE

Richard II; *The Iceman Cometh*; *Lost in Yonkers*; *National Anthem*; *Long Day's Journey Into Night*; *Hurlyburly*; *Ghosts*

FILM

Beyond the Sea; *The Life of David Gale*; *United States of Leland*; *The Shipping News*; *Pay It Forward*; *American Beauty*; *Midnight in the Garden of Good and Evil*; *L.A. Confidential*; *Albino Alligator* (director); *The Usual Suspects*; *Swimming with Sharks*

Meryl Streep

AWARDS

Oscar, Best Performance by an Actress in a Leading Role, for *Sophie's Choice*; Oscar, Best Performance by an Actress in a Supporting Role, for *Kramer vs. Kramer*; Golden Globe Award, Best Performance by an Actress in a Motion Picture (Drama), for *Sophie's Choice* and *The French Lieutenant's Woman*; Golden Globe Award, Best Performance by an Actress in a Motion Picture (Musical or Comedy), for *The Devil Wears Prada*; Golden Globe Award, Best Performance by an Actress in a Supporting Role in a Motion Picture, for *Adaptation* and *Kramer vs. Kramer*; Golden Globe Award, Best Performance by an Actress in a Mini-series or a Motion Picture Made for Television, for *Angels in America*; Emmy Award, Outstanding Lead Actress in a Miniseries or a Movie, for *Angels in America*; Emmy Award, Outstanding Lead Actress in a Limited Series, for *Holocaust*; Nominee, Oscar, Best Performance by an Actress in a Leading Role, for *The Devil Wears Prada*, *One True Thing*, *A Cry in the Dark*, *Out of Africa*, *Silkwood*, *The French Lieutenant's Woman*, *Music of the Heart*, *The Bridges of Madison County*, *Postcards from the Edge*, and *Ironweed*; Nominee, Oscar, Best Performance by an Actress in a Supporting Role, for *The Deer Hunter* and *Adaptation*

MILESTONES

STAGE
The Seagull; *Alice in Concert*; *The Taming of the Shrew*; *Happy End*; *The Cherry Orchard*; *Measure for Measure*; *Henry V*; *27 Wagons Full of Cotton*; *Trelawny of the "Wells"*

FILM
The Devil Wears Prada; *A Prairie Home Companion*; *The Hours*; *Adaptation*; *The Bridges of Madison County*; *The River Wild*; *Death Becomes Her*; *Postcards from the Edge*; *Out of Africa*; *Silkwood*; *Sophie's Choice*; *Still of the Night*; *The French Lieutenant's Woman*; *Kramer vs. Kramer*; *Manhattan*

Dianne Wiest

AWARDS

Oscar, Best Performance by an Actress in a Supporting Role, for *Bullets Over Broadway* and *Hannah and Her Sisters*; Golden Globe Award, Best Performance by an Actress in a Supporting Role, for *Bullets Over Broadway*; Emmy Award, Outstanding Guest Actress in a Drama Series, for *Road to Avonlea*; The Actor, Outstanding Performance by a Female Actor in a Supporting Role, for *Bullets Over Broadway*; The Actor, Outstanding Performance by a Cast in a Theatrical Motion Picture, for *The Birdcage*; American Comedy Award, Funniest Supporting Actress in a Motion Picture, for *The Birdcage* and *Bullets Over Broadway*;

Chicago Film Critics Association Award, Best Supporting Actress, for *Bullets Over Broadway*; Clarence Derwent Award, for *The Art of Dining*; Independent Spirit Award, Best Supporting Actress, for *Bullets Over Broadway*; Los Angeles Film Critics Association Award, Best Supporting Actress, for *Bullets Over Broadway* and *Hannah and Her Sisters*; National Board of Review Award, Best Supporting Actress, for *Hannah and Her Sisters*; National Society of Film Critics Award, Best Supporting Actress, for *Bullets Over Broadway* and *Hannah and Her Sisters*; New York Film Critics Circle Award, Best Supporting Actress, for *Bullets Over Broadway* and *Hannah and Her Sisters*; OBIE Award, Performance, for *Serenading Louie*, *Other Places*, and *The Art of Dining*; Society of Texas Film Critics Award, Best Supporting Actress, for *Bullets Over Broadway*; Theatre World Award, for *The Art of Dining*

MILESTONES

STAGE

One Flea Spare; *Don Juan in Hell*; *Blue Light*; *Hunting Cockroaches*; *After the Fall*; *Othello*; *Hedda Gabler*; *The Art of Dining*; *Ashes*

FILM

The Horse Whisperer; *The Birdcage*; *Bullets Over Broadway*; *Little Man Tate*; *Edward Scissorhands*; *Parenthood*; *Radio Days*; *Hannah and Her Sisters*; *The Purple Rose of Cairo*; *Footloose*